Published by Straight Talk Books
P.O. Box 301, Milwaukee, WI 53201
800.661.3311 · timeofgrace.org

Unless otherwise indicated, Scripture is taken from THE HOLY BIBLE, NEW INTERNATIONAL VERSION®, NIV® Copyright © 1973, 1978, 1984, 2011 by Biblica, Inc.® Used by permission. All rights reserved worldwide.

Scripture quotations marked AMP are taken from the Amplified Bible. Copyright © 2015 by The Lockman Foundation, La Habra, CA 90631. All rights reserved.

Scripture quotations marked EHV are from the Holy Bible, Evangelical Heritage Version® (EHV®) © 2019 Wartburg Project, Inc. All rights reserved. Used by permission.

Scripture quotations marked ESV are taken from The Holy Bible, English Standard Version®. Text Edition: 2016. Copyright © 2001 by Crossway, a publishing ministry of Good News Publishers. All rights reserved.

Scripture quotations marked GW are taken from GOD'S WORD®. © 1995, 2003, 2013, 2014, 2019, 2020 by God's Word to the Nations Mission Society. Used by permission.

Scripture quotations marked KJV are taken from the King James Version. Text is public domain.

Scripture quotations marked MSG are taken from *THE MESSAGE*, copyright © 1993, 2002, 2018 by Eugene H. Peterson. Used by permission of NavPress. All rights reserved. Represented by Tyndale House Publishers, Inc.

Scripture quotations marked NLT are taken from the *Holy Bible*, New Living Translation, copyright © 1996, 2004, 2015 by Tyndale House Foundation. Used by permission of Tyndale House Publishers, Inc., Carol Stream, Illinois 60188. All rights reserved.

Printed in the United States of America
ISBN: 978-1-949488-98-2

TIME OF GRACE *is a registered mark of Time of Grace Ministry.*

DAILY PROMISES

Devotions for Every Day

JANUARY

"See, I am doing a new thing! Now it springs up;
do you not perceive it? I am making a way in the
wilderness and streams in the wasteland."

Isaiah 43:19

Made new
Katrina Harrmann

We recently remodeled our office. This involved new wallpaper and floor-to-ceiling bookshelves to create my dream library, as well as a space for my desk. It's so full of potential!

Let's face it, new stuff is fun. New houses are a blast . . . even new jobs hold the charm of potential. I even remember getting giddy over a new grocery store that opened in our town this past year. New things are fresh and exciting. "Newness" is full of possibilities.

When Jesus healed a leper, the man praised God in a loud voice, thrilled to be made new. David rejoiced after being forgiven of his sins—relieved and grateful to be made new. And countless Old Testament heroes praised God when they were given new lands (Abraham) or new promises (Isaac) or even a new name (Jacob). "New" is a reason to celebrate!

That being said, your "new" might not look like other people's "new." As we start the New Year, it's important to recognize ways in which our "news" are different . . . but also how they are the same. For instance, God makes *all* of us new. Every time we confess our sins and rely on God to turn our rotting nature into something new, God celebrates. As does all of heaven.

As we lean into the New Year, let's celebrate what it means to be made new in Christ: clean, forgiven, cherished.

"The old has gone, the new is here!" (2 Corinthians 5:17).

Prone to wander
Mike Novotny

A famous old hymn said, "Prone to wander, Lord, I feel it. Prone to leave the God I love." The author admitted that his heart had a tendency to stray from God.

Jesus would agree. When he said, **"I am the good shepherd; I know my sheep and my sheep know me"** (John 10:14), he was implying that we, like sheep, go astray. We are prone to wander.

Why? Sheep see something they want (like green grass) and pursue it without checking if that pursuit takes them far from their shepherd. In addition, their flocking instinct means they are prone to follow their friends, no matter how near or distant those friends are from the shepherd.

Sound familiar? Often we see something we want (the best education, athletic achievement, extra money, etc.) and pursue it without asking about its effect on our closeness to Jesus (think church attendance, prayer life, etc.). In addition, we tend to follow the example of people we respect, scheduling our lives in similar ways, even if they aren't seeking God's kingdom before all else.

Perhaps the wisest thing for sheep like us to do would be to ask, "Will _____ keep me close to Jesus? Even if _____ isn't inherently wrong or _____ is a pretty good person, will it/he/she keep me close to the protecting arm of my Good Shepherd?"

You know Jesus. You know he wants what's best for you. Therefore, listen to his voice, the loving call that will keep you close and overcome the temptation to wander.

Every day is the last day
Matt Ewart

"Therefore keep watch, because you do not know on what day your Lord will come" (Matthew 24:42).

I love my kids and all, but some days I can't wait for them to go to bed. When I leave their room after saying prayers, it's like walking into freedom. At last, some time to myself!

An article I read challenged me on that idea. It said you should say goodnight to your kids as if it is the last time they will ever see you.

After feeling convicted, I invited the challenge of re-evaluating my priorities. I spent the next night lingering in their room after our prayers. I lay on the floor in the dark, letting them talk about anything on their minds. We had some great conversations, and we all ended up with the giggles.

I wish I could do that every night.

God doesn't give us the exact day or hour when our Lord will come. In not telling us, he invites us to live as if every day is the last day. He invites us to pursue him and seek him, not in a last-moment effort to get our spiritual affairs in order but in a way that unleashes his power and love in everyday life.

So maybe tonight after you lie down, linger with him a little longer. Picture his presence as you open up whatever is on your mind. It might not give you the giggles, but it will fill you with joy.

The new you is hidden
Daron Lindemann

Some years my New Year's resolutions are clear and focused.

This year they're hidden, which actually makes them more impactful and hopeful. Here's how:

"Set your minds on things above, not on earthly things. For you died, and your life is now hidden with Christ in God" (Colossians 3:2,3).

Hidden in his cross. Hidden in his grave. Hidden in his perfect forgiveness, patient mercy, and eternal glory. Pursue the new you . . .

Not in being chosen for the band or chosen for the department promotion but chosen in eternity to be a child of God by grace.

Not in how many friends or followers you have but in how faithful Jesus Christ is, who calls himself your friend and invites you to follow him.

Not in biased news feeds but in the good news of salvation.

Not in winning the basketball championship but in your victory over the control of sin and curse of death.

Not in finally finding a relationship with someone decent or finding that future spouse but in the relationship you have with Jesus.

Dear Jesus, you promise that my fuller, more satisfying life is hidden in you. You call me to experience greater joy and peace by believing in you more than worldly things. Hide me more in you. Amen.

Following God's route
Katrina Harrmann

Our dogs are funny.

When we take them on walks, they try to lead the way because 1) they think they are in charge and 2) they walk the same route so often, they kind of know it by heart.

Sometimes we like to change the route just to throw them a curveball. As they step off a familiar curb and start to turn left, we guide them right. You can see the confusion in their eyes—the hesitation as they follow with a bit less bravado than before.

It makes them remember to trust us. It reminds them to be obedient.

Have you ever been walking through life, doing your usual thing, when a curveball comes along?

Maybe it's God taking you on a new walking route—reminding you what it means to trust him and be obedient to his will.

Sometimes we walk ourselves on routes that aren't good for us. That's when we need to tune in to the Savior's voice and let him guide us.

Of course, God doesn't have us on leashes. Unlike my sweet pups, he allows us to misstep. We can even wander off if we're not paying attention. When this happens, we need to be still and listen for his guidance. We may not understand where he is leading us, but it is *always* for our good.

"A person's steps are directed by the Lord. How then can anyone understand their own way?" (Proverbs 20:24).

The penalty is paid
Clark Schultz

OK, so I admit that I watched the trial of Johnny Depp vs. Amber Heard. This couple who was once in love slung mud at each other day after day. Witness after witness came forward, each supporting a side of the story. Text messages, decades-old but spanning their relationship, were drudged up and read publicly.

This got me thinking of my own emails and text messages from this past week or even farther into the past. Would I give a lawyer full cooperation and say, "Yes, please read all of them out loud"? Or would I cower and cringe and make excuses for the venom that spewed from my fingers?

"What does the Lord require of you? To act justly and to love mercy and to walk humbly with your God" (Micah 6:8). I haven't always been truthful. I haven't always been kind. I don't always act justly. In the courtroom of my life, I stand guilty.

Yet even though I fall short at times, Jesus never did. He always showed kindness. He always showed love. He even prayed for those who drove the nails into his hands and feet. He lived, died, and rose for me and you. Jesus the Suffering Servant put our sins on himself and happily served instead of being served. Because of him, court is over; the penalty of our sins has been paid in full. God sees us all as not guilty through Jesus!

Is Jesus disappointed in you?
Mike Novotny

A few years ago, I lost my voice and my car wouldn't start on the same day, so I ordered an Uber to give me a quick lift to work. A woman pulled up in an impressive, upgraded Jeep. Since she was talkative and I couldn't talk, we started a hilarious me-texting and her-talking conversation that kept us laughing the whole way to church.

That's when Jesus came up. She mentioned how expensive gas was, which prompted me to text, "Time for that Prius!" She laughed, and I joked, "It's what Jesus wants." But she suddenly turned serious and muttered, "It wouldn't be the first time I disappointed Jesus . . ." That was the exact moment when she pulled into the church parking lot, I got out, and our conversation ended.

I wonder how many of us feel, deep down, that Jesus is disappointed in us. It's not an illogical emotion since sin disappoints Jesus and we are all sinners. But let's not forget what Jesus did to deal with those feelings. **"He was delivered over to death for our sins"** (Romans 4:25).

For our sins—those three golden words explain why Jesus did what he did. To pay for our sins. To erase our sins. To send our sins as far from us as the east is from the west. Or to put it another way, to make sure that our sins don't leave us as disappointments in God's eyes.

Sinner, take heart. If you have Jesus, God isn't disappointed in you.

God is punctual
Daron Lindemann

Just 30 seconds. That's how much later I checked in for the flight online than all the other passengers reserving their boarding positions on the Southwest Airlines flight. It meant I was group C instead of group A.

Timing is everything. So what timing are you trying to manage right now? Persevering in new habits? Best moment for a career change or critical conversation?

Sometimes we want to speed things up when God is trying to slow them down. Or we want to slow down when God wants us to speed up. Or we worry too much about precise timing when God is good either way and wants us to focus on other things.

So how do you operate more on God's perfect timing?

"But I trust in you, Lord; I say, 'You are my God.' My times are in your hands; deliver me from the hands of my enemies, from those who pursue me. Let your face shine on your servant; save me in your unfailing love" (Psalm 31:14-16).

Focus less on timing and more on God.

Trust in God helps you better turn the calendar. Relationship with God helps with right decisions. Pursuing God's peace helps define your punctuality and productivity.

Open to Psalm 31 and complete these statements: I can trust in God completely because (verse 6) _____. I can live with more joy because (verse 7) _____. I can be more free from worry and fear because (verse 8) _____.

No weight limit on forgiveness
Mike Novotny

While most everyone agrees that forgiveness (the opposite of vengeance) is the right thing to do, there are three aspects to biblical forgiveness that offend human reason—the size, the amount, and the necessity. Let's think about the first offense:

The Bible doesn't have a weight limit on forgiveness. When someone sins against you, God doesn't send a team of instrument-carrying angels to measure the dimensions of the sin or calculate its weight. Instead, God categorically says, **"Bear with each other and forgive one another if any of you has a grievance against someone. Forgive as the Lord forgave you"** (Colossians 3:13).

You might not be able to forget about their sin, and there may be consequences for their sin, but God still calls you to forgive. Even if she bullied you brutally. Even if your father spoke to you abusively. Even if his affair broke your heart. Even if the divorce left you broken. There is no asterisk on this passage. Just a blanket statement to forgive.

Why? Because that is exactly how the Lord forgave you. Jesus didn't die for some sins or socially acceptable sins. No—thank God—he died for all sins and all sinners. You never have to wonder if God will get you back, no matter how big or ugly your sin, because God doesn't limit his forgiveness. No matter the size of your sin, you are forgiven by your Savior.

In light of the cross, may God give you the strength to forgive even *him*. Even *her*. Even *that*.

A new definition for patience
Matt Ewart

I recently asked a large group of people how many of them wished they had more patience. Rather than raising their hands, most of them just laughed at the question. Why? Because everyone knows that everyone wants to be more patient.

Why do we need it? Here's what we think:

The world is full of people who don't move at our pace. We just need more patience so they all have time to catch up.

The world is also full of people who can't meet our expectations. We just need more patience until they can meet our standards.

Quite often our idea of patience is just a glorified version of selfishness. It's awfully centered on *me*.

God has a different version of patience that he puts into practice and teaches us to practice. His patience is not about giving us time to catch up to him; nor does his patience give us more time to meet his standards. Those things would be impossible for us to do, even if we were given an eternity to do them.

God's patience required him to lower himself to our level and slow down to our pace. He holds out the gifts of his grace and equips us with the faith to grasp them. His patience was not for his benefit but for ours. Ask him to teach you this kind of patience too.

"Therefore, as God's chosen people, holy and dearly loved, clothe yourselves with . . . patience" (Colossians 3:12).

What you really need
David Scharf

The paralyzed man probably thought, "If I could only walk, then I'd be happy." Four friends carried him to the teacher. Jesus looked at him and knew that this man's greatest need was not to walk in this life but to walk with him in eternal life. So Jesus said, **"Son, your sins are forgiven"** (Mark 2:5).

How would you finish this phrase? *Jesus, if only I had _____, then I'd be happy.* Have you ever noticed that when you get the thing you think you want, another pops up in its place that keeps you from being content? The new job brings new stress. The longed-for spouse is only semi-perfect. You find retirement is not the key to fulfilment. You are free from cancer, but there is still something that nags at happiness.

Do you want to know what it is? Sin. The source of all your troubles is not outside of you but inside. Jesus sees that. He sees the sin that no one knows about but you can't forget. He sees the sin that paralyzes you from getting up and really living life. Jesus sees your real suffering. You come to him with a million wishes, but he loves you too much to grant all those. Instead, he gives you better. Whatever it is, take it to Jesus. He took care of your greatest need. He suffered the cross so he could say to you, "My child, your sins are forgiven."

Inadequate coverage
Liz Schroeder

I'm an average-sized person, but when I use a pool towel at one of those "budget friendly" hotels, I have to wonder if the staff gave me a washcloth by mistake. It barely covers one hip! It takes at least four minimalist towelettes to provide any real coverage, and that requires the use of both my hands and some creative tucking.

I am so glad God doesn't bestow forgiveness the way stingy hotels dole out pool towels. When I attempt to conceal my sin, it's even less effective than a washcloth trying to hide an adult human body. However, God's robe of righteousness—won with the blood of his Son, Jesus—covers me from head to toe.

King David wrote, **"Blessed is the one whose transgressions are forgiven, whose sins are covered"** (Psalm 32:1). David knew a thing or two about trying to hide sins. He tried to keep his affair with Bathsheba and the murder of her husband under wraps, and the secret nearly killed him. **"When I kept silent, my bones wasted away through my groaning all day long. For day and night your hand was heavy on me; my strength was sapped as in the heat of summer"** (verses 3,4). When the prophet Nathan confronted David with his sin, David confessed, and he couldn't contain his relief.

Exposing your sins can be scary. You might feel naked and vulnerable. Forget trying to cover up your sins yourself. Jesus is here to wrap you in the luxurious robe of his righteousness.

Lessons from Barry
Jason Nelson

I'm learning a lot from my friend Barry. He's a native New Yorker and very devoted to his Jewish faith and heritage. He and his wife have led interesting lives and have been very successful. They enjoy helping others and have felt the slap of anti-Semitism personally. In the context of current events, they asked me to explain some things about Christianity that they didn't understand. I was **"prepared to give an answer to everyone who asks you to give the reason for the hope that you have"** (1 Peter 3:15). I pointed to Jesus as the Messiah in the prophecies Barry and his wife already knew.

Barry showed me the symbol on packages that certifies a food product is *parve*, which means it is kosher because it assures it was not prepared mixing milk with meat (see Deuteronomy 14:21). When they asked my wife and me over for dinner, he said, "I assume you say grace before you eat." I said, "We do." He asked me to offer a prayer and then said he would say one after I did. I prayed in Jesus' name, and he said a prayer in Yiddish that I asked him to translate. He thanked God for the food we were about to eat. When we hosted dinner, we made sure the food we served was *parve* out of respect for them.

This is unfamiliar territory for this old dog. But my life has been enriched because I made a new friend. I hope Barry can say the same.

Confused by your suffering?

Mike Novotny

If you've ever questioned God because of your pain, listen to what Jesus said in John 15: **"I am the true vine, and my Father is the gardener. He cuts off every branch in me that bears no fruit, while every branch that does bear fruit he prunes so that it will be even more fruitful"** (verses 1,2).

If branches could talk, I imagine they would accuse gardeners of assault. Gardeners snip and chop and take away, leaving branches with open wounds. But Jesus reminds us what every good gardener knows—that pruning produces more fruit. In fact, a friend of mine who owns a vineyard says that the biggest mistake grape growers make is not pruning their vines enough!

That's essential to remember when suffering leaves you confused. If God's goal for you is the "fruit" of faith, pruning makes complete sense. Sometimes if all you have is success, you end up arrogant. Sometimes if you've never suffered, it's hard to feel compassion or sympathy for people in pain. Sometimes you have to go through the fire before you have something valuable to say to people who are in the fire.

So even if you can't see the fruit just yet, don't be confused by your pain. God is pruning you, not punishing you, taking away your health, your dreams, your plans for the future for the sake of a greater future. In all things God is working for your good. Believe that and you won't be confused. You'll be more fruitful than ever before.

Short but sweet
Andrea Delwiche

Twenty-nine words; that's the entirety of Psalm 117. Frankly, it's so short and so like other psalms that we might brush past it without contemplating what the words ask of us and the claim they make.

"Praise the Lord, all you nations; extol him, all you peoples. For great is his love toward us, and the faithfulness of the Lord endures forever. Praise the Lord" (verses 1,2).

What if we ask the Holy Spirit to help us let this psalm sink in? What comes up if we quiet our minds and focus on it?

"Praise the Lord . . . extol him . . . for great is his love toward us." Where does God's *great love* show itself in your life? What blessings can you picture? What small miracles of life have you witnessed this week?

Perhaps it's helpful to jot down a list—something tangible and visible to help you remember.

"Praise the Lord . . . extol him. . . . The faithfulness of the Lord endures forever." How is God's faithfulness obvious to you? Are you perhaps struggling to name ways in which God's faithfulness leaves footprints in your life?

This psalm invites us to join with all God's people to praise him. If this seems impossible in your current circumstance, that's okay. God is with you in the struggle as well as in times of praise. Cling to God with your questions, and ask the Holy Spirit to bring glimmers of understanding and trust to still your soul.

The last word

Jan Gompper

I recently watched a national news anchor interview a potential presidential candidate. The news commentator iterated to the presidential hopeful a laundry list of all the things he's worried about in our country. China, rising inflation, foreign wars, national debt, energy independence, border issues, and woke agendas were among the things that were keeping him up at night.

The soothing balm for all his worries seemed to lie in political change—namely, a new president.

Granted, who sits in the White House *can* help effect change, but whether that change is for the "better" is a matter of what lenses we wear, isn't it? Our past indoctrinations and biases are embedded in our preconceptions, so much so that it's difficult, if not impossible, for any of us to see the future clearly.

But you know who can? God. He has known what will happen in our world, our country, and our lives from day one, and **"nothing and no one can upset [his] plans"** (Job 42:2 MSG).

This doesn't mean we shouldn't go to the polls, but it does mean that we don't need to throw up our hands in despair if we don't like the outcome. Rather, we'd do better to reach our hands up in prayer, confidently trusting in God's all-knowing leadership.

Don't lose sleep. **"Mortals make elaborate plans, but God has the last word"** (Proverbs 16:1 MSG).

Open your eyes
Clark Schultz

There's a story about a man who waited on the roof of his house during a flood. The waters kept rising, and he waited so long that he drowned. This happened after a boat, a helicopter, and more tried to save him, but he refused each attempt, saying, "I'm waiting for a sign from God."

Once in heaven, the man questioned God, "Why didn't you save me?"

God replied, "I sent a boat, a helicopter, and . . ."

Psalm 119:18 says, **"Open my eyes that I may see."** What signs are you and I ignoring? A friend confides in you that his marriage is in danger of unfaithfulness, and yet he goes right back to texting/meeting that non-spouse for the thrill. The near sideswipe of a car on a snowy road jump-starts your heart, but within two miles or less you're back to texting and driving. The promiscuous couple at school flaunt their ways, and soon a pregnancy is announced.

The problem with wake-up calls is NOT the call; it's when we ignore or hit snooze on them, thinking they aren't meant for us. We can laugh about the guy on the roof, but we are no different. If you're reading this and you've erred, take comfort that God has forgiven you. If you are a person who needs a wake-up call, listen to the sound advice from the family and friends God has put in your life. Finally, God bless those who do get us to open our eyes and turn to Jesus.

Jesus' love is for anyone . . . that's you!
David Scharf

The Bible says something touching just before Jesus feeds a crowd of five thousand people: **"He had compassion on them, because they were like sheep without a shepherd. So he began teaching them many things"** (Mark 6:34). Jesus gave the people what they needed most: his Word to feed their souls. Then with five small loaves of bread and two fish, he gave them what their bodies needed: food. What a miracle!

It's what God does for the world every day, including what we need most. He provides for our souls. He gave his Son to die on a cross to pay for the sins of the whole world! Yes, Jesus' love is for you, but it's also for *everyone* and *anyone.*

I love the word *anyone,* especially when my wife says it. My weakness is chips. When my wife gets home from the store, my eyes sift through the bags until I see that bright orange Doritos bag. My eyes get big, but I've learned to wait to open the bag until Beth gives clearance. "Who is it for?" I ask. She might break my heart. "It's for taco salad for the party tomorrow. Don't touch it!" Or, "I want to use it in the kids' lunches. Stay away." Or she might throw open the door of delight and say, "Anyone." And since I qualify as "anyone," those Doritos are for me! What's the point? Jesus is for anyone . . . that includes you!

The cautionary tale of Stan the stick
Mike Novotny

Once upon a time, Stan the branch was stuck on the trunk of a thick oak tree. Stan's leaves were beautiful, but sometimes as he looked down on the world, he wondered what it would be like to go wherever and do whatever he wanted. That's why when a fierce wind whipped through the air, Stan leaned into it until—snap!—he broke free from the trunk. He dropped into a soft bed of green grass and laughed as the wind rolled him to places he had never been before. That night Stan fell asleep in his plush bed with stars twinkling overhead. It felt thrilling to be free.

But in the morning, Stan felt . . . dry. Thirsty. Weak. Days passed, and the thirst got worse. His back tightened up, and his fingers turned brittle. One day a man walked up to Stan and saw not a branch but a dried up, leafless stick, good for little else than to be burned in a fire.

Jesus, full of truth and love, told a similar story to his friends: **"If you do not remain in me, you are like a branch that is thrown away and withers; such branches are picked up, thrown into the fire and burned. . . . Now remain in my love"** (John 15:6,9). Branches are not independent beings. They die in their independence. We do too. That's why Jesus wants you to remain in his love, in his Word, to stick now and forever to his unchanging truth.

Please don't become a stick. Instead, stick with Jesus!

A spiritual routine
Katrina Harrmann

My youngest child recently got her driver's permit. For her first drive, we deliberately picked the biggest, most empty parking lot we could find. It was perfectly safe. But as she sat behind the wheel and attempted to tap the gas for the first time, she hadn't even reached 1 mph before she engaged the brake. She curled her hands up over her eyes and moaned, "Ahh! I can't do this! I'm gonna kill someone!"

And yet, the very next day, she had her first official driving lesson with an instructor and confidently walked into the kitchen afterward and announced, "I'm a *REALLY* good driver!"

What a difference a day makes.

Sometimes repetition is all it takes for us to improve—or at least to FEEL really confident about doing new things, which is almost just as important. Repetition is often the key to *significant* improvement.

Now think about your spiritual life. If you're like me, I often forget to nurture this relationship on a consistent basis. Sometimes I go whole seasons neglecting my relationship with God.

How much better would we be at prayer or devotions or trusting God if we checked in daily? Imagine the confidence that would instill in us as Christians! The assuredness! Perhaps we'd even begin to witness and more readily pray for others.

Let's pray that the Spirit would encourage us in the daily routine of spirituality. **"Come near to God and he will come near to you"** (James 4:8).

God leaves room for faith
Nathan Nass

The Bible tells us that faith is being sure of what we cannot see. So do you know what God often does? He hides himself. He hides his blessings in the most un-likely places, where we'd never expect to find them. Why? God leaves room for faith.

Take Abraham, for example. God promised Abraham that he would have a son. Great, right? Except it didn't happen. For years. For decades. Abraham waited year after year. What was God doing? Why was God taking so long? Had God stopped caring?

No. God left room for faith. The longer God waited, the more God hid himself, the more Abraham had to rely solely on the Word of God, and the more his faith grew. The Bible says, **"Abram believed the Lord, and he cred-ited it to him as righteousness"** (Genesis 15:6).

If Abraham was going to be saved, there was only one way: by faith. Just like if you and I are going to be saved, there's only one way: by faith in Jesus Christ. If we're go-ing to be righteous, there's only one way: by faith in Jesus.

So don't be surprised when God leaves room for faith in your life. Don't be surprised when God's promises seem hidden behind silence or trial. What is faith? Being sure of what we cannot see. Trust in God's promises. We have a God who loves to leave room in our lives for faith.

Owen rocks!
Jason Nelson

My little grandson Owen has a way about him that commands attention. He's not naughty. He's just cute. For instance, his favorite Christmas song is "Jingle Bell Rock." With his deep voice and adorable speech, he orders it up. *"Awexa, play jingle bell wock."* Alexa obeys; Owen sings right along and—yes—he rocks.

Jesus showed us how to respond to little boys like Owen. He showed us how to value all children. He took them in his arms and blessed them (Mark 10:16). That can be our prayer as parents and grandparents: "Lord Jesus, please take our little ones in your arms and bless them."

This world will never be a perfect place. But I pray it can be a better place for Owen. Maybe in years gone by I wasn't paying attention, but I don't remember the threat level for children being as high as it seems now. It's not just crossing the street that puts kids at risk, but danger enters our homes in too many ways. The survival skills children are forced to learn at an early age shatter their innocence and breed anxiety in their tender souls. All the noise they hear and images they see frighten them. And there is nothing they can do about it. But we can. And we must.

A starting point is placing them regularly in the arms of Jesus. Bringing his love and teachings into our homes is the blessing they need now more than ever.

Light in dark places
Andrea Delwiche

Important words sometimes lose their freshness and impact when they become overly familiar. We stop paying attention to or taking joy in the thoughts and emotions expressed.

Think about a question we ask or respond to out of habit: *How are you?* How about the most crucial words of all: *I love you?*

Even favorite Scripture grows stale, and we need to contemplate it again: **"Your word is a lamp for my feet, a light on my path"** (Psalm 119:105).

Scripture's word pictures flowed from their author's lived experiences. Led by the Holy Spirit, they wrote as they wrestled with their daily lives. Whoever wrote *these* words perhaps first had the idea as they navigated the pitch-black darkness of a long-ago Middle Eastern night.

I'm thinking about a Wisconsin campground where my family and I have camped. After dark we rely on electric lamps, less than two feet off the ground, to keep us out of the weeds and gopher holes and on the firm, packed path. Yet sometimes in that dark countryside, I've been able to walk just by the light of God's stars.

When have you benefitted from lights in dark places? When have the dark paths of your daily life been illuminated by God's words and guidance?

Are there ways to rely on the light of God's kingdom wisdom more than you currently do? What if you stopped fearing the darkness of uncertainty and trusted that Jesus' teachings would light your uneven foot path and bring you unexpected, well-lit surprises in your daily life?

Grace brings you from the back to the front

Nathan Nass

My wife and I once purchased tickets to a magic show. As we usually do, we bought the very cheapest tickets in the back row of the theater. When we got to the theater, however, we were in for a surprise. The usher looked at our tickets and said, "How would you like a better seat?" Then she ushered us down to the very front row. We got to watch the show front and center, right at the feet of the magician.

Grace brings you from the back to the front.

When that happened, I couldn't help but think of God's grace—God's undeserved love—for us. We didn't deserve to sit in the front row. We hadn't paid nearly enough to earn it. It was given to us freely, as a gift. Like God's grace. In his undeserved love for us, God takes us from the back and brings us to the front. He takes sinners, forgives us through Jesus' death on a cross, and gives us eternal life in heaven. He takes sinners, washes us through the power of Baptism, and makes us into the children of God.

The apostle Paul learned to say, **"But by the grace of God I am what I am"** (1 Corinthians 15:10). Isn't that the truth for you and me too? Grace brings you from the back to the front. Thank you, Jesus!

The arc of history
Jason Nelson

Dr. Martin Luther King Jr. is credited with saying that the arc of the universe bends toward justice. I think that's true because God is perpetually bending the arc of history toward himself. But it takes a long, sometimes very long, view of history to have that confidence. The arc of history doesn't bend without resistance from forces of evil no matter how much pressure God is putting on it. But it will bend justly under the influence of courageous doers of good.

A student of history can name notable instances where justice has been realized in the story of humanity. That is why we can have hope that better days are always coming. Good eventually wins because God is good and wants the best for his dearly loved children.

It follows that the arc of history also bends toward reconciliation between his dearly loved but wayward children and himself. There was that moment **"when the set time had fully come, God sent his Son, born of a woman, born under the law"** (Galatians 4:4). So we measure the sweep of the arc in terms of ages before that moment to the ages after it.

It was in that moment **"that God was reconciling the world to himself in Christ, not counting people's sins against them."** Ever since, all believers in Jesus have a distinct role in history. **"He has committed to us the message of reconciliation"** (2 Corinthians 5:19). May we embrace our place in history.

God's system is best
Mike Novotny

Our gut reaction, especially if we are Americans, is to hate submission. When the Bible commands, **"Submit yourselves for the Lord's sake to every human authority"** (1 Peter 2:13), we cringe.

But we shouldn't. According to my dictionary, the word *submit* simply means "to yield to the authority or will of another person." That idea—yielding—isn't cringeworthy. It's wise.

Think of that flashing yellow arrow that tells drivers in the turn lane to yield to the traffic in the oncoming lanes. Does that offend you? I would guess not. Does that flashing arrow imply that you are an inferior driver? Not even close. Yielding is a way to avoid confusion and destruction. It's a submission-based system that tells certain people to put others first so everyone can remain safe.

Our wise Father in heaven has ordered his world the same way. He knows that a submission-less, always-trying-to-get-my-way world would be filled with relational wreckage. If we all expected everyone else to hit the brakes so we could do what we wanted, families, churches, and nations would implode! Some, sadly, do.

That's why God sets up a system of submission in society, in the home, and in the church. He commands those in authority to lead with love, humility, and justice. He commands those under authority to yield to the final decision instead of insisting on getting their way.

As challenging as it can be, I see the wisdom of God's system. Are you starting to appreciate submission too?

Competition or cooperation
Matt Ewart

The following two statements are true:

Possessions are a blessing from God. Possessions are a burden to manage.

Abraham and his nephew Lot had made a community together. Their families, livestock, and workers lived side by side. And God blessed them.

He blessed them so much that their blessings became a burden to manage. Worker arguments began to erupt as they competed over food and water for their animals. And then: **"Their possessions were so great that they were not able to stay together"** (Genesis 13:6).

If God has blessed you with many possessions, you know the burden that Abraham and Lot were carrying. They were trying to maintain their relationship while also maintaining their empires. In the end, they had to part ways because no space was big enough for them both. Even if God hasn't blessed you with a surplus, you know the competition that can erupt when someone else's stuff crosses your side of the fence.

Whether God has blessed you with much or with little, he has created a space big enough where all can come together and be one in full cooperation without any competition. He calls this his church. It's where the message of sin shows how all stand condemned before God. And it's where the message of grace shows how that condemnation was placed on Jesus instead of us.

Set aside the competition today. Reach out in cooperation to help a fellow soul for whom Jesus died.

Adultery? Don't!

Mike Novotny

Of the 55 uses of the word *adultery* in the Bible, the very first one that shows up is this: **"You shall not commit adultery"** (Exodus 20:14). Our Father is that blunt for a reason. Even though an affair can feel like a lifeline for a spouse stuck in an unhappy marriage, breaking your vow will not lead to life but instead to death.

In 1941 a woman from the Soviet Union was put in a Nazi concentration camp where she witnessed murders, lost family members, and endured Hitler's horrors. But she survived, got married, and sadly was cheated on. And this Holocaust survivor said that the affair was the most painful experience of her life.

Maybe you or someone you know is aching for love, attention, or affection. If so, please remember that adultery butchers God's blessings. It takes the "one flesh" of marriage and rips it in two. Committing adultery, as one author says, is like hosting a picnic with the people you love on an interstate. Eventually your sin will smash into your life like a cement truck, and the carnage will take years to heal.

If you have committed adultery, run to Jesus for salvation (John 8:11). If the thought has only crossed your mind, run to Jesus for protection. Plead with him, "Lead me not into temptation!" That's a prayer he loves to answer with strength and self-control.

How adultery happens
Mike Novotny

Few Christians see themselves as the kind of people who would commit adultery. Yet it happens.

Here's a common pattern: First, deprivation. A spouse feels deprived of love/respect/attention/intimacy at home. Second, attraction. The deprived spouse notices someone and is drawn to them. Third, intention. You make an intentional effort to be with/impress the person you're attracted to. You stop by the party that he'll be at. You dress up for the Zoom call she is on. Fourth, emotion. You share emotional, personal, and vulnerable things with the object of your attraction, often about your own struggling marriage. Finally, connection. You physically connect. A touch, a hug, which rushes into something much more.

In his famous teaching on adultery and lust, Jesus said, **"If your right eye causes you to stumble, gouge it out and throw it away. It is better for you to lose one part of your body than for your whole body to be thrown into hell"** (Matthew 5:29). Jesus' point? It's better to take a drastic step now than end up with a devastating ending then.

Maybe God has you reading these words for a reason. You haven't cheated, but you see yourself in that pattern. You haven't physically connected, but you are definitely attracted and intentional about crossing paths with a particular person. Consider this devotion your warning from God before it is too late. Do whatever you need to do to avoid the catastrophe of adultery.

How to heal from infidelity
Mike Novotny

I interviewed a number of couples from my church that had been through and healed from an affair. I then developed an equation to describe how healing happens: Healing = Time x Work x Work.

Time—Adultery is like getting hit by a bus. There's no shortcut to getting back on your feet. You can work on yourselves and work with a professional counselor, but if time equals almost zero, your healing will be minimal. Many experts suggest that one to two years are needed for most couples to start to trust each other and feel hopeful about the future.

Work—The one who cheated must work. In 4,000 different ways, you will have to be humble. Like telling the whole truth. And talking when he wants to talk (even if you'd rather not). And giving her the passwords to all your accounts (even if it feels intrusive). And accepting a break from intimacy for the time being. You must do the holy work of humility.

Work—And the one cheated on must work too. Work to forgive, to serve, not to use the sin as an excuse for your own sin. 1,000 x 1,000 x 0 = 0, a reminder that the work you do matters too.

While you work and wait, you can walk with God. His grace will save you when you feel unforgivable or unworthy. His strength will sustain you when you feel like you can't do it another day. **"The Lord is my shepherd, I lack nothing"** (Psalm 23:1). Nothing. Even while healing from adultery.

Hope after an affair
Mike Novotny

I sat down with a woman a few years after her husband's affair. After recounting the pain and struggle, she told me about the healing and positive changes she had seen in her husband. Then I asked another couple this dangerous question: "Can you see any ways that the affair has made you stronger or closer than before?" He said, "Pretty much all of it." She added, "He really, really wants to bring joy to me. And we really didn't have that before." Then I heard a similar story from another couple. They both went from complacent, lazy, me-first spouses to attentive, loving, you-first partners. These people are proof that there's hope after an affair.

I know it doesn't always happen that way. Jesus was honest about adultery's ability to divide the "one flesh" that was made in marriage (Matthew 19:6). Sometimes the trust doesn't return, and it is okay for a Christian to walk away. But I also know that when Jesus is at the center of it, when friends and family give grace and truth, when two people work and wait, miracles can happen. As an angel once said to a virgin who saw zero possibility of being a mother: **"For no word from God will ever fail"** (Luke 1:37).

Your almighty Father can bring beauty from these ashes. Maybe not today and maybe not tomorrow, but he can restore what sin has broken. Pray that every couple reeling from an affair can fix their eyes on the only One capable of doing impossible things.

FEBRUARY

Now these three remain: faith, hope and love.
But the greatest of these is love.

1 Corinthians 13:13

The real problem with submission
Mike Novotny

Why do so many people hate the biblical idea of submission? Perhaps because authority can be awful. If you have suffered under the abusive authority of a corrupt government, a monstrous husband, or a pastor with selfish motives, I can understand how triggering the passages on submission must be.

But—can we be honest?—much of the time the real problem is not a dictator or an abuser or a pastor who is a monster. The problem is that we just don't want to submit. Paul explained, **"The mind governed by the flesh is hostile to God; it does not submit to God's law, nor can it do so"** (Romans 8:7). The flesh is that selfish part of us. When it governs our minds, it never hits the brakes. It does not submit to what God says. It cannot.

Isn't that often the real issue? You would submit to God, but he tells you to be nice to the most annoying person you know. You would submit to the government, but they tell you to report all your income. You would submit to your husband or your pastor, but they aren't using their God-given authority to do what you want.

One of the vital purposes of God's commands is to help us see our own sin. As painful as the call to submit can be, we can be thankful that it immediately exposes the ugliest part of us, prompting us to repent and pointing us to Jesus as our only hope of salvation.

Stand firm in Jesus
Clark Schultz

I recently had the opportunity to go on a police ride along. I was amazed to find that the time in the squad car was a series of highs and lows. One minute we were like people passing time on a road trip, counting cars with heavy eyelids. Then in the blink of an eye, the lights were flashing and we were racing down a highway at 90-plus miles per hour with hearts pumping. The ride along was a mix of chasing shoplifters up a snowy hill to knocking on the doors of a senior living facility to assure all were safe. Once our hearts and blood pressure came back to a reasonable level, we were back to the quieter activity of sitting in a day care parking lot as a symbol of peace and assurance to those parents picking up their precious cargo.

What a picture of life—the constant highs and lows! One minute we're in moments of life that are quiet, trying to stay awake. Boom! Then there's a death, a family crisis, an argument at work that causes our hearts to pump wildly. During these highs and lows of life, Paul encourages us, **"Be on your guard; stand firm in the faith; be courageous; be strong"** (1 Corinthians 16:13). We can stand on more than our cell phones, our reputations, or our wealth; all that is temporary and shifting. Instead, we stand on Jesus. We focus on his protection and service, and we enjoy the ride!

Jesus is *the* way
Mike Novotny

Recently, I took my first-ever hike through the beautiful desert of southern Arizona. Think prickly pear and towering saguaro cacti, multicolored mountains, and a Wisconsin boy escaping the March snow of his native land for the southwestern sun. There was only one problem—I got lost. Apparently, I left the official hiking trail and ended up in a thick mix of pokey plants and burrowed holes that looked like venomous snakes might be hiding within them. Oops.

It turns out that not every way is a good way. In fact, some ways are downright dangerous. This is what Jesus meant when he said, **"I am the way"** (John 14:6). Jesus made it simple, declaring himself to be the one and only way to a relationship with God.

Lose sight of Jesus and you'll get lost in thoughts of your own worthiness—am I really good enough to go to a better place like heaven? Deviate from the path of his promises and you'll put yourself in danger of that ancient serpent, the devil, who will strike with the venomous accusation of your failures (there are plenty). But stick to *the* way, that is, believe in Jesus, and you will be safe.

Your heavenly Father wants you to know, beyond a shadow of a doubt, that you are heaven bound. He wants to free you today from fearing anything in your future. That's why he sent his Son to show you the way.

Lamb over me

Daron Lindemann

I was studying the Bible with a Chinese friend at our church. We were looking at the word *righteousness*, and one of the Bible verses was this: **"Look, the Lamb of God, who takes away the sin of the world!"** (John 1:29).

Jesus is the Lamb of God, whose innocent blood was shed on a cross as the perfect sacrifice for us. His righteousness becomes ours in Baptism and remains ours by faith forever.

My friend's face lit up. With big, bright eyes, he grabbed his pen and started drawing for me. Chinese characters took shape on the paper. Two of them, one above the other.

He pointed to the bottom Chinese character and said that it means "me." He pointed to the top one and informed me that it means "lamb." Then he announced, "This is the ancient Chinese word for righteousness."

Lamb over me. Right with God because of Jesus.

Have you seen the insightfully theological and delightfully playful poem by Marv and Marbeth Rosenthal called "Mary Had the Little Lamb"? I've used it a few times to help people connect the dots of Jesus' saving works. Search for it online. Share it with a friend. Here are a few lines:

Mary had the little Lamb, obedient Son of God;
Everywhere the Father led, His feet were sure to trod.
(John 6:38)
Mary had the little Lamb, crucified on the tree.
The rejected Son of God, He died to set us free.
(1 Peter 1:19)

The shadow of death
Katrina Harrmann

Here's a funny question: Would you rather get hit by a boulder or the shadow of a boulder?

It really doesn't take a master's degree in physics to figure out which would be easier to survive. I can't imagine Indiana Jones in his iconic boulder chase scene trying to evade a mere shadow. After all, the one might weigh 5 tons and crush the life out of you, while the other is made of darkness and air and wouldn't even cause a puff of wind against your skin.

Shadows are funny things. They are a loose interpretation of the things that are casting them but much less substantial, threatening, or able to inflict any kind of damage.

Here's another question: Would you rather experience death or the shadow of death?

In Psalm 23, King David wrote, **"Even though I walk through the valley of the shadow of death, I will fear no evil, for you are with me"** (verse 4 ESV).

Jesus defeated Death once and for all. Death with a capital *D*. The main event. Because he has done this mighty thing, we only need to walk through the shadow of death. Because death doesn't get to win. Ever. It doesn't get the final say because of what our Lord has done.

Yes, our earthly bodies WILL die, but then . . . BUT THEN! We enter the perfect life of heaven. The valley of the shadow of death holds no final power over us. It has been reduced to a shadow. Thanks be to God!

Failing to be somebody
Matt Ewart

The desire to be a somebody can lead people to do crazy things.

I will spare you my own foolish stories from high school. Thankfully the Bible is full of examples. Leah and Rachel were sisters. They shared more than the same set of parents. They also shared a husband, Jacob. But when Leah gave birth to four children and Rachel gave birth to none, Rachel began feeling like a nobody. So she did what nobodies do.

She got desperate.

She had her female servant sleep with Jacob. When the servant became pregnant and gave birth to a son, Rachel said, **"God has vindicated me; he has listened to my plea and given me a son"** (Genesis 30:6).

She wanted to give her husband a son, and she found a way to do it. The irritating part is that she interpreted her "success" as a sign that God approved of her method.

That's the funny thing about success. It can fool you into thinking you're somebody that you're not.

Success is way overrated. God celebrates our failures when failures are the result of doing the right thing for the right reason.

You don't need success to be a somebody. When Jesus died, it seemed like he had failed to establish the kingdom he had talked about so much. But it was through this "failure" that God succeeded in changing you from a nobody to a somebody who belongs with him.

Care to the last detail
David Scharf

His baby was sick. In fact, she was dying. Those of you who have gone through something like this know there is no greater pain. You would do anything and everything to help your child. Jairus, the synagogue ruler, knew where to go. He approached Jesus through the crowd and cried out, "Hurry! My little girl is dying! You have to come." So Jesus went. Jairus' daughter was already dead, but that didn't stop Jesus. **"Little girl, I say to you, get up!"** (Mark 5:41). And she did! As incredible as that is, I want to focus on a different aspect of the story. It's what happened after.

After raising Jairus' daughter from the dead, the Bible includes the most beautiful little line: Jesus told them **"to give her something to eat"** (Mark 5:43). Isn't that beautiful? Don't you think her parents knew to feed their daughter? Of course, but Jesus wanted to ensure she had EVERYTHING she needed.

Jesus cares for you down to the last detail. Do you feel like there are some things too small for his attention? Your Savior, who hung on a cross to win salvation for the world but also just for you, is not just concerned with the "big things" or the "important people." The one nobody notices, Jesus notices in the least detail. What a comfort. He cares for you down to the last detail!

We need Jesus
Clark Schultz

A daily ritual in our home is that Dad makes breakfast. Occasionally, number-three son (yes, I grew up watching Charlie Chan) asks, "Dad, can I help you?"

I do not "need" his help. In fact, it takes longer and can be more of a mess with five-year-old fingers assisting in the pancake-making process. However, to give my son a tablespoon of self-worth along with a cup of confidence, I answer, "Yes, I need your help."

"Go to the village . . . you will find a donkey tied there, with her colt by her. Untie them and bring them to me. If anyone says anything to you, say that the Lord needs them" (Matthew 21:2,3). Jesus *did not* need the disciples or *need* a donkey. He's God. He could have ridden into town on Seabiscuit. But like the breakfast analogy above, he wanted to give his disciples a cup of confidence that he was here to fulfill *all* prophecy. What's awesome to see is that the disciples obeyed Jesus' command.

Jesus asks us to do the same with his commands. At times we've made more than a mess in the kitchen of our lives: "God I *need* this (insert earthly treasure that will fade here) to keep me happy." Sometimes God allows a mess to happen, to show us *we need him.*

We have nothing if we don't have God. But with him we have more than we need. Grab the syrup or applesauce and chew on that thought!

God's forgiveness is limitless
Mike Novotny

Biblical forgiveness is not like the express checkout at your local grocery store—maximum 15 items. Instead, God calls you to forgive and forgive and forgive and forgive, followed by more forgiveness, after which comes additional forgiveness, which . . . well, you get the point. Biblical forgiveness is without limit.

Peter had an express-lane mentality when he asked, **"'Lord, how many times shall I forgive my brother or sister who sins against me? Up to seven times?' Jesus answered, 'I tell you, not seven times, but seventy-seven times'"** (Matthew 18:21,22). There is some debate whether Jesus' original words should be translated "77" or "70 times 7," but the point of Jesus' hyperbole is the same: "Peter, stop counting. Just keep forgiving."

We might give a sinner a second chance or a third strike, but God pushes us to forgive much, much more. Vengeance is never a Christian option, no matter how serial the sinner. The day will never come when God says, "*Now* you can get them back!"

Why would Jesus push us to such extremes? Because his forgiveness for us would be just as extreme. At the cross, Jesus didn't cover your first 7 sins or your first 77 sins but instead removed every last trace of your sinfulness. Even that sin you have struggled with your whole life. Even that habit you hate but so often find yourself flirting with. The blood of Jesus covers a multitude of sins!

Thank God for the limitless forgiveness of our Savior!

Foolish convenience
Matt Ewart

Jesus told a parable about ten virgins who were part of a wedding celebration. Because the celebration went past sundown, they needed to bring lamps both to light their way and so others could see who they were. But Jesus noted that five of them were foolish, and here's why: **"The foolish ones took their lamps but did not take any oil with them"** (Matthew 25:3).

Because they had no extra oil with them, their lamps went out, and they weren't allowed into the party.

Good thing we'd never do something that foolish, right? Hold on. The point is that there's a fool in all of us.

Extra oil would have been inconvenient. It would have been another thing to plan out and carry along. So they settled for what was convenient.

As you seek to reflect God's love in your life, do you settle for what is convenient? You are willing to wait . . . but only for so long. You are willing to give . . . but only if you get back. You are willing to love . . . but only if it is appreciated.

Jesus set aside all convenience for you. He willingly gave everything to make you fit for God's presence. It was inconvenient for him to say the least, but to him, you were worth it.

So today, see if you can do one thing to reflect the lavish love that Jesus showed you. You may have to go out of your way, but the inconvenience will be worth it.

Work is not a four-letter word
Liz Schroeder

If you have time off from work or school, maybe you aren't too eager to return. You sigh as you take a shower and swing by Starbucks on the way to your fully furnished office. I feel your First World pain.

Instead of working for the weekend or hanging on until the next vacation, what if there were a better way?

"Whatever you do, work at it with all your heart, as working for the Lord, not for human masters" (Colossians 3:23).

The late Pastor Timothy Keller left behind a treasure trove of teachings on the gift of work. Chew on this quote from one of his sermons: "Work is a gracious expression of creative energy in the service of others."*

When you hear *gracious expression*, think of a spring-fed river. The love God has shown to us through Jesus bubbles out of this spring and overflows to feed plants and bring forth life. We're not designed to be reservoirs; our work gives us an outlet for the geyser of grace we have received.

Because we were created in the image of our Creator-God, we have an abundance of *creative energy*. Work is an outlet for this creative energy.

Finally, our work is to be *in the service of others*. Far from a four-letter word, work has been redeemed and elevated as we serve the Lord instead of ourselves.

* Timothy Keller, "Work and Calling," July 7, 1996, Gospel in Life and Redeemer Presbyterian Church of New York, https://podcast .gospelinlife.com/e/work-and-calling/.

When life goes wrong
Mike Novotny

If you're like most humans, most of your emotions are connected to five "f words": *family, friends, finances, fitness* (physical health), and *faith*. When something goes wrong in one or more of those five areas—a sick father, a stressed friendship, an unexpected car repair, breast cancer, a struggle with trusting God—it's easy for joy to move out and trouble to take up residence in your heart.

This is why Jesus looks you in the eyes and says, **"Do not let your hearts be troubled. You believe in God; believe also in me"** (John 14:1). "You believe in God," Jesus reminds us. "You aren't atheists. You believe that God exists, that God cares, that God controls all things. You aren't unbelievers who have to sit around and hope it gets better. No, you believe in God; believe also in me."

The phrase Jesus uses here in the original Greek of the Bible is interesting. The word "in" from "believe in" has the idea of direction, like you're looking toward or at something. Jesus is saying, "You are people of faith, people who believe in God." So turn toward him. Look at him. Put your attention in his "direction."

In this world you will have many troubles, even with those five words that mean the world to you. When trouble comes, don't just sit there and take it. Instead, look in Jesus' direction and take heart, remembering that Jesus has overcome the world, your troubles included.

Hey, Dad! You awake?
Katrina Harrmann

My kids used to wake me up in the night when they were small. "Hey, Mom! You awake?" It was for a variety of things: They needed a glass of water, they had gotten sick, something looked scary in the darkness of their bedroom, they had a bad dream . . . the list goes on.

As a parent, you learn pretty quickly to develop an inner well of (mostly) inexhaustible patience. You get up. You soothe the child and clean up the mess or investigate the "monster" in the closet. You lay curled around your kid in their tiny twin bed while they calm down and fall back to sleep.

Only kids are bold enough to demand this kind of no-holds-barred attention in the dead of night, right? They ask, and they receive. Only kids have that kind of access to a parent's inexhaustible love and commitment.

Guess what? You're one of God's kids. So am I.

And here's the real gem: We have that kind of access to the Creator of the world. **"In him and through faith in him we may approach God with freedom and confidence"** (Ephesians 3:12).

We get to come to God with Every. Little. Problem. Every monster in our closet. Every thirst for water. Every little thing, big or small, real or imagined—we can wake him up with a nudge in the dead of night (not that he ever sleeps!): "Hey, Dad? You awake?"

And his answer? "Always." His arms open wide to calm and soothe us.

Jesus submitted for us
Mike Novotny

There is a beautiful, handmade cross that hangs over the entrance to my church's gathering place for worship. My friend Tom crafted it back in 2014 during a sermon series that attempted to redeem one of American's least favorite words—*submission*.

That cross is engraved with these words of Jesus: **"Not my will, but yours be done"** (Luke 22:42). Jesus, in this vital moment before his arrest, submitted. He expressed his desire (**"take this cup from me"**) but then yielded to the final decision of his Father. The New Testament later says, "[Jesus] **was heard because of his reverent submission"** (Hebrews 5:7).

Before we assume the worst about the "s-word," let's remember that you and I were saved through an act of submission. Jesus prepared a place for us in his Father's house by submitting. He accomplished his mission through submission, and the result was our salvation. For all those moments when we put ourselves first, Jesus put himself second. He didn't try to get his way, and now there is a way for us to spend forever with God.

You can't hate a word that saved you! You can't call it dirty if it made you clean. That is why the Holy Spirit was not ashamed to inspire the writers of the New Testament to write *submit* again and again and again. *Submission* is a beautiful Bible word. Looking at our selfless Savior, don't you agree?

The problem with being human
Mike Novotny

According to Jesus, the problem with being human is that humans are like sheep.

Sheep, despite all they offer our world (wool, milk, meat), have a fatal flaw—they can't conquer wolves. Even a varsity sheep can't outrun a JV wolf, and once caught, a sheep can't fight back. It has no bearlike claws or sharklike jaws. No protective scales or tail. Sheep without a shepherd are dead meat.

Some people make the mistake of thinking they don't need Jesus because they are, by comparison, pretty good people. That might be true, as true as some sheep being faster than others, but that doesn't deal with their/our fatal flaw. Without a Shepherd/Savior, we are dead meat. We are unable to fight back against the reality of our sin and the soon-to-come judgment of God. We don't have the perfection required to defend ourselves before the holiness of heaven.

But that is why we sheep love our Good Shepherd. Jesus affirmed, **"I am the good shepherd"** (John 10:14), and with those words he offered us his protection. A shepherd can fight back against a wolf, striking with staff, sling, and rod; Jesus fought back against our sin, conquering it with his life, his cross, his blood.

Our problem has a solution. His name is Jesus, our Good Shepherd and great Savior.

Badwater Basin
Nathan Nass

The lowest, hottest place in the United States is Death Valley National Park in California. At the lowest place in the valley, there is a pool of water. Try to imagine this: As you descend into the valley, all you see around you is dusty dry mountains, cracked earth, and rocks. It's a dead, barren desert. But there, down at the bottom, you see sunlight reflecting off a pool. Water! You almost want to run to it!

Except, you can't drink it. The water in that pool, just like the entire floor of Death Valley, is filled with salt. That's why the earliest explorers called it Badwater Basin. It looks so good from a distance, but it has nothing to offer a thirsty traveler.

That's how the Bible describes false teachers and their false promises. Peter writes, **"These people are springs without water"** (2 Peter 2:17). Have you learned this lesson yet? Sin looks good, but it never delivers. Sex, money, and power promise pleasure, but they lead to disaster. Like Badwater Basin.

There is only One who can truly fill you. There is only One who can truly quench your thirst for meaning and purpose in the desert of life. It's Jesus! He promises, **"Whoever drinks the water I give them will never thirst. Indeed, the water I give them will become in them a spring of water welling up to eternal life"** (John 4:14).

Watch out for Badwater Basins. You already have living water in Jesus!

A little taste of home
Andrea Delwiche

In Reagan International Airport, I unexpectedly ran into someone from home. Had we *been* at home, we would not have greeted each other in the way we did, with excited exclamations and hugs. People nearby smiled. They understood the joy of the familiar amid uncertainty.

Something similar seems to be at work in these words from Psalm 119:54: **"Your statutes have been my songs in the house of my sojourning"** (ESV). Another translation substitutes the word "pilgrimage" for "sojourning." Still another reads, "Your statutes have been my songs wherever I make my home."

God's *statutes*, the commands he's given to govern our lives, are *songs* to bring familiar comfort wherever we make our home. How?

Aren't our entire lives a traveling toward deeper understanding and following of God and his ways? As we grow as believers, God's ways provide unshakeable comfort even in strange or frightening stopovers.

Oftentimes God's statutes don't seem like songs that bring peace or like a little taste of home. Yes, we often turn away stubbornly from God. But some of us grew up with a picture of a vindictive God with arbitrary rules to catch or shame his creation. Perhaps we've never seen God as a loving Father whose guidelines suit our needs.

Sit with the Holy Spirit and ask for new insight, healing, and joy in your relationship with your good Father. What if you start praying that in unfamiliar places, God's guidelines would be a comfort of home, a welcome and familiar sight, and a favorite song to sing?

Hand in hand
Jan Gompper

Every Sunday, Bob and Alice walk hand in hand to our church's café counter to buy a single donut. Bob is 92. Alice is 87. They have been longtime members of our congregation.

Recently, they were asked to share their faith journeys at a church event. Bob's eyes twinkled as he expounded: "When we were first married, Alice and I held hands because we were so in love that we couldn't let go of each other. Later in our marriage, we held hands because if I let go, she'd go shopping. Now we hold hands because if we don't, one of us will fall down."

Obviously, his story got a big laugh, but it resonated on a spiritual level as well. King Solomon encouraged: **"Two are better than one, because they have a good return for their labor: If either of them falls down, one can help the other up. But pity anyone who falls and has no one to help them up"** (Ecclesiastes 4:9,10).

Solomon's words not only point to the value of being married; they also reinforce the importance of Christian community. Married or not, believers in Christ are to hold one another's spiritual hands as they continue on their faith journeys. Congregation members can pay particular attention to those who are single or widowed, making sure they do not fall with "no one to help them up."

Bob and Alice's story is a testament to their love and to their commitment to walking hand in hand with God. May we learn from their example.

100% saved
Mike Novotny

Imagine if you lived an average American life (77 years or 28,207 days) and you only had to be good 1% of the time to make it to heaven. By my math, 1% would be .77 years or 282 days. Think you could do it?

What if God forgave you for 99.9% of your sins and you only had to obey .1% of your life? That would be .077 years or 28.2 days. Love God and others perfectly for the month of February and you're in! You in?

Fine, what if God did 99.99% of the forgiving and you only had to do .01% of the loving? That would be 2.82 days. Love God and others perfectly Monday, Tuesday, and most of Wednesday and you're saved! Sound good?

If not, what if God did 99.999% of the forgiving and you only had to do .001%? That calculates to 6.8 hours. Just be perfectly patient, kind, trusting, believing, forgiving, gentle, joyful, and at peace for one day at school/one shift at work/one day at home with the kids and you get to be with God forever.

Isn't that crazy? Even if God did 99.999% of the work of forgiving you, it still wouldn't be enough.

That's why Jesus didn't do 99.999% of the work. He did it all. "[Jesus] **is the atoning sacrifice for our sins, and not only for ours but also for the sins of the whole world**" (1 John 2:2).

Thank God for giving us a Savior who did 100% of the saving. That's what makes the gospel such incredibly good news.

Unwind or rewind
Matt Ewart

Picture it's the end of a long day. In addition to being a long day, it has also been a long week. You have no responsibilities tomorrow—you don't even need to take a shower if you don't want to. What do you do? The phrase I hear in my mind is this: *Time to unwind.*

Unwinding is a perfectly fine thing to do. It implies that you have been "wound up" for a while, going full pace to accomplish what needed to be accomplished. Rest is a welcome thought, so it is time to unwind.

Just be aware of how you unwind.

Rest is not an excuse to let loose. The recognition that you've done a lot of hard work does not justify slipping into what the Bible refers to as "darkness."

"Have nothing to do with the fruitless deeds of darkness, but rather expose them" (Ephesians 5:11).

After professional athletes do an intense workout, they do not consume a ton of junk food and say, "I need to unwind." They rest in a way that restores their bodies because what happens after the hard work is just as important as the hard work.

The same is true of you. God has an incredible purpose for you, and it is more important than any professional athlete. You get to be his ambassador and reflect his love.

Rest is not just an opportunity to unwind. It is an opportunity to rewind and be ready for what God has prepared for your tomorrow.

Number our days
Liz Schroeder

Did you get a new planner for the new year? Oh, that clean calendar feeling! Nothing but blank space for as far as the eye can see. Depending on your season of life, there are no exam weeks or due dates for term papers, no prenatal visits or job interviews, no orthodontist appointments or weekend tournaments, no prostate exams or mole checks—nothing.

My planner is so basic that I have to write in the name of the month and actually number each day. It's not hard to see why this verse came to mind: **"Teach us to number our days, that we may gain a heart of wisdom"** (Psalm 90:12).

How is a heart of wisdom gained by learning to number our days? Because I can write my husband's birthday on the calendar, but it does not guarantee he will be alive to celebrate it. We can plan our 25th anniversary adventure on the Mediterranean Sea, but that doesn't mean a worldwide health scare couldn't shut it down. Since 2020, I think we all learned to write our plans in pencil.

A heart of wisdom acknowledges that each day is a gift of God's grace—not something we are owed. We thank the Giver of that gift by faithfully stewarding every moment he has entrusted to us. When I acknowledge that my time is not "Me Time," I can hold my plans with an open hand, trusting the Lord to give and take away as he sees fit.

Every spiritual blessing
Mike Novotny

When I read all 389 Bible passages that use the word *bless/blessed/blessing*, I noticed a distinctive shift from the Old Testament to the New. In the Old Testament, physical blessings get the vast majority of the attention, but post-Jesus, things change. While the apostles are more than grateful for daily bread, good friends, and the gift of family, they tend to reserve the word *blessing* for the spiritual gifts that are ours through Jesus.

The apostle Paul summarized that sentiment when he wrote, **"Praise be to the God and Father of our Lord Jesus Christ, who has blessed us in the heavenly realms with every spiritual blessing in Christ"** (Ephesians 1:3). Every last spiritual gift is yours through Jesus. You want to go to heaven? Yours. You want to be forgiven? Yours. You want God to be with you, for you, beside you, behind you, all around you? Yours! You want God to listen, to care, to do something important with your life? Yours. You want God to call you his friend, his beloved, his child? Yours, yours, yours!

This is why Christians, when we stop and consider our spiritual situation, feel so blessed. We can't complain for all that long when every (not a few, not some, not most) spiritual gift is ours through the name of Jesus. Fix your thoughts on Jesus today, and you will feel truly blessed.

Checking in
Katrina Harrmann

As a parent, one of the most common things I find myself saying, other than, "Make smart choices!" is this: "Call me when you get there, and let me know if you end up going somewhere else."

In other words: "Check in! I want to know where you're at!"

My kids nod and head out the door. Often—especially on road trips—I wait by my phone with slight unease until I get the text: "I've made it safely."

Sometimes they forget, which is hard on a mama!

In my relationship with my children, I often find myself thinking of my own parent/child relationship with God and applying a lot of these life lessons to my faith life.

This got me thinking: Maybe God would like us to check in more often? Maybe, instead of only coming to him with our highest highs and lowest lows, we should be checking in far more often with what we consider to be the mundane details of day-to-day life. Because just like an earthly parent, he's interested in all that stuff. Maybe it's as simple as saying: "Dear Father, here is where I'm at today. Lead me where you would have me go."

Our heavenly Father LOVES it when we pray and lean on him. This dependency makes us spiritually strong so we are better able to withstand the attacks of the devil when they come—and they WILL come—further down the road.

"Devote yourselves to prayer, being watchful and thankful" (Colossians 4:2).

God's spacious place
Andrea Delwiche

"When hard pressed, I cried to the Lᴏʀᴅ; he brought me into a spacious place. The Lᴏʀᴅ is with me; I will not be afraid. What can mere mortals do to me?" (Psalm 118:5,6).

What makes you feel hard pressed? Do you feel weighed down by others' expectations and judgments or burdened by having to maintain cultural standards of living for yourself or your family? Do you, like me, ever feel hard pressed by your own fallibility? *What will it take for me to finally change and be the person I want to be?* Sometimes I feel hard pressed by the abounding skepticism and unbelief directed toward our good God.

Suddenly, I understand why these verses ring so clearly for me. I, too, need to stand unburdened. I, too, long for God's spacious place.

Jesus was hard pressed by friends and adversaries alike. But he walked with his heart fixed on his Father, and so his joy was unquenchable. God's love and approval gave him an endlessly spacious place to stand, regardless of outward circumstance. Jesus' perspective can be summed up with these words from Psalm 16:6: **"The boundary lines have fallen for me in pleasant places; surely I have a delightful inheritance."**

You and I have God's love and approval. Think about that, and let the burdens of judgment and criticism start falling from your shoulders. You can stand up straight and breathe. Can you envision life under the spacious tent of God's love?

Already clean
Mike Novotny

If you struggle to believe that God likes you due to the overwhelming evidence of your sinfulness, listen closely to Jesus. He told his friends the night before he died, **"You are already clean because of the word I have spoken to you"** (John 15:3).

How could Jesus say that? The guys in the upper room were hours away from denying Jesus and abandoning Jesus, so how could they be "already clean"? Jesus told them, "Because of the word I have spoken to you." The word of Jesus, his message of forgiveness and salvation, had the power to make them clean. When God looks at a Christian, because of the blood of Christ, he declares with authority: "Already clean!"

"But, Pastor Mike, what if I have a record, have done time behind bars, am on parole?" *Already clean.* "But what if I'm still struggling with the same sins I did a year ago?" *Already clean.* "But what if I was a rebellious kid who did shameful things?" *Already clean.* "But what if I messed up my marriage?" *Already clean.* "But what if I said . . ." *Already clean.* "But what if I . . ." *Already clean.* "But what if . . ." *Already clean.* "But what . . ." *Already clean.* "But . . ." *Already clean!*

Do you regret your sins? Me too. Do you wish you could go back and redo parts of life? Me too. But Jesus shed his blood to make sure that there is no condemnation, that you are, right now, *already clean.*

The Lord does all these things
Nathan Nass

The Lord controls all things. Do you believe that? Sometimes it's hard. My city was hit this past summer by severe thunderstorms with 100+ mph winds. Days later, thousands of people still didn't have electricity. Life was messed up. It was hot. Are you saying that God was in control of that?

Yes! Here's what God says: **"I form the light and create darkness, I bring prosperity and create disaster; I, the LORD, do all these things"** (Isaiah 45:7). Every blessing in life is a gift from God. And so is every disaster. *"I, the LORD, do all these things."*

Why? We often don't understand. We're not God. We can't see the big picture. We can't see the spiritual struggles happening behind the scenes. But God can. God knows. That's enough. If God knows, that's enough.

Because we know who the Lord is. He's the God who sent his own Son, Jesus, to die for our sins and win for us eternal life. He's the God who loves us even when we don't deserve it. The cross proves that the Lord is full of compassion and grace.

So in the light and in the darkness, we find comfort in this: The Lord does all these things. In prosperity and disaster, we find strength in this: The Lord does all these things. When our eyes tell us a different story, our faith believes in God's promises. Even in disaster, the Lord does all these things.

Glob remover
Matt Ewart

Ever feel like there's something wrong with you even when you didn't do something wrong? Lewis Smedes helps put that feeling into words in his book *Shame & Grace*. He wrote:

"Guilt was not my problem as I felt it. What I felt most was a glob of unworthiness that I could not tie down to any concrete sins I was guilty of. What I needed more than pardon was a sense that God accepted me."*

Many followers of Jesus wrestle with this. They believe God forgives them, but they wrestle with how God could love someone like them. They believe their guilt has been taken away, but a general feeling of shame might not go away. Maybe you feel "a glob of unworthiness."

When that happens, you and I need God to provide a glob remover—*grace*.

The apostle Paul was an excellent example of what grace can do to guilt and shame. He wrote: **"Christ Jesus came into the world to save sinners—of whom I am the worst. But for that very reason I was shown mercy so that in me, the worst of sinners, Christ Jesus might display his immense patience as an example for those who would believe in him and receive eternal life"** (1 Timothy 1:15,16).

Grace is given, not when it is deserved but when it is needed. When the glob of unworthiness begins to settle in, remember that God's grace was designed for people like you.

* (San Francisco: HarperOne, 1993), p 80.

Jesus didn't run
Mike Novotny

If you know the geography of Jerusalem, you realize that Jesus could have run. On the Thursday night that he was arrested, Jesus was praying in the Garden of Gethsemane on the east side of the city. The garden was right on the edge of the Judean wilderness, the cave-filled desert that was ideal for escaping from your foes. Judas was leading a group of soldiers from the west, and Jesus knew it, which meant he had the perfect chance to flee to the east and save his own life.

But Jesus didn't run. Here's why: **"I am the good shepherd. The good shepherd lays down his life for the sheep. The hired hand is not the shepherd and does not own the sheep. So when he sees the wolf coming, he abandons the sheep and runs away. Then the wolf attacks the flock and scatters it. The man runs away because he is a hired hand and cares nothing for the sheep. I am the good shepherd"** (John 10:11-14).

Unlike some selfish shepherd who only "serves" for his own self-interest, Jesus served for the sake of others. In order to save us from the wolf of sin, he was willing to lay down his life. What a sacrifice!

The next time you read about Jesus in Gethsemane, think about how he could have escaped. Then marvel at the love that held him in place until the work of saving you was done.

MARCH

Praise be to the God and Father of our Lord Jesus Christ!
In his great mercy he has given us new birth
into a living hope through the resurrection
of Jesus Christ from the dead.

1 Peter 1:3

Yielding to authority
Mike Novotny

When I looked up every Bible passage that mentioned the word *submit/submission*, I found out that our Father has ordered his world in a specific way, asking five groups of people to yield to the authority placed above them.

First, residents submit to their government: **"It is necessary to submit to the authorities"** (Romans 13:5). Second, employees submit to their bosses: **"Slaves, in reverent fear of God submit yourselves to your masters"** (1 Peter 2:18). (Please note that first-century slavery was more like modern employment than the slavery of the American South.) Third, wives submit to their husbands: **"Wives, submit yourselves to your own husbands as you do to the Lord"** (Ephesians 5:22). Fourth, Christians submit to their pastors: **"Have confidence in your [church] leaders and submit to their authority, because they keep watch over you as those who must give an account"** (Hebrews 13:17). Finally, everyone submits to God: **"Submit yourselves, then, to God"** (James 4:7).

The first four examples teach us that while we can and should share our desires, ideas, and preferences, we yield to the authority of others for the sake of order. (If that seems like a bad system, read the book of Judges where everyone did what they wanted. Hint: It did not end well.) The final example reminds us that our ultimate submission is to God, which means we yield to him even if our government or our church leaders would ask us to sin (read Acts 5:29).

What would a humble, submissive life look like for you this week?

You have to forgive
Mike Novotny

Are you familiar with the Lord's Prayer, the prayer in which the Lord Jesus urged us to ask God for forgiveness as well as the strength to forgive those who sin against us? If so, do you know what Jesus said right after that prayer? **"For if you forgive other people when they sin against you, your heavenly Father will also forgive you. But if you do not forgive others their sins, your Father will not forgive your sins"** (Matthew 6:14,15).

You have to forgive. *Have to.* It's a necessity for every true child of God. While you may struggle to do it and fall short every other time you try, no Christian can live in (a.k.a. continue in, a.k.a. persist in, a.k.a. not repent of) bitterness, vengeance, and a lack of forgiveness. Christians care about Christ's teaching. The Holy Spirit within us moves our hearts to follow Jesus, even when the commands of Jesus are far from convenient.

If you have refused to forgive someone, repent of disobeying the clear command of God. If you are trying to forgive but failing as often as you try, thank God that he has mercy on his sincere children who are weak. If you have made and continue to make the choice to forgive, praise God for helping you treat others as Jesus first treated you—with grace.

Child of God, you have to forgive. And because of Jesus' forgiveness, I know you want to.

Stop trying and start training
Matt Ewart

Has anyone ever asked you why you aren't doing better at something? Maybe your doctor asks why you aren't making better health decisions. Or your financial planner asks why you aren't spending more wisely. Or your friend asks why you aren't more patient with a certain person. Or your pastor asks why you aren't better at reading your Bible more.

If you're like me, you've probably given this answer more than once: "I'm trying."

"I'm trying to be nicer, but you don't know how difficult this person is!" "I'm trying to eat healthier, but my coworker keeps bringing donuts to work!" "I'm trying to read the Bible more, but I just don't have the time!"

It's easy to get stuck in the trap of trying. The apostle Paul encouraged a young leader named Timothy to take a different approach:

"Train yourself to be godly. For physical training is of some value, but godliness has value for all things" (1 Timothy 4:7,8).

To run a lengthy race, you don't go into trying. You go into training.

To perform a complex operation, a surgeon doesn't just show up and try. He or she goes through extensive training.

The most important things in your life are too important to leave it up to trying. Stop trying. Start training.

If you try and end up failing, that makes you a failure who may never try again. If you train and end up falling short, that makes you a learner who can keep going.

Staffing shortage
Jason Nelson

You may have heard that our society is plagued by staffing shortages. There aren't enough nurses, pastors, pilots, or tradespeople to go around. People who need or want a variety of services are delayed or denied in receiving them because there are not enough providers. I've seen people wait to be seated in restaurants, not because there weren't open tables but because there weren't enough servers and cooks to fill orders. So we have to reimagine ways to cover all the bases that need to be covered. That generally means asking fewer people to do more, older people to put off retirement, and admitting more skilled immigrants to America. Eventually, the dynamics of money and work and forces of supply and demand will rebalance things, at least for a while.

Seems like an ancient problem. Jesus once said, **"The harvest is plentiful but the workers are few"** (Matthew 9:37). He told his disciples that his kingdom was missing opportunities because of staffing shortages. Afterall, he did everything he could. He taught everywhere he went, he proclaimed the good news of his kingdom, and he healed the sick. Crowds followed him, and he had compassion on them because they were lost like sheep without a shepherd. He would die trying to meet their spiritual needs. He said, **"Ask the Lord of the harvest, therefore, to send out workers into his harvest field"** (verse 38). He gave opportunities to help then. And he offers opportunities to help now. Let's get to work.

When Jesus' cross disappears
Daron Lindemann

One Ash Wednesday morning, I was preparing ashes to apply to hands or foreheads in a special worship service to begin the Christian season of Lent.

I struggled with the particular recipe as I mixed ashes and olive oil. As I tested it, the ash mix wouldn't shape a clear, defined black cross. It smudged, smeared, and after a few hours dissolved and disappeared.

I was a bit frustrated until I remembered this verse: **"I have been crucified with Christ and I no longer live, but Christ lives in me"** (Galatians 2:20).

Later, when applying the ashes to others, I spoke the verse God provided. I said that the smudging and blurring of the cross on their foreheads or hands meant that the death of Christ was dissolving into them, into their bodies, their souls, their identities, their problems, their eternity.

When your boss or boyfriend treats you unfairly, you are not a victim who must beat yourself up with guilt, but you are a victor alive in Christ.

When your family or friends let you down—or you let them down—you don't have to punish yourself with blame and shame, because all punishment for sin already took place in Christ crucified, who is alive in you.

When you can't find enough time to pray or read your Bible more, you're not dead to God or worthless as dirt, but you're as precious as his own Son, Jesus.

Christ lives in you.

Our Father
Liz Schroeder

How a letter is addressed has the power to completely change the tone of the message, doesn't it? Consider how you'd feel receiving these different types of correspondence: "Hey, friend!" vs. "Dear Parent or Guardian of Alexander" vs. "To Our Valued Customer at 1313 Mockingbird Lane." The way a letter is addressed reveals the closeness of the relationship.

How telling, then, that when Jesus showed his disciples how to pray, he opened with, **"Our Father"** (Luke 11:2 KJV).

Jesus could've said, "Our King," because it is true that God is our King. He could've said, "Our Almighty Creator," because he is. But Jesus said, "Our Father" to emphasize the close, familial relationship we have with the Almighty Creator-King through Christ.

It is said that knowing God as our King makes us tremble, knowing God as our Creator makes us humble, but knowing God as our Father makes us marvel. When we understand God as our Father, we can enter the throne room of the King. Instead of bowing and scraping, we can boldly approach the throne and crawl up onto his lap.

Looking at the Lord's Prayer through this fatherly lens gives nuance to each petition. Is a toddler shy about asking his daddy for a snack? Nope. Does a good father know what's best for his child? Yup.

The next time you pray the Lord's Prayer, imagine yourself curled up on the lap of your heavenly Father. He who formed the galaxies and knit you together bends his ear to hear every whispered petition.

God's got this
Mike Novotny

Not long ago, my friend was facing a serious legal situation that had immense implications for his future. A judge was about to decide if he would be free to change out of his orange jumpsuit or if he would spend decades in prison. He was afraid of 20 years behind bars. Honestly, I was too. I thought he should be set free, but the state of Wisconsin wasn't asking my opinion.

Just before the verdict, my friend wrote me a letter, updating me on the case as well as how he was holding up under the uncertainty. But on the bottom of his letter, he wrote three words that proved that he wasn't just sitting and waiting; he was trusting and believing. He wrote, "God's got this."

What faith! You, like my friend, might be facing a serious situation that has immense implications for your future—a college application, a job interview, a scan for cancer, an important election, etc. As a Christian, however, you don't have to twiddle your thumbs or hold your breath. You can trust. You can believe. Like my friend, you can declare with hope: "God's got this! God can fix this! God can change this! Even if it goes 'wrong,' God will use this! My God has got this!"

The famous proverb says it best: **"Trust in the Lord with all your heart and lean not on your own understanding"** (Proverbs 3:5). Don't fear, my friend. God's got this!

Heirlooms
Katrina Harrmann

Last spring, an old neighbor of my grandmother's passed away, and it turned out she had a bench that used to be on my grandmother's farm. My grandma has been gone for a long time, so when I got the chance to take that bench home, I was grateful.

But when I saw it—the wood splintering and the feet rotting off—I was overwhelmed. It needed some serious TLC! My dad and I spent many spring afternoons power washing it, sanding it, putting in new screws, and finally painting it with a lovely natural finish. In the end, the formerly decayed bench glowed with new life.

One of my friends said to me, "Sit quietly, close your eyes, and you'll hear conversations from 50 years ago." What a thrilling thought!

Heirlooms are like that. They speak to us of who and what has gone before. They evoke memories, and we treasure them far more than their actual material worth.

The same can be said of the heirloom our Lord has passed down to us. The Bible. It's been passed down carefully from generation to generation. It speaks to us of those who have gone before.

It's priceless . . . far beyond the material cost of paper and binding glue.

And if you're very quiet while you're reading and close your eyes, you'll definitely hear conversations from countless years ago.

What a precious heirloom indeed! **"The grass withers and the flowers fall, but the word of our God endures forever"** (Isaiah 40:8).

Some people don't want our prayers
Daron Lindemann

Some people find prayers valuable, while others would actually pay to avoid them.

Two sociologists studied residents who survived a hurricane, asking them to describe their hardships. Then they made an offer of a prayer and tied the offer to money.

What did they discover? Christians valued prayer from a stranger, but others said they would pay more than $3.50 to *avoid* a Christian stranger's prayer.

Wait . . . what? Who doesn't want prayer? People who see the offer of prayer as a warm and fuzzy platitude that is not tied to actual action, a bailout.

"Suppose a brother or a sister is without clothes and daily food. If one of you says to them, 'Go in peace; keep warm and well fed,' but does nothing about their physical needs, what good is it?" (James 2:15,16).

Let's admit this. "I'll pray for you" sometimes means, "I'll delegate your problem to God. He'll take care of you while I go take care of me."

Giving others' problems to God is good. Not being part of the solution is bad.

Consider these loving actions. Instead of saying, "I'll pray for you," pray right there, on the spot, with the person (even on the phone or in a text message).

When you say, "I'll pray for you," grab your phone right there, on the spot, and enter the person's name and request into your notes so you don't forget.

Don't just pray but also act. Don't just act but also pray.

Feet like a deer
Nathan Nass

I once saw a bighorn sheep in the wild. It was amazing! The bighorn sheep was galloping on rocky cliffs. There were so many cracks and crevices, so many rocks and boulders. But that bighorn sheep? He didn't mind at all. He jogged with his head held high, not one bit afraid as his hooves skipped along the rocks.

Wouldn't it be great to live like that? Confident. Unafraid. Unfortunately, that's often not how I feel. I face the cracks and crevices and rocks and boulders of life with doubts instead of confidence, with fear instead of courage. I think, "There's no way. It's too hard for me!"

Except, it's not just me. Life is not just me trying to find my way. It's me and God. It's you and God. Do you know what God does for us? David writes, **"It is God who arms me with strength and keeps my way secure. He makes my feet like the feet of a deer; he causes me to stand on the heights"** (Psalm 18:32,33).

Hear that? It is God who gives us strength. It is God who keeps our feet secure. It is God who enables us to walk through the cliffs and crevices of life without fear or anxiety. It is Jesus and his forgiveness that enable us to face rocks and boulders with heads held high. Self-confidence is overrated. True confidence comes from God. He makes our feet like the feet of a deer . . . or a bighorn sheep!

Your reality
Clark Schultz

It's interesting how perspectives can be misunderstood. Take church during a February blizzard, for example. If services are held in the snowy conditions: "How dare you expect me to drive in this!" But only a few years ago a government mandate shut the doors of churches. "How dare you take away my right to worship!" Or how about the person in the hallway who doesn't return your hello? "Oh, they must hate me."

Perspective? Or reality? We are the masters of our own storylines. We love to be the stars and too often the victims. Let's take some perspective from our Savior. A woman in Nain had just lost her only son: **"When the Lord saw her, his heart went out to her"** (Luke 7:13). Jesus didn't tell this widow to suck it up buttercup. Instead he understood exactly how she was feeling.

Empathy is putting yourself into the shoes of the other person. Instead of launching a tirade of when and in what conditions we worship, we can focus on the One we are worshiping. Instead of assuming someone who doesn't return our hello doesn't like us, we can offer empathy—turns out she's hurting after losing her father. She needs our prayers vs. our "woe is me."

Let's dim the light on our stars and focus more on a Savior who despite his star status **"did not consider equality with God something to be used to his own advantage"** (Philippians 2:6).

You are loved and forgiven. That's not a perspective but a reality you can share.

Count your blessings from God
Mike Novotny

If you want to increase your level of gratitude, a habit that has incredible spiritual and emotional benefits, check out some research I recently did on everything the Bible has to say about being blessed. There are 389 passages in the Scriptures that use words like *blessed* or *blessing*, and in the Old Testament, God's good gifts are almost always physical blessings.

One of the first examples from the first page of the Bible reads, **"God blessed them and said to them, 'Be fruitful and increase in number.'"** And a few pages later, **"Isaac planted crops in that land and the same year reaped a hundredfold, because the LORD blessed him"** (Genesis 1:28; 26:12). A new baby or a successful business are both, according to God, blessings, and you are so blessed when you count your own blessings, connecting everything good to a generous God.

When we think about being blessed, we often start from a perfect life and subtract all the good things we don't have. Instead, God wants us to start from nothing and notice every good thing that we do have. Even if you have a car payment, you have a car. Even if exams are coming up, you have a good education. Even if your husband left his socks on the floor (again), you are blessed with a husband. Even if your wife is mad about your hamper-less socks, you have a wife!

Every good gift from God is a blessing. Count them all today, and you will soon count yourself as someone who is truly blessed.

Renewing our minds
Jan Gompper

You can tell a lot about a society by what they read. The first issue of *LIFE* magazine was published in 1936. It was a humor and general interest publication, focusing on photojournalism that captured the essence of significant world events and people.

In 1923 and 1933, *TIME* magazine and *Newsweek*, respectively, hit newsstands. Each examined current events from its own political perspective.

The 1970s brought a focus shift in journalism. *People* and *US* hit newsstands. Stories and photos of Hollywood celebrities and other "elites" were their nucleus. In 1979, *Self* brought self-help articles on health, fitness, food, beauty, finance, relationships, and sex.

Today selfies and opinions streamed via social media have all but replaced objective, researched media forms.

With each passing year, we've turned more inward, focusing on our own importance. With such self-absorption, it's no wonder that today many think they can define their own identities and determine their own truth. All the while Satan smiles because he knows the more narcissistic we become the less we will see a need for God.

No wonder the apostle Paul warned, **"Do not conform to the pattern of this world, but be transformed by the renewing of your mind. Then you will be able to test and approve what God's will is—his good, pleasing and perfect will"** (Romans 12:2).

How do we renew our minds? By getting our information from the most trustworthy media source—the Word of God.

God works wonders
Andrea Delwiche

God waters our souls with nourishment, direction, and clarity in many unique ways.

One evening, I sat with a group of believers, and we slowly read through the 175+ verses of Psalm 119. We took our time. We began with a bit of reluctance, as if we were about to endure a cross country race that we didn't feel equipped to run. We finished silently, cherishing a sense of intimacy with God and each other. Shepherded by the Spirit's gentle leading and read aloud with a beloved community, the psalm spoke to us, first individually and then collectively, as we discussed our experience.

God drew us into a live-action version of a Christian spiritual truth—that God's Word is alive, active, and useful.

"Open my eyes so I can see what you show me of your miracle-wonders. I'm a stranger in these parts; give me clear directions. My soul is starved and hungry, ravenous!—insatiable for your nourishing commands" (Psalm 119:18-20 MSG).

It's good if we can approach each encounter with the Word anticipating "miracle-wonders" and direction from God. But even when we are too shortsighted to do so, God still works wonders.

Whether lifelong followers or tiptoeing around a newfound love of Jesus, we are all "strangers in these parts." Our souls are starving, and God longs to fill us with the goodness of his kingdom day after day.

How can we put ourselves in a place to experience God's working?

You need only to be still
David Scharf

It's easy to trust God's promises when we see the blessings, but it is much harder when we see challenges. God freed his Old Testament people by sending ten plagues on Egypt. Pharaoh chased and trapped the Israelites at the Red Sea. What do we do when we see Pharaoh's army at our backs and the Red Sea of challenges standing between us and the Promised Land?

We remember what Moses told the Israelites: **"Do not be afraid. . . . The Lord will fight for you; you need only to be still"** (Exodus 14:13,14). Who fights for you? The Lord, who created and sustains the universe. The One who has saved his people repeatedly and shaped all of world history to keep his promise of sending a Savior for this world. Doesn't that put your "impossible" problems into perspective? When the impossible in life meets God's promises, remember that it is the Lord who will fight for you.

Are you worried about your sin? You need only to be still. Look at the cross and see the Lord fight to the death for you. Are you worried about sickness? You need only to be still. Look at the empty tomb, and see the Lord defeat death for you. Are you worried about having enough? You need only to be still and see Jesus' ascended hands raised in blessing over you. When the impossible in your life meets God's promises, know that the Lord will fight for you. You need only to be still.

Editing and pruning
Katrina Harrmann

Editing hurts.

I say that as a writer who has experienced it.

Recently, I was asked to cut a manuscript down by 15,000 words—I nearly swooned! How could I DO this?

Another example involves the peach trees in my yard. Every spring when the peach blossoms fade and are replaced by stalwart little fruits, there comes a time when I must "thin" them. Thinning means I have to get rid of all the fruit that's too close together. Because if I let them ALL grow, it will get too crowded, and the peaches will stay small and hard. But taking all those lovely little peaches and throwing them to the ground is SO hard!

How do we handle it when the Great Editor or the Great Gardener tells us to cut something out of our lives? Something we may see as harmless or even beneficial but may not be what God has planned for us?

Wow, is it ever hard! We struggle and sometimes fight back, don't we?

Here is the remarkable thing: When I cut 15,000 words, my project ended up better than ever. And the remaining peaches that grew on that tree with plenty of space? They were gorgeous and delicious three months later.

God edits and prunes us for a reason, even if we can't always see it clearly. **"Every branch that does bear fruit he prunes so that it will be even more fruitful"** (John 15:2). Trust his methods and his love.

The marvelous motivation of our Good Shepherd
Mike Novotny

Why do shepherds shepherd? Why would anyone choose to spend those long days and weary nights watching the flocks and searching for the strays? Simple answer—for themselves. Despite the work, sheep provide shepherds with wool, milk, and meat, which provide clothing, meals, and paychecks. Like any other job, shepherding brings home the bacon (in this case, the mutton ☺).

But this is what makes Jesus so marvelous. Why did Jesus become our Good Shepherd? Did he come down from heaven because he needed clothes? No, he was clothed in glory. Was he hungry? No, he spent all eternity at the feast of heaven. Was he broke? No, the sheep on every hill belonged to him as true God.

So why did Jesus do it? Here's why: **"I am the good shepherd. The good shepherd lays down his life for the sheep"** (John 10:11). For the sheep. Have you ever read such marvelous words? Jesus came down to be the Shepherd "for the sheep." His motivation was not self-preservation but your soul's salvation. He wanted to clothe you in holiness, feed you with his goodness, and enrich you with God's presence.

No one in history has even been motivated by such selfless love. That's why we love the name of Jesus, our Good Shepherd.

Start talking to yourself
Matt Ewart

"Set your mind on things above, not on earthly things" (Colossians 3:2).

Within your mind, you have an inner voice—a constant internal dialogue that only you can hear. Sometimes it will say things like, "Oh, that's pretty!" when you see some flowers in bloom.

But it can also flood your mind with negative thoughts: "I'm so stupid. They must hate me. I can't believe I said that. Why can't I be more like them?"

What do you do when your inner voice bothers you? Take a moment to think through last week. When your inner voice bothered you, what did you do to make it go away? Or what did you do to make yourself feel better? If you are ready for a change, here's what you need to do:

Stop listening to yourself, and start talking to yourself.

Instead of listening to your inner voice, start talking to it. Correct it when it is wrong. For example, tell yourself that

- you are wise for salvation through Jesus Christ.
- God declares you are worthy of his love.
- your sins do not make you a failure, because you are forgiven in Christ.
- your unique gifts mean that God has a unique purpose just for you.

What would happen this week if you stopped listening to your inner voice and instead started talking to it? Give it a try. Just be sure to let your words be guided by God's truth.

You can't clean a fish you haven't caught

Jan Gompper

My older brother loves fishing. He enjoys the peace and tranquility of being on a lake, patiently waiting for a fish to bite. For him, it's all about the catch.

When I go fishing, I focus on the messy part—cleaning the fish. As a result, the joy of experiencing a nibble on my hook eludes me because I'm envisioning scaling and gutting the fish.

It's pretty silly, isn't it—to think about cleaning a fish before even catching one?

Sometimes Christians put the knife before the hook with people too. We want to clean them up before we've caught them. When we meet people who are not Christ followers yet, we may get offended by their language or lifestyles and think that our first job is to get them to scrub off the scales of sin they're covered in. Worse yet, we may deem them "uncleanable" and not even cast our line in their direction.

Thankfully, Jesus didn't fish this way. He understood the importance of the catch. He knew he would never be able to clean up our sinful hearts without getting us on the hook. He didn't tell us to gut the sin out of our lives first and then follow him. He simply said, "Follow me," because he knew that when we do, we are clean forever.

How did Jesus bait his hook? With empathy and compassion, with gentle words and generous acts—and always with love.

"'Come, follow me,' Jesus said, 'and I will send you out to fish for people'" (Matthew 4:19).

Forgiveness beyond human expectations
Mike Novotny

In the 1950s, Jim Elliot wanted to bring the good news of Jesus to the Huaorani people of eastern Ecuador. For years, Jim studied their language. For months, he made cautious contact by dropping gifts from an overhead plane. Jim and his friends even made face-to-face contact with a small group of Huaorani warriors, which was a friendly and hopeful encounter. But before Jim and his friends could deepen the relationship, the tribe attacked and murdered the men.

But what happened next caught the attention of the world. Elisabeth Elliot, Jim's widowed wife, after two years of studying the Huaorani language as she grieved Jim's death, went to live with the tribe that killed her husband. She was so gracious that when her story was turned into a movie, the scriptwriters insisted on making the family less forgiving and more vengeful. Why change the truth of the events? The scriptwriters explained to Elisabeth's family: "Your mom trusted God. But most people in the world don't have that."

The forgiveness of Jesus goes beyond human expectations. The gospel forgives more people for more sins more often than the world would ever imagine. And, once believed, that same gospel compels us to forgive more people for more sins more often than the world could ever script.

Is there a sin you're holding on to today? A sin you committed? A sin committed against you? **"Forgive as the Lord forgave you"** (Colossians 3:13).

The stress of the nurturer
Jason Nelson

Where is the stress in your life? I don't mean what is causing you angst. But what are you focused on? This is a critical question for all of us who roll up our sleeves and help others grow. It can be exhausting and the outcomes disappointing. In 1 Corinthians 9, the apostle Paul cues us in on the stress of a nurturer.

"Am I not free? . . . Have I not seen Jesus our Lord? Are you not the result of my work?" (verse 1). *I could do other things, but I choose to serve Jesus by helping you reach your potential.*

"I have made myself a slave to everyone" (verse 19). *I refuse to assert my rights or emphasize what I need. You are my priority now.*

"I have become all things to all people" (verse 22). *You are unique. I want to put myself in your place and understand you.*

"Run in such a way as to get the prize" (verse 24). *I'm competitive. I don't want to lose you. And I want you to be a winner.*

"I strike a blow to my body and make it my slave" (verse 27). *I have to take care of myself if I'm going to be there for you. I'm working hard on self-discipline.*

"I myself will not be disqualified for the prize" (verse 27). *We share in the gospel. I want both of us to be in heaven.*

The stress of the nurturer is relieved by what the nurturer stresses.

The purpose of storms
Matt Ewart

You know that feeling you get when you know someone is angry with you? It feels a little like guilt or shame, but there's also a sense of separation between you. No matter what you call it, the feeling isn't good. Especially when you did something to deserve whatever anger is directed your way.

Ever wonder if God is angry with you? With people, the signs are usually clear—they scowl at you, yell at you, ignore you, or do some other bad thing to you. But if God was angry with you, how would you know?

We might think that when bad things happen to us, that's a sign that God is angry with us.

But that wasn't the case for Jonah. This runaway prophet had denied God's call to share a message to the people in Nineveh. He got in a boat and went the opposite direction, so here's what God did:

"Then the Lord sent a great wind on the sea, and such a violent storm arose that the ship threatened to break up" (Jonah 1:4).

The storm was not designed to get back at Jonah. It was designed to bring Jonah back, both to God and his calling.

Bad things in your life are not signs that God is angry with you. Jesus received all the anger toward our sin when he was on a cross. God can use storms and other things that seem bad to accomplish something eternally good.

A beautiful picture
Clark Schultz

When you look at a group photo that you're in, what's your first reaction? If you're like me, you go immediately to your face and pick apart your flaws in the photo: "My glasses are dirty. My shirt collar is sticking up."

In Luke 15, Jesus told his listeners the story of the prodigal son. When we read that account and think about the picture it portrays, we can get caught focusing in on the sons and their flaws. The younger son says, "Dad, I want you dead; give me my inheritance." He leaves home to blow an entire fortune only to hit rock bottom. The older son also feels entitled and cheated that he doesn't get a party or a steak dinner with his friends.

But our focus is off. In this picture, we are those brothers. We run from God. We go wild in sinful actions. We blur the truth: "We would never live like that!" Like the Pharisees of Jesus' day, we feel because of all we've done, God owes us. The unfiltered truth is that we are owed hell!

Thankfully we can take a second glance to see someone else—the father and his continued looks to the horizon for the wayward son. He shows compassion and underserved love for BOTH sons. That, my friends, is our Father! By punishing his Son, grace, love, and compassion are ours. What a beautiful picture! **"See what great love the Father has lavished on us, that we should be called children of God! And that is what we are!** (1 John 3:1).

It is finished
Clark Schultz

"The Boxer" is a song that was recorded by the American music duo Simon & Garfunkel on their fifth studio album, *Bridge Over Troubled Water*. To avoid being sued by one of the best duos of folk rock, I will attempt to summarize a stanza without using the exact words.

The song depicts a fighter who is against the ropes; he's taken punches, and yet he is still standing. Despite leaving the ring, he is still a fighter. *I will give you a second to sing the refrain that follows. . . . Okay, back to the devotion.*

On the cross, Jesus said, **"It is finished"** (John 19:30). Some have compared Jesus' fight to save us to a boxer in a ring. Agree or disagree? You can agree in the fact that Jesus went into the ring, went toe to toe with the old evil foe, and defeated him. He delivered a knockout punch to Satan, death, and our sins: "It is finished."

You can disagree because a boxer wins one fight and soon has to defend his title or fight again. With Jesus this was a *one-time* fight to save humanity. The Greek word for our verse above carries with it the idea that it was a one-time sacrifice with ongoing effects. This means your fight, dear reader, is over; the battle is won. Jesus experienced the cuts, the anger, the shame, and he is NOT leaving you. The fight is over, but the Savior and his presence still remain. Cue the refrain . . .

Confusing to be a Chreaster
Mike Novotny

Pastors have a nickname for church members who only show up to worship on Christmas and Easter—Chreasters. We love them and would love to see them more, which is why most Christmas and Easter sermons include a plea to come back before the next major holiday.

Last Easter, however, it dawned on me how confusing Chreasters would have been to first-century Christians. If Jesus really is the God who died and rose in order to save us from eternal punishment, then visiting your church as often as you visit your dentist simply doesn't make sense. If Jesus was an ancient influencer or brilliant philosopher, perhaps, but if he is your Lord and Savior, your Prince of peace, your King, and your Friend, then surely he deserves a primary place in your schedule.

Let me nudge you and those you love off the fence. If Jesus didn't die and rise for you, do whatever you want on the weekends. But if you believe, like I do, that Jesus gave up his life so you could live and conquered death so you wouldn't die eternally, then love him with your heart, soul, mind, and schedule. **"Let us consider how we may spur one another on toward love and good deeds, not giving up meeting together, as some are in the habit of doing"** (Hebrews 10:24,25).

God wants to spur you on toward a greater love and use you to spur others on toward that same goal. That's why we gather for Christmas, Easter, and all the Sundays in between.

You are not controlled by sin
David Scharf

People will sometimes say, "I'm struggling with my demons." In a way, it's true. Evil is behind every sin, and it feels controlling, like a demon wrapping its talons around your soul.

One story from Mark 5 makes the hairs on your arm stand on end. A demon-possessed man, naked and screaming and bleeding, tells Jesus, **"My name is legion, for we are many"** (verse 9). Talk about struggling with your demons! Demons are powerful, yet they left the man. Do you know why? Jesus told them to. That's how much stronger he is.

What demons are controlling you? Addiction? Anger? Selfishness? Jesus wants to cast out those demons too, because he wants to make his home in your heart. Jesus said, **"The coming of the kingdom of God is not something that can be observed, nor will people say, 'Here it is,' or 'There it is,' because the kingdom of God is in your midst"** (Luke 17:20,21). Jesus wants to cast those demons out of your heart so he can live there . . . and he has.

Jesus came into this world and battled the devil. The devil lost. Jesus freed you from all the sins the devil accuses you of by living a perfect life, dying for your sins, and rising from the dead. Jesus crushed the devil's head forever by stepping out of the tomb alive on Easter morning. The devil does not control you, nor does your sin. Jesus lives to cast the demons out of your life and to dwell in your heart. You win!

You're going to die
(a.k.a. Happy Easter!)
Mike Novotny

My youngest daughter didn't want me to tell you that you're going to die. I gave her a preview of my upcoming Easter sermon, the one that the pastor's family gets each spring, but she wasn't a fan. "Maya," I said, "I think I'm going to start the Easter sermon with, 'You're all gonna die.'"

She objected, "Dad, it's Easter. It's supposed to be happy."

"But how can I talk about the resurrection of the dead unless I talk about death?" I explained.

"Dad," she repeated, exasperated with my logic, "it's Easter."

She's probably right, but for real, you're going to die. From small earthly losses to your big final breath, death is something we all have in common. I know we'd rather not think about that, but seriously, what do you do with that? How do you cope with that? How do you have hope in that?

That's where Easter comes in. Instead of avoiding or denying death, Easter offers hope on the other side of death. You don't have to pretend like you're not getting older or losing those you love. Instead, with Christian hope, you can look to Christ and know that your story ends in glory, just like Jesus' earthly story didn't end with a cross but with an empty tomb.

Yes, you're going to die. But yes, you're going to live forever. **"The one who believes in me will live, even though they die"** (John 11:25).

Sans everything, with joy
Liz Schroeder

In ninth grade, I had to memorize Shakespeare's "All the world's a stage" speech from *As You Like It*. In it, the Bard describes the seven ages of man, from infancy to death—man's entrance and exit. The poem ends with the line, "Last scene of all, / That ends this strange eventful history, / Is second childishness and mere oblivion; / Sans [without] teeth, sans eyes, sans taste, sans everything."

Now there's a cheery thought! What do you have to look forward to before you die? Dementia, dentures, cataracts, and Ensure. Wahoo!

God has let my husband and me live long enough to see signs of old age in our parents. At first, it's painful to witness your mom and dad losing their faculties. You used to have to run to keep up with your dad's long strides; now you hold his hand to keep him steady. You listen patiently—but not patronizingly—to a story your mom already told you minutes before.

God has also given us the grace to see the pleasure that this third act gives to our parents. **"I have no greater joy than to hear that my children are walking in the truth"** (3 John 1:4). When their kids and their families take up four rows at church while visiting the grandparents, there's no greater joy. Likewise, when our parents get to celebrate the Christian baptisms, confirmations, and weddings of their grandkids, they rejoice.

And for the grandkids who've strayed, they pray fervently that God will delay bringing the final curtain down.

Honoring the dishonorable
Jan Gompper

I had lunch with a childhood friend I hadn't seen in years. Our families spent lots of time together when we were growing up. Sadly, we had lost touch.

As we reminisced about "the good old days," my friend also shared some old pain—her father's verbal abuse about her physicality (ironically, she resembled him) and his favoritism of his youngest son over her and her other brother.

I witnessed some of her father's behavior, but at the time chalked it up to "teasing." It went much deeper, and his verbal abuse was harsher behind closed doors.

Tears welled in her eyes as she talked about wanting to obey God by "honoring her father" in his old age, particularly now that her mom is gone. Unfortunately, he continues to treat her in ways that are *less* than honorable.

If you also struggle with this dilemma, remember that God's directive for parent/child relationships is twofold. True, God tells children to honor their parents, but he also commands, **"Fathers, do not provoke your children to anger [do not exasperate them to the point of resentment with demands that are trivial or unreasonable or humiliating or abusive; nor by showing favoritism or indifference]"** (Ephesians 6:4 AMP).

When parents don't live up to what God asks of them, children can still honor them by praying for them and ensuring their needs are met, without remaining the target of their abuse.

By doing so, your heavenly Father promises, **"It may go well with you"** (Ephesians 6:3).

God knows the end
Nathan Nass

When you look out the window of an airplane, you can't see what's in front of you. Have you noticed that? It's beautiful to see what's on the side, but you can never see what's coming next. You also can't see what's behind you. When you look out the window of an airplane, all you can see is the side.

Isn't that true in life? We can't see where we're going. All we can see is right now. We also can't see where we've come from. The past quickly flies from our minds. All we see is the present. That's hard. Do you want to know the end? The end of the trouble? The end of the pain? The end of this waiting? I do! But all we see is what's happening right now.

Remember this: God knows the end. God says, **"I make known the end from the beginning, from ancient times, what is still to come. I say, 'My purpose will stand, and I will do all that I please'"** (Isaiah 46:10). Unlike us, God doesn't just see the present. He sees the past—even ancient times! And he sees the future—the very end! God knows the end. We can trust in him.

So take a deep breath. The God who knew you before you were born . . . the God who sent his Son to die for you . . . the God who has prepared a home for you in heaven—he knows the end.

Jesus suffered for you
Mike Novotny

In 2017, 60 miles north of London, archaeologists discovered the ancient remains of a man who had been crucified by the Romans, proven by the two-inch iron nail smashed through and still stuck in his right heel bone. Scientists detected signs of trauma on the decomposed body, but the most disturbing detail was the indentation next to the nail hole. Apparently, the Romans tried to drive the nail through his foot, but it lodged in the bone, so they ripped it out and tried again nearby. Search for "Fenstanton cross," and you'll see the disturbing details of a Roman crucifixion.

Jesus died like that. **"They crucified him"** (Mark 15:24). It is easy to gloss over those words when you live so far in time and space from the cross. Sometimes it takes an archaeological discovery to remind us just how brutally Jesus suffered.

But glimpses of the cross give us glimpses of God's love. Despite the immense cost, Jesus was willing to pay that price, enduring the nails, the thorns, and the scorn of the crowds. God's passion to save you was so profound that even the shame of the Romans would not stop him from finishing the job and declaring you free.

Marvel with me at the cross of Jesus. No one has ever or ever will love you like that. This is why, no matter how simple or complicated your life might be, you have every reason to praise Jesus today!

APRIL

In the same way, the Spirit helps us in our weakness.
We do not know what we ought to pray for,
but the Spirit himself intercedes for us
through wordless groans.

Romans 8:26

Proving facts
Jon Enter

Army veteran John Crabtree was wounded in Vietnam and received military benefits due to his disability. One day he opened an official notification from the government that stated he had died! John wrote and called the government, showing he was very much alive! Nothing changed; they didn't believe him.

Billions of people right now are convinced that Jesus is still dead. Or they've convinced themselves he never existed; he's a fairy tale, a legend, a myth. How do you know Christ's death and resurrection are true? Your eternity depends on it! **"If Christ has not been raised, your faith is futile; you are still in your sins"** (1 Corinthians 15:17).

God's Word declares that Easter happened. **"By his power God raised the Lord from the dead, and he will raise us also"** (1 Corinthians 6:14). This is all we need to prove the eternity-changing truth of Easter! Sadly, some reject the Bible. So point them to the eyewitnesses of Christ's resurrection, his disciples. If the resurrection was a lie, a pact made by the disciples to sell Bibles and gain fame, then why were they willing to die proclaiming that Christ rose? It cut short their lives. Peter and Andrew were crucified. James was stoned. The apostle Paul was beheaded. These men were willing to give their lives because they knew—saw with their own eyes—that Christ conquered death. Through their witness and through inspired Scripture, so do you. Christ is risen! That truth changes everything.

Words we know "by heart"
Katrina Harrmann

When my daughter was little, we often sang the Davy Crockett song. One time we got to the line about how he killed a bar (bear) when he was only three years old.

My little girl looked up at me and asked, "What was he doing in a bar when he was only three?"

"What?" I asked, baffled.

She explained: "It says he was killed in a bar when he was only three!"

I stifled a laugh and explained the REAL lyrics, wondering what she'd been thinking as she sang these odd lyrics over and over for years. It reminded me of a time when I was little in church, singing a hymn about a feast of victory for the Lord. I always thought the congregation was saying, "This is the beast . . ." I *never* understood it!

Funny stuff, indeed! But how often do we rip through the "lyrics" of an age-old prayer or song without even CONSIDERING the words—the *meat*—of what we're saying, promising, or offering as praise to God?

It's easy to rattle things off without stopping to think about words we've recited a thousand times. But when we actually stop and think about what we're saying, it can be a complete game changer and offer us new and insightful ways to connect with our worship, worship we *thought* we knew by heart but maybe didn't after all!

"May these words of my mouth and this meditation of my heart be pleasing in your sight, Lord" (Psalm 19:14).

Dying would be easier
Jason Nelson

I was waiting to be called for a cardio rehab session, and I noticed a lady being wheeled in by a companion. It was clear she was not feeling well. When her name was called, she struggled to her feet and mumbled to herself, "Dying would have been easier." I could empathize with her. I've had times in my life when dying would have been easier. Maybe you have too.

It seems Job felt that way and with good reason. The piling up of hardships put a big damper on his life. **"The groans of the dying rise from the city, and the souls of the wounded cry out for help"** (Job 24:12). As we age, suffering can have a cumulative effect. There is no way to sugarcoat it. Each blip on an EKG or each dark spot on a CT scan causes a tug-of-war with Satan himself. Do we give up, or do we fight to keep going? We can even feel guilty that we may have ingested something we shouldn't have. **"But God charges no one with wrong-doing"** (Job 24:12).

It takes a well-tested faith to survive severe testing of faith because

Earth's joys grow dim; its glories pass away.
So hold thou thy cross before my closing eyes;
Shine through the gloom and point me to the skies.
Heaven's morning breaks, and earth's vain shadows flee;
In life . . . especially in life . . . O Lord, abide with me!

("Abide With Me," by Henry F. Lyte, adapted)

Cover the cost
Matt Ewart

"From that time on Jesus began to preach, 'Repent, for the kingdom of heaven has come near'" (Matthew 4:17).

I ask God for forgiveness so often that I often forget the weight of what I am really asking him to do.

When a fellow human being forgives me, it usually means that they have decided to overlook one of my indiscretions. Forgiveness means they agree not to be angry anymore, or at the very least it means they will refuse to act on their anger. To give forgiveness is often a form of self-restraint.

But when we ask God to forgive us, we are not asking him to overlook our indiscretions or restrain his anger. We are asking him to take the debt that our sin incurred (death) and transfer it to somebody other than us (Jesus).

Every time you pray to God and ask for his forgiveness, you are asking Jesus to cover the cost of your sins. And the cost was not small. When Jesus said to repent in our verse for today, he was saying that the lives of believers are lives of repentance.

Jesus loves you so much that he invites you to lay your sin on him. He invites a daily repentance by which you continually ask him to cover the cost of all your sins. The amazing thing about his grace is that while you and I might hesitate to stop forgiving someone, he never refuses to cover the cost.

How many questions do kids ask?
Daron Lindemann

"Why is that man homeless? What's that noise? Why can't I stay up late? Why aren't there any dinosaurs at the zoo?"

Do you know how many questions kids ask per day? Experts say about 450, depending on their age and environment. Asking questions is a healthy and important practice for kids' development. Asking questions is how they learn and understand.

The authorities who arrested and crucified Jesus **"questioned Jesus about his disciples and his teaching"** (John 18:19). Their questions, like those from a well-trained lawyer, were meant to lead toward a verdict that they had already decided.

Jesus got tired of their questions and in silence didn't answer most of them. Not because they asked but because they didn't want his answers.

Can you trust Jesus—who gave his life for you? Can you trust Jesus—whose knowledge is supreme? Can you trust Jesus—who loves you eternally and will be with you forever? Can you trust Jesus—who took great pains and made extreme sacrifices to fulfill every prophecy's detail about him and still intends to keep his every word to you.

Then stop putting Jesus on trial. He is faithful, right, and true. **"The word of the Lord is right and true; he is faithful in all he does"** (Psalm 33:4).

Ask Jesus questions in faith and believe him like kids do. You'll learn and understand so much more.

Good answer!
Liz Schroeder

Do you remember Richard Dawson, the original host of the game show *Family Feud*? When he would tell a contestant to "name something you would bring on a camping trip," the player would think for a moment and respond, "Toilet paper!" or, "Sleeping bag!" Then his or her teammates would cheer, "Good answer!" The bar was set fairly low, to be honest. As long as the player didn't blurt out something like, "A Jacuzzi," the teammates would shout, "Good answer!"

When the apostle Paul was arrested, he appealed to Caesar, as was his right as a Roman citizen. As Paul sat in jail, God lined up meetings for him with various leaders. At one, Paul shared his conversion story with King Agrippa and a court of high-ranking military officers and bigwigs of Caesarea (Acts 25:23). After they listened to Paul's testimony, Paul asked Agrippa if he believed what the prophets had written.

"Then Agrippa said to Paul, 'Do you think that in such a short time you can persuade me to be a Christian?' Paul replied, 'Short time or long—I pray to God that not only you but all who are listening to me today may become what I am, except for these chains'" (Acts 26:28,29, see also Acts 25:23-26:23).

Good answer! When God gives you the opportunity to share your conversion story, do it. What will that person do with it? God's grace demands a response. By the power of the Holy Spirit, may they too give a good answer.

Measuring up to her
Matt Trotter

I have a Proverbs 31 wife. Worth more than rubies (verse 10), stays up late to provide for her family (verse 18), no fear of snow or the snowblower (verse 21), and her daughters are ready for what's next (verses 26,28).

But have you read the first half of Proverbs 31? It's a great leadership teaching by a mom raising a good son, challenging him to ignore distractions and speak up:

"It is not for kings, Lemuel—it is not for kings to drink wine . . . lest they drink and forget what has been decreed, and deprive all the oppressed of their rights. Speak up for those who cannot speak for themselves. . . . Speak up and judge fairly; defend the rights of the poor" (verses 4,5,8,9).

Consider these verses for King Lemuel versus those about a woman set about her work vigorously with her strong arms?! Ah! This feels like accountability. Moderate my living so I can help people? It's hot in here . . .

If, like me, you are not perfect in this regard, look to Christ, who identified the people we are to aid. Read his Sermon on the Mount (Matthew 5–7) and let the people he holds in highest regard become your next volunteer gig. Reach out to a shut-in member of your congregation. Listen to those who can't vote at the next congregational meeting and consider their input in casting your vote. If all that tricky work with adults isn't your thing, remember Jesus held up children and said to let them come!

Thwarting apathy
Matt Ewart

Apathy is when you aren't moved by something that you should be moved by. In Jesus' parable of the good Samaritan, a helpless traveler was left for dead. Two travelers walked right by him without helping him. They were apathetic. They should have been moved to help, but they weren't.

Apathy is a major issue in today's world. There are two things working against us:

1. The world population is higher than ever. While that means a lot of good things, it also means that the number of tragedies and heartaches is increasing by the second.

2. News travels faster now than ever. If war or a natural disaster ravages the other side of this planet, you are notified of it within minutes.

Those two things, multiplied together, equal something that human beings cannot cope with. A necessary ability is to disengage our feelings from the things that we can do nothing about. But once we develop the ability to feel nothing about some things, it can be tempting to feel nothing about important things.

The biblical writer Paul encouraged people living in Rome with these words: **"Never be lacking in zeal, but keep your spiritual fervor, serving the Lord"** (Romans 12:11).

While you will never have the capacity to give the world what it needs, Jesus did. He refused to let apathy deter him from loving and saving you. So while you aren't moved by every tragedy, don't lose your fervor to love and serve those whom God brings into your world.

Let's talk about your sins
Mike Novotny

In late 2021 a song shocked the world. No one expected this quirky bilingual song to sell three million copies, but that is exactly what "We Don't Talk About Bruno" did. Ever heard it? From the animated movie *Encanto*, this song is about a certain member of a certain family whom they don't talk about. The family members feel comfortable talking about most things but not *that* thing.

Is that true for you? Is there something, most likely a personal struggle with an embarrassing sin, that you don't talk about? Does anyone in your world know about how inferior you feel when you scroll on social media or how instinctively you fall apart at one person's critical words or how often you are the first to order a drink and the last to stop drinking? Is anyone in your church family praying, encouraging, and spurring you on to fight your longtime battle against needing the last word or buying things you really can't afford? Does anyone truly know what kind of sinner you are?

The book of Proverbs teaches us, **"Whoever conceals their sins does not prosper, but the one who confesses and renounces them finds mercy"** (28:13). Few people make progress by keeping secrets. Maybe that's why God wants you to bring your fiercest spiritual battles into the light so that fellow believers can fight by your side.

Looking for mercy? It might be one honest confession away.

Flowers . . . again!
Katrina Harrmann

When the long Michigan winter finally lets go, I notice little shoots in my garden—even as the snow is still melting.

Usually it's the daffodils and hyacinths that are among the very first flowers brave enough to poke their heads through the soil into the cool sunlight.

There are years when they get snowed on as a reward. I have many photos of tulips and hyacinths bowing their pretty pink heads under the snow. But still, they push forward. It never ceases to amaze me to see life coming back to my garden after months of darkness and snow.

By now, I should be used to it, right? I see it every year, and yet something still thrills me.

I like to think it thrills God as well. Our God never gets tired of making miracles, miracles we get bored with that he never finds tiring—the sun rising, the stars shining—all of it is a daily miracle!

And he displays his love for us in the beauty of his creation. **"As long as the earth endures, seedtime and harvest, cold and heat, summer and winter, day and night will never cease"** (Genesis 8:22).

Let's exult in the returning of springtime—a miracle of God!

God's love for *you*
Mike Novotny

If you are one of those people who loves to learn and can't go to church without taking notes, this devotion is for you.

"The LORD said to Moses, 'Tell Aaron and his sons, "This is how you are to bless the Israelites. Say to them: 'The LORD bless you and keep you; the LORD make his face shine on you and be gracious to you; the LORD turn his face toward you and give you peace.'" So they will put my name on the Israelites, and I will bless them'" (Numbers 6:22-27).

In Hebrew, the three lines of the blessing are intentionally crafted. The first line contains three Hebrew words, the second line five Hebrew words, and the third line seven Hebrew words, as if the blessing is trying to expand and increase your soul's realization of God's good gifts.

The sacred name of the LORD shows up three times in those three lines, a hint, perhaps, of the Trinity. The Father blesses us. Jesus is gracious to us. The Spirit gives us peace.

But my favorite part is how personal this blessing is. It is meant for the masses but is worded in the singular—"the LORD bless *you*." Hebrew has different words for *you* (singular) and *you all* (plural), and this is the singular in every single line. It's like God is looking right at you, saying, "You are so blessed."

Ah, isn't Hebrew grammar the best?! May you grasp today the height and width and depth of God's love for *you* (singular) in Jesus.

Let God catch you
Katrina Harrmann

My dog is obsessed with the bunnies in our garden. She stands at the door constantly, waiting to go outside. And when she's outside, she spends all her time stalking through the flowers, looking for rabbits. It's an addiction.

The other day I even had a treat for her and was trying to chase her down and get her attention. But she had a bunny in her sights and would NOT be distracted!

Author L.M. Montgomery once wrote in her book *Emily Climbs*, "If we don't chase things, sometimes the things following us can catch up."

I love this quote. Sometimes the things following people are bad things. But inexplicably—like me with my silly dog—the things chasing after us are sometimes *good*.

Sometimes we run from good things without knowing it because we're so stubborn! Sometimes we *know* it's goodness chasing us down but that it will still be uncomfortable when it happens—because it requires change, or a reckoning, with how we've been living. When the good things catch up, it's not always easy.

Remember Jonah and the big fish? When Jonah finally stopped running, God "provided" a fish to swallow him whole. Like it or not, the thing following Jonah (God) had "caught up." And whether Jonah realized it at the time or not, it was a GOOD thing. A GOD thing.

Sometimes we need to stop chasing the things of this world and let God catch us.

"Seek the Lord while he may be found" (Isaiah 55:6).

At the foot of the cross
Linda Buxa

Our friends went on an adventure of a lifetime. After retiring from the military, Angie and Bryan embarked on the Camino Portuguese—a two-week hiking pilgrimage that took them over 180 miles from Sé Cathedral in Porto to Santiago de Compostela in Spain.

Before they left on the trip, they etched their names on some rocks and brought them along, knowing that many pilgrims place rocks at a monument along the way. This is a way of symbolically letting something go. After carrying that extra weight for 13 days, they left their rocks at the foot of a cross—and then kept walking.

What a beautiful picture of the reality for everyone who believes in Jesus. When you approach Jesus' cross, you get to leave your pain, hurts, sins, and the weight of the troubles you face there, all because Jesus said, **"It is finished"** (John 19:30). His pilgrimage on earth and his sacrifice on a cross have brought you peace with God.

When you leave all that at his cross, you get to spend more time thinking about the empty tomb, knowing that **"I have been crucified with Christ and I no longer live, but Christ lives in me. The life I now live in the body, I live by faith in the Son of God, who loved me and gave himself for me"** (Galatians 2:20).

When you leave your old self at the foot of Jesus' cross, you spend the rest of your pilgrimage walking by faith.

Being content
Clark Schultz

Our oldest son reached a milestone in his third-grade advanced reading course. As a reward, he asked for the entire set of *Diary of a Wimpy Kid* books—17 books to be exact. He was the happiest camper until a week later when he said to me, "Dad, what would really make me happy is the complete set of *Big Nate* books."

My reaction? I was angry, not at my son for his lack of contentment but at myself. How was I modeling contentment? Our 48-inch mower isn't big enough; we need the 52-inch deck. My cell phone doesn't have the three cameras; it only has two.

"But godliness with contentment is great gain. For we brought nothing into the world, and we can take nothing out of it. But if we have food and clothing, we will be content with that. Those who want to get rich fall into temptation and a trap and into many foolish and harmful desires that plunge people into ruin and destruction. For the love of money is a root of all kinds of evil. Some people, eager for money, have wandered from the faith and pierced themselves with many griefs" (1 Timothy 6:6-10).

It's not wrong to want or even have nice things. The problem begins when wanting nice things becomes more important than God. Practice being grateful to him for what you have. As a friend once reminded me, it's hard to be thankful and angry at the same time.

Is hell real?

Mike Novotny

In 1741 Jonathan Edwards, pastor and future president of Princeton, preached a sermon about hell. Entitled "Sinners in the Hands of an Angry God," his message had an explosive impact in the American colonies. Two hundred and seventy years later, in 2011, another famous American pastor, Rob Bell, wrote a book about hell. Entitled *Love Wins*, his message claimed that hell doesn't exist; that God is a loving God, not an angry one; and hell must be a human invention.

It appears that Americans, more and more, are less persuaded by Edwards' sermon and more influenced by Bell's book. The concept of hell feels unfair, exaggerated, perhaps invented by the church to control sincere people of faith.

But what did Jesus say? According to Jesus, does hell exist? If so, what is it like, and who goes there and why? And how can we escape it? Believe it or not, Jesus had a lot to say about hell, which is what I want to share with you in the upcoming devotions. Eighty-five percent of the times that *hell* appears in the Bible, it is a direct quote from the lips of Jesus.

There are lots of ideas, opinions, and conjectures about hell. Let's listen to the Lord who came down from heaven, the One who knows the whole truth about hell. **"Whatever I say is just what the Father has told me to say"** (John 12:50).

Three truths about hell
Mike Novotny

You can learn a lot about hell from Jesus. He once said, **"But I will show you whom you should fear: Fear him who, after your body has been killed, has authority to throw you into hell"** (Luke 12:5). Here we find three important truths about hell:

First, hell exists. Hell is not something that a bunch of old church guys made up to scare and control people. While it's true that some sinful church leaders use hell in a sinful way, talking about hell cannot be sinful, because a sinless Jesus talked about it. In fact, tons of Jesus' parables (or stories) talk about heaven and hell, eternal life and eternal fire, this guy goes to paradise and that guy goes to punishment.

Second, hell happens after death. We sometimes say, "It was hell. We went through hell." According to Jesus, that isn't true. If you were alive, that wasn't hell. It might have been insanely hard, but it wasn't hell. Hell happens after death, not before it.

Finally, God has authority to throw you into hell. When you die, you don't get to decide where you go. Your friends and family don't get to vote. Only God has that authority. He, and no one else, will make a judgment about your forever future. That's why Jesus says you should fear God.

Jesus wants to show you the truth about both heaven and hell. Listen to his words. Fear God, lamenting the seriousness of your sin and trusting that Jesus came down from heaven to save you from hell.

What hell is like
Mike Novotny

Years ago I was on a bus with a pastor friend and met a very extroverted woman who was very proud to tell us that she did not agree with our biblical beliefs. We weren't preaching or pushing her. She was driving the conversation about salvation, and at one point she said, "I know you guys think I'm going to hell, and I'm okay with that, because all my friends will be there."

No. I'm sorry, but that's not true. Not according to Jesus. He once told a story about a man in hell who screamed, **"I am in agony in this fire"** (Luke 16:24). Agony. Torment. A place where you weep and gnash your teeth. That's what hell is like.

Please, please believe Jesus when he speaks about hell. There's no happiness in hell. No good days. No friendship. No love. No one who cares. There's nothing good when you are separated from God. That's what hell is like.

We, perhaps even those who attend church, have downplayed a message that Jesus frequently preached. But if hell is as bad as Jesus says and heaven is as glorious as Jesus claimed, we must keep our focus on the life to come. In the end, all that truly matters is whether or not we will be with God.

So repent of your sins, and trust in his Son. Know that through Jesus, this life is as close to hell as Christians will ever get.

Every sinner needs a Savior
Mike Novotny

Who goes to hell? Who ends up in the fire that Jesus so often talked about? Ask the average American, and the answer is: "Hitler, serial killers, school shooters, and child abusers." But what did Jesus say?

A lot. In Matthew 18 Jesus threatened those who hurt children with a punishment worse than drowning. In Matthew 23 Jesus threatened church leaders who use God's name in order to use people and line their own pockets. In Matthew 5 Jesus said that anyone who gives in to anger and snaps at their brother is in danger of the fires of hell. In that same chapter, he made the same claim about those who look at a woman lustfully. Then in Matthew 25, Jesus explained that the damned will be damned because **"whatever you did not do for** [the hungry, the thirsty, the strangers, the sick, the imprisoned]**, you did not do for me"** (verse 45).

Sin condemns people to hell—the sin of abusing a child or shooting up a school or getting revenge or sneaking a lustful look or doing nothing when your fellow man is in need. If you disagree with that sentence, please know I have tried very, very hard simply to quote Jesus. You and I don't know better than the King of heaven when it comes to the truth about hell.

The truth is that every sinner needs a Savior to save them from the agony of hell. Me. You. Your grandmother. Your friend. Thankfully, **"Everyone who calls on the name of the Lord will be saved"** (Romans 10:13).

Jesus keeps you out of hell
Mike Novotny

How do you avoid the agony of hell? If Jesus truly said that angry, lustful, and selfish people (and not just serial killers and child abusers) are in danger of eternal fire, how can any of us be saved? Ask the man hanging on the cross next to Jesus. The Bible called him a "criminal," a word that means "evildoer" or someone who "customarily does what is wrong." But then something happened in this man's heart. He realized he was a sinner. By the power of the Holy Spirit, he came to see that Jesus was the Savior, the King who came down from heaven to help him avoid hell. That's why he cried, **"Jesus, remember me when you come into your kingdom"** (Luke 23:42). And what did Jesus say to this monster on death row? **"Jesus answered him, 'Truly I tell you, today you will be with me in paradise'"** (verse 43). Today. You. Paradise. That man is the paradigm of how sinners end up in paradise. Repent, believe, and you will be saved.

Without Jesus, the smallest sin would send us to hell. With Jesus, the biggest sin can't keep us out! Through repentance and faith, you are connected to Jesus. That means the sins that would damn you are dead and gone. That means the righteousness you need to be close to God is yours. That means that whenever your life on this earth ends, your future is set—you will be with God in paradise.

What must I do?
Jon Enter

In 1715 King Louis XIV of France died after a reign of 72 years. He called himself "the Great" and made certain his funeral was equally spectacular. As his body lay in a golden coffin, orders were given that the cathedral be dimly lit with a big, bright candle set above his coffin to dramatize his greatness. At the memorial service, Bishop Massillon began to speak, slowly reached down and snuffed out the candle, and said, "Only God is great." And he was exactly right! Only God is great! King Louis XIV forgot that truth. He's not alone.

The devil is so good at drawing our attention to those who fail God *more* than we do. When that's our focus, we develop a false sense of spiritual security. The devil is a pro at getting us to self-inflate our accomplishments and faithful living. "I'm better than I used to be." When that becomes our focus, Jesus isn't.

The apostle Paul warned the Romans about the devil's tricks, saying, **"No one will be declared righteous in God's sight by the works of the law"** (Romans 3:20). Our best isn't good enough. Bishop Massillon was right. *Only God is great.*

The beautiful truth of God's Word is that Christ's greatness, his perfection, is ours through faith. This life is not about making your mark like King Louis XIV; it's about trusting Jesus' hands, feet, and side are marked by his eternity-changing love for you. Trusting the power of Jesus' love, that's truly great!

Forever people
Nathan Nass

Every person you meet today will be around forever. Do you realize that? Every person you talk with today is going to be around forever either in heaven or hell. Every person you see today is on a path to experiencing either the most unimaginable joy forever with Jesus or the most severe punishment imaginable without him. Every person you meet today will be around forever. Do you realize that?

Too often, I don't. I treat people like they will be around for the next five minutes. I look out the window and have as much concern for the people driving by as for the ants racing around the sidewalk. Instead, my mind is on my tasks. On my work. On sports. On politics. On food. On stuff.

But do you know what's going to fade away? Tasks. Work. Sports. Politics. Food. Stuff. Do you know what's going to be around forever? People. Every person you meet today will be around forever.

Jesus realized that. So Jesus had grace for everyone. Every person was on Jesus' mind as he urgently preached repentance for the forgiveness of sins. Every person was on Jesus' mind as he died on a cross to win eternal life. What grace for all! For us!

Every person you meet today is going to be around forever. How does that change how you think about them? **"Be kind and compassionate to one another, forgiving each other, just as in Christ God forgave you"** (Ephesians 4:32).

The stories people tell
Matt Ewart

What will people say about you after you die?

While thinking about your death isn't among the most cheerful thoughts, being mindful of the finish line does affect how you run the race. I'm sure you know that you aren't just remembered for what you did on your best days. You are remembered for how you lived most days.

Most people, when they near their finish line, have some amount of regret. They could have had a different life and a different outcome if they had only lived in a different way.

Everyone will occasionally wonder what his or her life could have looked like if it hadn't been for certain regrets. Even right now you might grieve the life that *could have been* were it not for the mistakes you *did make*.

Never let your thoughts end with regret. Let every thought lead you to Jesus. His perfect life is credited to you. Your regret-filled life was put to death on his cross. Your story is not limited by your regrets; it is expanded by the power of grace.

Someday when I die, that's what I want people to remember about me. My life is not defined by my best moments or my worst regrets. It is defined by Christ's grace for me.

"Christ redeemed us from the curse of the law by becoming a curse for us" (Galatians 3:13).

What is it?

Mike Novotny

The word for *confess* in the Greek New Testament is ἐξομολογέω (*ex-homo-logeo*). *Logeo* often means "to speak or to say." *Homo* means "the same" (like a *homo-sexual* is attracted to the *same* sex). And *ex* frequently means "out" (like an *exit*). Put it all together, and the word means "to speak the same thing out."

That's what some brave souls did with John the Baptist. **"People went out to [John the Baptist] from Jerusalem and all Judea and the whole region of the Jordan.** *Confessing* **their sins, they were baptized by him in the Jordan River"** (Matthew 3:5,6). Tax collectors and prostitutes and all kinds of sinners had committed all kinds of sins, so they said exactly what they did out loud.

It is incredibly tempting to share (if you share at all) a sanitized, edited, filtered, less embarrassing version of your sins. But that's not true confession. Confession speaks of sin in all its ugliness, allowing others, like John the Baptist, to respond with forgiveness in all its beauty. If you choose for the sake of your own reputation to hide your sins, you will never get to bask in the moment that follows true confession, namely, when a fellow Christian who knows how bad you are still tells you how good grace is.

Confess to someone today. Say the same thing out loud. That truth will set you free.

We are so blessed
Mike Novotny

In the late 1970s, in a valley just southwest of Jerusalem, excavators stumbled upon some ancient burial caves. Inside, alongside the pottery and the bones, archaeologists found two tiny silver scrolls, measuring around an inch wide and a few inches tall. Written on both of the scrolls was the oldest surviving example of the Bible, dating back to the 600s B.C. A few lines and letters were broken off and missing, but the remaining words were clear: **"The Lord bless you and keep you"** (Numbers 6:24).

I have seen those little scrolls with my own eyes at a museum in Israel. You can see them with a quick search for "Ketef Hinnom Scrolls," but every believer has seen that blessing in their own life. The Lord blessed us when he gave us a Savior from every one of our sins. And then the Lord kept us from eternal danger by giving us the gift of faith day after day. Think of it: There are billions of people on the planet who do not repent of their sins or trust in Jesus as their Savior. If you do, by God's grace, you are truly blessed.

Some scholars called those tiny scrolls one of the most important discoveries ever made for biblical studies. I just call them a reminder of why we are so blessed. The Lord blessed us. And the Lord kept us. And God's keeping is one of our best blessings.

Four little improvements for praying
Daron Lindemann

Lots of people want to pray better but don't know how. Here is a model prayer from Nehemiah 1. It breaks down into a helpful teaching tool that has improved my own praying.

Start by praying more about God than you. Invoke characteristics and works of God more than your problems. Say things such as "Our Father," "God, you are good all the time," or "Jesus, you're human, so you get this."

It focuses your faith like it focused Nehemiah's: **"Lord, the God of heaven, the great and awesome God, who keeps his covenant of love"** (Nehemiah 1:5).

Nehemiah also confessed his sins (verse 6). His confession led to repentance, which is the catalyst for real, heartfelt change. And personal change is the path to changing the world. Start with the person in the mirror.

Even though God knows everything, he wants you to ask in prayer. When you ask, you will pay attention more closely for the answer. So ask like Nehemiah: **"Give your servant success"** (verse 11).

Prayer, however, must not be a way of getting things from God, as if he's a vending machine. Nehemiah spoke the word *servant* 8 times in these 11 verses. He wasn't praying as if he was the lord or the master; that's God. He was praying as a servant. It's all about God.

There's a name for this teaching tool. It's called P-R-A-Y. Praise. Repent. Ask. Yield. Use that outline for your praying this week.

Destroy the snares
Linda Buxa

The Israelites were about to enter the Promised Land. Moses gave a series of farewell speeches that are recorded in the book of Deuteronomy, which literally means "words." Using almost 788,280 words (the name of the book seems pretty appropriate, doesn't it?), Moses repeated the laws for the people who had been younger than 40 years old when the journey started.

Included in these sermons was wisdom he learned from 40 years of watching the Israelites follow God, then rebel, then repent, then follow God, then rebel. He applied that to his cautions for the next generation as they prepared to meet the current residents of Canaan: **"Do not look on them with pity and do not serve their gods, for that will be a snare to you"** (Deuteronomy 7:16). They didn't take that wisdom to heart, and the Bible tells about a whole host of problems that followed.

Even though we live 3,500 years later, it's easy to think that God's priorities about our money, time, sexuality, or words are restrictive. Then we look at the people around us who don't know God, love God, or follow his commands, and we might be tempted to follow them. Sometimes their lives look easier, their priorities seem more fun, and they don't seem to suffer any consequences.

But that's a shortsighted view, and you and I need to take Moses' caution seriously. Once we destroy the snares, then we can follow the advice from Solomon: **"Do not let your heart envy sinners, but always be zealous for the fear of the Lord"** (Proverbs 23:17).

My favorite *sola*
Jason Nelson

One of the great catchphrases in history lingers among us in the old Latin language: *sola fide* (faith alone), *sola scriptura* (scripture alone), *sola gratia* (grace alone). Taken together these discreet elements are the motto of Christianity. Each is preeminent in our belief system, and yet they depend on each other. **"For it is by grace you have been saved, through faith"** (Ephesians 2:8). How do I know? The Bible tells me so.

I like them all, but grace is my favorite *sola* because of what you can't do with it. You can't legalize it. You can't weaponize it. You can't beat people down with it. There's no confusion over it. By contrast, faith can be found on a continuum of weak to great. People can be made to feel theirs isn't developed enough. That causes doubt within us. The interpretation of the Bible gets debated and can cause controversy, which leads to divisions among us. But grace can never be misused. It is always the unencumbered expression of God's love for us. It is his essence. He demonstrated it in that while we were still sinners, Christ died for us. Not some of us. Not just the strong ones. Not only the confirmed in the faith. He died for all of us, and none of us deserved for that to happen. Grace is never ambiguous.

So I plead with you to anchor your faith in Jesus and on grace alone.

The desert will bloom
Nathan Nass

Have you ever seen the desert? The real desert? I once drove through the Mojave Desert in the middle of summer. Do you know what it's like? Dead. Dry. Empty. Hot. No flowers. No trees. Just desolation.

That lonely drive made me appreciate one of God's promises: **"The desert and the parched land will be glad; the wilderness will rejoice and blossom. Like the crocus, it will burst into bloom; it will rejoice greatly and shout for joy"** (Isaiah 35:1,2). Here is God's promise: The desert will bloom! That's how powerful God is. God is able to make even the desert bloom!

Sometimes I feel like a desert inside. Do you know what I mean? Because of my sins, because of other people's sins, I feel dead inside. Dry. Empty. Desolate. I feel like there's no hope. Like nothing could grow. Not here. Do you ever feel like that?

Then remember this: God can make even the desert bloom! The God who can turn dry, desolate wastelands into fields of wildflowers can take your heart and make it new. He can take your life and make it bloom.

When Jesus died on a cross, he washed all your sins away. When you were baptized, God gave you new life in Christ. When you hear God's Word, the seeds of faith and hope are planted in your heart. I know life can feel like you're driving through a desert, but trust this: God can make even deserts bloom!

The best time to prune
Liz Schroeder

Get out your pruning shears! According to horticulturalists, spring is the best time to prune a tree so that it maintains its structural integrity. You'll want to trim it back before the growing season—nip it in the bud, so to speak. Failure to do so will produce a gangly tree that is prone to come crashing down during a storm.

In Christ's illustration of the vine and the branches, he talks about how the owner of a vineyard ensures a bumper crop by getting rid of unfruitful branches and by pruning the fruitful ones.

"Every branch in Me that does not bear fruit, He takes away; and every *branch* that continues to bear fruit, He [repeatedly] prunes, so that it will bear more fruit [even richer and finer fruit]" (John 15:2, AMP).

If you are going through a time of pruning in your life—if it seems that every comfort is being stripped away—rejoice that you are found worthy of pruning. By the grace of God and power of the Holy Spirit, you are bearing fruit: love, joy, peace, forbearance, kindness, goodness, faithfulness, gentleness, and self-control (see Galatians 5:22,23). Getting more of those things in your life—have you ever prayed for patience?—requires the painful process of pruning.

Now is the best time for God to prune you. As the heavenly harvest approaches, now is not the time to allow self-control and faithfulness to wither. Instead, may the Lord produce in you a bumper crop of peace that will weather any storm.

Church size matters
Mike Novotny

If you want to live your best church life, please don't miss this essential truth—church size matters. The number of people who call your church their "church home" matters.

Just ask Moses. When the megachurch we call the people of Israel escaped from Egypt, Moses was single-handedly trying to pastor a metropolis worth of people. But when his father-in-law took one look at the weary look on Moses' face and the impatient looks on Israel's faces, he stated, **"What you are doing is not good. You and these people who come to you will only wear yourselves out"** (Exodus 18:17,18). Thankfully, Moses came to accept that church size matters (read the rest of Exodus 18 for the resolution).

Imagine you were a member at a church of ten people and your best friend was a member at a church of ten thousand people. Would you expect talented musicians to lead worship at each church? personal access to call the pastor whenever to talk about whatever? well-organized programs for new moms, teens, young professionals, retirees, and recovering addicts? a place where everybody knows everybody else's name? It depends! Neither big churches nor small churches are better according to the Bible, but it is important for you to know what kind of church you are.

Your Father in heaven wants you to have a great spiritual life. By thinking through the size of your church (with all its pros and cons), you will be one step closer to loving the church you call home.

MAY

Surely God is my help;
the Lord is the one who sustains me.

Psalm 54:4

Your spiritual gift?
Mike Novotny

If you had to give yourself a letter grade for confrontation, which letter would you pick? That was one of the questions I emailed to our ministry staff, curious to see how many of them were honest with others in their lives. "C+" one woman wrote, explaining that her big, harmony-loving heart made it difficult to speak the truth. "D+," another admitted, "I RUN from confrontation." "B," an experienced Christian added, "with practice, it gets easier."

How about you? Maybe your boyfriend gets angry over a hundred things that don't really matter. Or your sister, who says she loves Jesus, is saying stuff on social media that Jesus doesn't love. Or your buddy says things about other ethnic groups that make you cringe. Or your son moved in and started a family together with his girlfriend, as if sex *after* marriage was just his mom and dad's idea.

Have you talked to them? Or, like most of us, are you just talking *about* them? If you're flunking freshman confrontation class, God wants to help you in the days to come through his inspired Word. **"All Scripture is God-breathed and is useful for teaching, rebuking, correcting and training in righteousness, so that the servant of God may be thoroughly equipped for every good work"** (2 Timothy 3:16,17).

Scripture is useful for comforting those who confess and confronting those who don't. So let's open God's Word and see how our Father can equip us for the agonizing but essential work of confronting one another.

God is with you
Mike Novotny

I bet you would rather not confront the sinners in your life. Not only is the conversation itself often awkward, but most people are too proud and defensive to receive biblical correction. There's a reason why the prophets were not the most popular kids in Old Testament times!

But confrontation is essential because unconfronted sin is like cancer. It grows and gets worse and gets dangerous. If no one says anything about her drifting from Jesus, she will end up very far from Jesus, perhaps for all eternity. If no one stops the pastor who uses his authority to bully his congregation into submission, people will walk away from organized Christianity once and for all. If you don't speak up courageously about his drinking or her flirting or their lifestyle, there will be heartbreaking consequences, both physical and spiritual, right now and potentially forever.

God is saying to you what he said to Joshua: **"Have I not commanded you? Be strong and courageous. Do not be afraid; do not be discouraged, for the LORD your God will be with you wherever you go"** (Joshua 1:9).

Don't let fear or discouragement keep you from humbly, biblically, and lovingly confronting a fellow Christian. It may not be a walk in the park, but it is the best option when someone God loves is caught in a sin.

Be strong, brother. Don't be afraid, sister. God will be with you wherever you go, even if you are going into a confrontation today.

Who should confront?
Mike Novotny

Does God want you personally to confront, call out, and judge other sinners? Jesus' answer is, "Depends." He preached, **"Why do you look at the speck of sawdust in your brother's eye and pay no attention to the plank in your own eye? You hypocrite, first take the plank out of your own eye, and then you will see clearly to remove the speck from your brother's eye"** (Matthew 7:3,5).

Jesus doesn't want you to call others to repentance if you haven't repented yourself. Don't express your concern about your friend being gay if you are living/ sleeping with your girlfriend. Don't yell, "Stop yelling!" Don't accuse someone of stubbornly trying to win an argument because you're trying to win the argument. First, look into the mirror of God's Word and see your own sinfulness. Repent.

But if you are repentant, you are called to confront. "Then you will see clearly," Jesus said, "to deal with your brother's sin." You don't have to be perfect to say something, just repentant.

If someone gets defensive and throws your sin back in your face—"Who are you to talk?!"—you can say, "You're right. I sin too. But I'm sorry for that sin. Are you?"

Please don't assume that confrontation is just for the pastor or the boldest members of your church. It's part of your calling, a crucial way that God keeps his children from straying so that they can spend forever with him (and you) in heaven.

How do you do it?
Mike Novotny

If you see someone caught in a sin and know God is asking you to say something, please don't forget the Golden Rule of Confrontation: Confront them like you'd want them to confront you.

Jesus taught us, **"So in everything, do to others what you would have them do to you"** (Matthew 7:12). "Everything" includes confrontation. In other words, if the tables were turned, how would you prefer to be confronted?

I bet you'd want the truth. As much as we want our doctors to tell us we're as healthy as ever, we would prefer the true diagnosis if there was something concerning on the scans. In the same way, give someone the truth about their sin. Bring a Bible, open it to the passage that applies, and give them examples of where you see a pattern of behavior. Don't let them weasel out with their feelings or opinions. Keep the Bible open and your finger pointing to the passage that is your cause for concern. Give them the truth.

While you're giving them the truth, speak in love. Love is kind, talking to the sinner instead of about the sinner, so don't gossip with others about it. Love listens, willing to accept information that you might not have known about the situation. Love is patient, giving the sinner some time and space to process your concern. Love isn't easily angered when sinners get defensive.

Truth and love. That's how you confront others in a way you would want to be confronted.

What could go right?
Mike Novotny

When it comes to having hard conversations with people we love, our anxious minds immediately rush to worst-case scenarios. He'll get defensive. She'll shut down. He'll blow up. She'll never be my friend again.

While those aren't illogical thoughts, make sure you also think of what could go right. He could repent. She could thank you for getting her back to God. He could reconnect with the truth. She could be with you in heaven. That could happen. Many times that does happen.

Not long ago, I heard about a woman who confronted her sister who was saying some unbiblical things, caused by the pain of losing the love of her life. With patience and courage, the woman pointed out her sister's sin, and—thank God—the sister humbly received the rebuke. In fact, the sister who got called out emailed me to say, "Now I am back on track. I thanked my sister for her courage. I still have a long road ahead, but at least now I see that I am on the right path."

Jesus said such wonderful things could happen! **"If your brother or sister sins, go and point out their fault, just between the two of you. If they listen to you, you have won them over"** (Matthew 18:15).

It's not foolish to prepare yourself for what might go wrong, but please don't forget to consider what might go right. You might win them over. You might win them back for God. Angels will rejoice with you when they come back.

Faith + mountains
Matt Trotter

I toured the Holy Land a few years ago with my friend Mike. One day he said, "Let's start our day with a six-mile run up and down a mountain. It'll be worth it; I promise." He also promised one other thing about our trip. He said that I would return home and find that reading the Bible would be different—3D, full-color different. It wasn't long after returning that I was reading the Great Commission in Matthew 28. One word shocked me that I had missed countless times before: **"Then the eleven disciples went to Galilee, to the *mountain* where Jesus had told them to go. When they saw him, they worshiped him; but some doubted. Then Jesus came to them and said, 'All authority in heaven and on earth has been given to me'"** (verses 16–18).

Did Mike run me up that mountain? It's possible. We ran up Mount Arbel. From there we could see all of Galilee and perhaps farther. There were huge caves that could have hosted 11 disciples easily. I'm not sure if the mountain in this passage is the same one I was on, nor do I know if you'll ever make it to Galilee. But I would challenge you to meditate on *every word* you read in the Bible. Slow down and draw it all in. Every word has been placed by the Holy Spirit and made to connect you to the ancient Scriptures that promise a Messiah and to your role of sharing the gospel with others.

To whom should you confess?
Mike Novotny

In a world where plenty of people are gossips and plenty of others are terribly judgmental, to whom should you confess the whole truth of your sinfulness? Good question. The Bible's answer? Start with your pastor.

After encouraging struggling Christians to **"call the elders of the church"** (a.k.a. the pastors, James 5:14), James writes, **"Therefore confess your sins to each other and pray for each other so that you may be healed"** (5:16). God doesn't want to be the only one to hear your confessions. He wants your pastor(s) to truly know you so they can truly pray for you.

This isn't a requirement to sit in a confessional booth but an opportunity to find freedom in the gospel. The man whom God called to (1) know the gospel and (2) care for your soul is in the perfect position to offer you Jesus when shame is dragging you down. As a pastor myself, I can tell you that I am totally unequipped to answer most people's questions about their careers, college choices, etc. I am, however, incredibly equipped to offer grace to those who are drowning in guilt.

Pastors aren't the only ones, of course, who can share the gospel with you. But they are a wonderful place to start. So if you don't have a pastor, start searching for a faithful church home today. If you do, let your pastor know the real you. That just might be the way that God heals you and helps you move forward with his grace.

More than a glimpse
Matt Ewart

There was a first-century man named Zacchaeus. Not many people liked him, not even his own people.

The reason not many people liked him was because he decided to spend his life supporting the empire that was oppressing his own people. Zacchaeus was a tax collector, siphoning taxes from his fellow countrymen to support the Roman Empire. And as a "chief" tax collector, Zacchaeus was known for being good at what he did.

But one day Zacchaeus became known for something else.

Jesus was coming through his town. I'll let Luke tell the story:

"[Zacchaeus] **wanted to see who Jesus was, but because he was short he could not see over the crowd. So he ran ahead and climbed a sycamore-fig tree to see him, since Jesus was coming that way"** (Luke 19:3,4).

Have you ever felt like Zacchaeus? Maybe you felt like you were not worthy to be loved or even seen by Jesus, so you just went to get a glance. Maybe your version of "getting a glance" meant trying out a church for the first time or asking a friend about their faith or clicking on an online devotion.

I hope that what happened to Zacchaeus will happen to you. He just wanted a glance of Jesus, but he ended up getting Jesus as his guest. And from that moment on, Zacchaeus' life was changed forever. (Read Luke 19:1-10 for the full story.)

Praise the Lord!
Clark Schultz

When we gather in church to worship, we are worshiping the Creator-God. He's the MVP, the One and Only, the triune God who deserves our best and our respect.

But sometimes when we worship, we're far from our best. Perhaps we go into a tailspin if a new hymn is played or the baptismal font is moved 1/8 of an inch out of place. Defiance captures our hearts over something different. Perhaps church is too crowded or not crowded enough, and that leads to grumbling over numbers. Maybe the pastor's sermon hits close as he calls out a pet sin, and resentment takes the place of respect.

Depending on your stage in life, does the mention of eternity comfort, bore, or even make you afraid? Psalm 111 reminds us to simply **"praise the Lord"** (verse 1). The psalmist reminds us of all God's blessings to us.

Heart-check time: Stop and think of all the blessings God has given you. Also answer this question: Is worship something you do for God or something God does for you? You and I have freedom to worship our awesome God. In church we have a place to worship him. We have a Savior who died for all our sins and gives us peace that they are forgiven. Jesus tells us he is with us always and will be with us when we are welcomed home into his loving arms. Now that's a reason to worship! Praise the Lord!

I'm glad he asked
Jason Nelson

Recently, a younger man who knows my difficult health story asked me a show-stopping question: "How have you made it this far?" *Hmm* . . . I paused to gather my thoughts and said, "I'm glad you asked me that." I knew we both needed to hear the answer to his question. How *did* I make it this far? I told him I didn't want to be overly dramatic or say something cliché. So I said, "Well, you just can't quit."

The Bible refers to "not quitting" as perseverance. We are directed to **"run with perseverance the race marked out for us"** (Hebrews 12:1). Each of us has a different race marked out for us. No two races are the same. But all races have this in common: **"The testing of [our] faith produces perseverance"** (James 1:3). Becoming *non-quitters* is a ripening fruit of the Spirit that persistently animates us in Christ's perseverance. This younger man was experiencing that himself. He still feels tempted to quit and has at times in the past. He has experienced the regrettable consequences of quitting. But he now recognizes that with God at his side, he is able to quit no more. He seems to understand that not quitting is the threshold to succeeding.

I suspect there are times when you feel like quitting too. Please don't. Take a deep breath and think about it. **"May the Lord direct your hearts into God's love and Christ's perseverance"** (2 Thessalonians 3:5).

Already yours
Jon Enter

Ali Hafed was a wealthy man who lived in ancient Persia. When he discovered the extreme value of diamonds, he suddenly wasn't content. He sold his expansive farmland and traveled the world looking for diamonds. His money ran out, and he never found a single diamond. Broken and depressed, he ended his life.

Meanwhile, the man who bought Ali Hafed's property saw a twinkle of light in a stream. It was a diamond! He found 10,000,000 carats of diamonds more! Ali Hafed had a literal diamond mine of fortune, but he overlooked the blessings he already had.

You are also blessed, wealthy beyond imagination! Wealth isn't always measured in bank accounts. The devil convinces Christians to overlook and underappreciate the grandness of the blessings God has poured upon them.

Do you have food in the fridge? You are blessed.

Do you have money saved in a bank? You are blessed.

Do you have a home that safely locks and is climate controlled? You are blessed.

Do you have access to health care? You are blessed.

Do you have the ability to worship Jesus freely? You are blessed.

Do you have your past forgiven and your future in heaven secured? Yes, you do! You are blessed.

Because of these truths, **"rejoice always . . . give thanks in all circumstances; for this is God's will for you in Christ Jesus"** (1 Thessalonians 5:16,18). What blessings from God have you overlooked? Today, give thanks!

Unsure or unwilling
Jason Nelson

One of Jesus' disciples damaged his personal brand forever by being skeptical. Thomas was missing when the resurrected Jesus appeared to the other disciples. When they told Thomas they had seen the Lord, he said, **"Unless I see the nail marks in his hands and put my finger where the nails were, and put my hand into his side, I will not believe"** (John 20:25). Thomas was willing to die with this man he believed was the hope of Israel. But he was traumatized and disillusioned by the gruesome execution of his beloved Messiah.

Jesus later appeared to his disciples, including Thomas. How did Jesus treat a man who needed to touch God for himself? Jesus held out his hand and drew Thomas to his side and said, **"Stop doubting and believe"** (verse 27). Jesus understood that doubt isn't the same as unbelief, that being unsure isn't the same as being unwilling.

I can only speak for myself, but I too have moments of doubt and have needed Jesus to extend his hand to me in a very personal way. Those times of doubt have agitated me and energized me to reach out and rediscover the Savior I so desperately want to believe in. Christianity is a faith that grows when God validates what we know about him through our unique experiences with him. That is how he gets us to stop doubting and confess over and over again, **"My Lord and my God!"** (verse 28).

They tried to bury us
Daron Lindemann

Have you been stepped on, leaving you feeling flattened and unappreciated, down and out? Have you been denied an opportunity you desired, crushing your dream? Have you buried a talent or passion because you're afraid of expressing it fully or afraid of failure?

These words by Greek poet Dinos Christianopoulos came into my inbox and made me pause: *"They tried to bury us. They didn't know we were seeds."*

Various political and social movements have claimed that statement as a rally cry. Better than that, the truth behind it can be found in the Bible.

"What you sow does not come to life unless it dies. When you sow, you do not plant the body that will be, but just a seed" (1 Corinthians 15:36,37).

Those words are from the Bible's great resurrection chapter that proclaims victory because Jesus rose from the dead. Jesus was buried, but he came back to life like a seed.

Jesus is the one with the power, not the executive board, not the city council, not the consultants, not the accountants, not the social media comments or even your own delusional feelings that convincingly call you a loser.

They don't know you're a seed. Live victoriously today because of Jesus!

Homework: This secular saying about seeds is a life principle that those who don't yet believe in Jesus can understand. Talk about it with a friend who needs something greater than secular hope—the life-saving power of Jesus. Their name. Right now. Say it. Pray it. Don't delay it.

You are like Roman concrete
Linda Buxa

In Rome, the famous Pantheon, which was completed around A.D. 128 and has an unreinforced concrete dome, still stands. Some ancient aqueducts are still used today as well. And in these structures, if cracks develop, they heal themselves. For years, researchers were stumped. How did ancient engineers come up with a material that has not only survived for thousands of years but has actually gotten stronger—even structures built in harsh conditions like seawalls or sewers or in areas that are seismically active?

Finally in 2023, researchers from MIT, Harvard University, and laboratories in Italy and Switzerland published a paper in the journal *Science Advances* sharing that they discovered the reason: hot mixing and lime casts. (Google it. I'm not an engineer, and I'll mess it up if I try to explain it.)

However, because I am a devotion writer, I get to share that people who believe in Jesus are like Roman concrete. Instead of getting your strength from hot mixing and lime casts, you get it from God. As you grow closer to him, you **"live a life worthy of the Lord and please him in every way: bearing fruit in every good work, growing in the knowledge of God,** *being strengthened with all power according to his glorious might so that you may have great endurance* **and patience"** (Colossians 1:10,11).

This means that whatever harsh conditions you face, you have great endurance. Whenever the cracks happen that inevitably come from living in a broken world, God's glorious might heals you. When the world feels like it's shaking, he gives you strength to keep standing.

What's in it for you?
Matt Ewart

For some people, following Jesus can extol a great price.

For business owners, Christ-like love means you quote an honest price even when you know there isn't any competition.

For employees, it means giving your employer your best effort even when it isn't reciprocated.

For husbands, it means being ready to lay down your life even when you aren't respected.

For wives, it means being willing to follow even when the direction isn't what you would choose.

If you were a follower of Jesus in the first century, you could have been rejected by your family, fired from a job, imprisoned, or killed. But even in those circumstances, Jesus held out this promise:

"'Truly I tell you,' Jesus replied, 'no one who has left home or brothers or sisters or mother or father or children or fields for me and the gospel will fail to receive a hundred times as much in this present age: homes, brothers, sisters, mothers, children and fields—along with persecutions—and in the age to come eternal life'" (Mark 10:29,30).

Nobody can take away the eternal life that Jesus secured for you. But even in this life, there is a promise. Following Jesus puts you in the company of many other people who are following him too. So even if following Jesus means you lose something, you will gain much more through the multitude who follow Jesus with you.

Hi, my name is . . .

Liz Schroeder

This will not come as a shock, but Jesus is better than a 12-step program. I have the privilege of serving as a Resilient Recovery group facilitator, and many of the women in the program have gotten sober with the aid of Alcoholics Anonymous. While I am grateful for the help they received that kept them alive long enough to hear the gospel, there is a degree of reframing that needs to happen in the area of identity once they know Jesus.

Even if you've never stepped foot in AA, you've seen it on TV: "Hi, my name is Taylor, and I'm an alcoholic."

"Hi, Taylor."

Really? Thirty, forty, fifty years of a person's life can be summed up by classifying their pet sin? These are mothers, sisters, entrepreneurs, students getting their GEDs or tech certifications. They've experienced unimaginable loss and redeeming love. They are survivors, storytellers, and breakers of generational strongholds. But most of all, they are children of God.

"Alcoholics" might be what they were, but they've been given a new identity. As Paul writes, **"Neither . . . thieves nor the greedy nor drunkards nor slanderers nor swindlers will inherit the kingdom of God. And that is what some of you** *were.* **But you were washed, you were sanctified, you were justified in the name of the Lord Jesus Christ and by the Spirit of our God"** (1 Corinthians 6:9–11).

What about you? Would you rather introduce yourself as the pet sin of your past or who you are in Christ? Live in that new identity today.

Hungry for the right stuff
Katrina Harrmann

One night my son ate the following over a span of 5 hours: 2 cookies, 2 bowls of chicken pasta, chocolate milk, 24 wontons, 2 hamburgers, a pickle, a milkshake, and a bowl of cereal. It was like watching *The Very Hungry Caterpillar* in real time!

He laughs when we joke about his "hollow leg," which is a completely normal thing for a healthy, active, growing teenage boy. (Boy, do they eat!)

But it made me think about how sometimes in life we ingest unhealthy combinations of consumables that AREN'T food: the movies we watch, the company we keep, the habits we form, the books we read, the mindless scrolling on our phones. We ingest and consume and devour, and it isn't all good and healthy stuff.

And we're all guilty.

It's easy to ingest too much junk, isn't it? Especially in this day and age with information at our fingertips designed to feed and encourage any and all habits, views, and lifestyles. The devil makes it even easier, telling us it's no big deal. But we blink, and all of a sudden we've strayed so far that we can't see our safe harbor and are in danger of drowning.

So keep an eye on what you consume! Milkshakes and pickles may be okay, but what you devote your THOUGHTS and most of all your HEART to is most important! Seek God in these moments!

"Above all else, guard your heart, for everything you do flows from it" (Proverbs 4:23).

God keeps you
Mike Novotny

In the famous blessing of Numbers 6, it says, **"The Lord bless you and keep you"** (verse 24). You can guess what it means to be blessed, but do you understand the miracle of being kept?

Think about a door for a second. Why do you have doors on your home? Answer—to keep you. Doors keep dangers out—strangers, animals, and elements like wind and rain. And if you have little kids, doors keep loved ones in.

What doors do for your family, God does for your faith. You and I, like curious kids, are prone to wander. Temptation is tempting, and sin is fun. Part of us wants it. There are friends, classmates, coworkers, websites, and more that want us to believe their messages too. "Be true to yourself." "Jesus is *a* way to get to heaven." "It's my right to say what I want!" The basic message of Jesus—repent of your sins, believe in God's Son, and be saved—is reconsidered every day. Not everyone stays. Not everyone keeps the faith.

And that is why your keeping is such a blessing. If your sinful nature hasn't led you out into the deadly road of no repentance, God has kept you! If you believe that truth belongs to God and not to your heart, God has kept you! If the devil hasn't convinced you that you are unforgivable and that you being in heaven is impossible, God has kept you!

God didn't just call you to faith back then. He has kept you in the faith until now. What a blessing!

Pray it forward
Jon Enter

Who causes you pain? Who breaks promises, repeatedly crushing your heart or knowing just what to say to hurt you? Who does regrettable things but doesn't regret them?

It's emotionally exhausting to be the collateral damage of someone's bad day and evil actions. Hurt people (you) tend to hurt people (them), but God's Word forbids revenge and retaliation. **"Do not take revenge, my dear friends, but leave room for God's wrath, for it is written: 'It is mine to avenge; I will repay,' says the Lord"** (Romans 12:19). This passage shows revenge is wrong, but it does say God brings the heat of fiery judgment.

So here's the big question: Is it okay to pray that God's justice falls upon those who've hurt you?

In Acts 7, Jewish leaders heard Stephen, a Christian, tell the truth that Jesus was crucified, rose from the dead, and stands next to the Father in glory. They dragged him outside the city and began to stone him. During that onslaught of deadly rock strikes, Stephen prayed *for* his attackers: **"Lord, do not hold this sin against them"** (Acts 7:60).

That prayer was answered! One of those who approved of Stephen's death was Saul, who became Paul, one of the greatest Christian missionaries ever. Stephen prayed *for* those who attacked him.

Want a better boss? Pray *for* your boss. Want a better relationship with a family member? Pray daily *for* that person. Pray *for* their restoration, not for revenge. Pray and watch what God does!

By grace
Clark Schultz

While gift shopping for my wife, I came across an ad that offered a free purse. Who doesn't like free? However, the fine print said, "Free with a $100 or more purchase." So basically, I needed to buy an overpriced item to get an item for free? Pass.

Ever heard of Christian Ludwig Scheidt? He wrote a hymn entitled "By Grace I'm Saved, Grace Free and Boundless." Every stanza starts with the words *by grace* and echo the apostle Paul's words in Ephesians 2:8,9: **"For it is by grace you have been saved, through faith— and this is not from yourselves, it is the gift of God— not by works, so that no one can boast."**

When it comes to your salvation, there's no fine print. It's a gift. This gift cost Jesus his life, but he gifts you with eternal life and the assurance that ALL your sins are forgiven. No tricks. No bait and switch. FREE.

This news needs to be shared! During the seventh inning stretch of a recent baseball game that I attended, a stadium worker donned an air gun that launched free T-shirts from the dugout clear up to the upper deck. It was wild to watch all the folks clamoring to catch a free T-shirt that was hurdling at them at high speed. Wouldn't it be cool if we, with the same zeal and speed, took this message of freedom, heaven, and sins forgiven and shared it with our neighbors, coworkers, and friends? No tricks. It's free.

Your "soil" matters
Katrina Harrmann

In early spring, I get my annual delivery from a local landscaping company. Most people would be offended if someone walked up to them and handed them a bunch of dirt, but nothing thrills me more than to see that dump truck pull into my driveway. As the truck's bed tips up, mounds and mounds of beautiful, fluffy black soil tumble out.

I call it black gold. It clumps up beautifully when you squeeze it and smells like green, growing things.

Soil matters. It's important to renew the nutrients of tired, old soil because if you don't, the plants that grow in it will be stunted and lack nutrients.

People are the same. If our "environment" is off and we don't nurture ourselves in the right ways spiritually, nothing we do will flourish.

Our environment, and the things we let into it or the things we let deplete it, can affect our faith and our lives.

One year I didn't bother with composting my garden because it takes time and effort, and I wasn't up for it. My garden was a sad, sorry mess and hardly produced any harvest.

The same holds true if we don't nurture ourselves with God's Word and create a spiritual environment rich in God's teachings. We wither on the vine instead of growing fruitful.

"Blessed is the one who trusts in the LORD, whose confidence is in him. They will be like a tree planted by the water that sends out its roots by the stream" (Jeremiah 17:7,8).

Unhealthy fears
Matt Ewart

"Do not let your hearts be troubled and do not be afraid" (John 14:27).

I had an unhealthy fear of law enforcement when I was starting to drive as a teenager. Even though I knew that police officers were there to help, I couldn't shake the fear that they could pull me over at any time.

One day I realized how unhealthy my fear had become. I was driving along a two-lane country highway. A car was approaching me from the opposite direction. When the vehicle was close enough for me to see the other driver's eyes, I realized that the other driver was a police officer. My automatic response was to slam on the brakes for fear that I was speeding (even though I wasn't). Thankfully I didn't lose control of the vehicle. But because of my suspicious driving maneuver, I did get pulled over.

What are some of your unhealthy fears? What has been consuming your attention to an unhealthy degree? Go ahead and think back to last week. What were some things that you were worried about? Did your fear fix any problems? Did it make you a better person to be around? Did your worries reveal a proper faith in Jesus?

It's no wonder that the Bible is filled with hundreds of commands and encouragements to "fear not." Today, start making a list of your unhealthy fears. Then you will see how a healthy fear of God puts to death every unhealthy fear.

An age of rediscovery
Jason Nelson

The 15th to 17th centuries are often referred to as the Age of Discovery. Columbus and other notables hoisted sails, caught prevailing winds, and discovered places people didn't know existed. I would like to suggest that we are entering an "age of rediscovery" just as historic because God is bound to keep his covenant **"for all generations to come"** (Genesis 9:12). An ascending generation of storm-tested travelers are claiming God's promises for themselves. They also see rainbows.

Like all good explorers, they are coming of age in turbulent times. Consider how stories of brazen scandals, a pandemic, school shootings, and political dysfunction have buffeted them nonstop from a spatter dash of social media. They seem to be leaning away from it all and searching for a better world. The pure kindness of Jesus' love is appealing to young people who have seen so much hate. They don't want their liberty and happiness manipulated by others because their entire adult lives are ahead of them. They want their planet to be livable. They see their neighbors as likable. Their future must be attainable.

I have decided to view life through the eyes of a select group of this generation—eight of them. They call me Papa. I could think in terms of what I want for them, but I will try to understand what they want for themselves. That is what I will advocate for. That is what I will vote for. That is what I will pray for. And I'll trust in God's promises to the end.

Exit interview
Liz Schroeder

Spring is marked by endings and exits. For people in the Northern Hemisphere, it's the end of the school year. Are you graduating? leaving home? getting married? If so, consider scheduling an exit interview with your parents.

Human resource departments in healthy businesses perform an exit interview when an employee leaves the company so management can learn how it can improve.

Healthy families might perform a type of exit interview when a child leaves home to provide an opportunity for parents and child to offer one another forgiveness. It's a chance to excavate any hurts that are buried and wrap them in grace. That will prevent the stench of unforgiveness from permeating the relationship. Just like you wouldn't pack dirty laundry for a trip, you don't want to move trauma or stinky memories into the next chapter of your life.

We are preparing for an exit interview with our oldest child, who will be getting married. I'm a little nervous about it. I know I've missed the mark as a perfect parent. I've modeled a lack of self-discipline, gentleness, patience, kindness, love . . . well, all the good fruit. But by the grace of God, I've also modeled repentance, forgiveness, and an utter reliance on the Lord.

I don't need to be nervous because **"if we confess our sins, he is faithful and just and will forgive us our sins and purify us from all unrighteousness"** (1 John 1:9).

Thankfully, my final review is not based on my performance but on Jesus' perfect one.

Contentment is great gain
Nathan Nass

An NBA superstar made the news for an unexpected reason: He drove a 21-year-old vehicle. That's not what anyone would expect. What should a millionaire basketball player be driving? Whatever is new and fast and expensive. Not this guy. He drove around town in his old, beat-up car.

I wonder if he's learned the truth of these words in the Bible: **"Godliness with contentment is great gain. For we brought nothing into the world, and we can take nothing out of it. But if we have food and clothing, we will be content with that"** (1 Timothy 6:6-8). To be content with food and clothing—and an old vehicle—is great gain!

That's easier said than done. My sinful heart struggles with contentment. It seems like the grass is greener everywhere else. It seems like my life would be better if I had more and accomplished more and got praised more and seemed more important in everyone else's eyes. Do you think that discontentment brings me happiness? Does your discontentment bring you peace? No way!

Instead, godliness with contentment is great gain. Your worth doesn't come from the kind of car you drive or the brand of clothes you wear or how impressive you look in the mirror. It comes from your Savior Jesus who was willing to give up everything for you to make you his own. There is no greater gain than finding contentment in Jesus, even with a 21-year-old car!

Why take the risk?

Mike Novotny

I get why most Christians have a sin they are not confessing. It feels too awkward, uncomfortable, and risky. Maybe it's better to keep certain sins between you and God, right?

Wrong. The reformer Martin Luther knew the unmatched power of being completely honest with fellow believers. He wrote, "As to the current practice of private confession, I am heartily in favor of it . . . for it is a cure without equal for distressed consciences. For when we have laid bare our conscience to our brother and privately made known to him the evil that lurked within, we receive from our brother's lips the word of comfort spoken by God himself" (*The Babylonian Captivity of the Church*, 1520). While there are countless benefits to true confession, Luther put his finger on the most powerful—comfort for your conscience. The devil would love to convince you that your sin, that sin, is too much for grace. But honest confession and the forgiveness that follows exposes the devil for the liar he is. You are forgiven, even for that.

John pointed to this benefit when he wrote, **"If we confess our sins, he is faithful and just and will forgive us our sins and purify us from all unrighteousness"** (1 John 1:9). God is faithful. God will forgive. God will purify us.

That's what you get when you share the whole story, your real story, with a brother or sister in Christ. You get Jesus. And Jesus is exactly what real sinners need.

Going home
Jason Nelson

My wife, Nancy, and I are feeling a little displaced right now. We have a nice roof over our heads and familiar furnishings around us. But it just doesn't feel right. Our cabin in the woods felt like home because we built it and lived there longer than we lived anywhere else. It was filled with cherished reminders of times with family and friends that can't be replicated anywhere else. I left in an ambulance and never returned. Nancy followed the ambulance and never returned. Now we drive past all the places we used to live looking for a place that feels like home.

Having a place that feels like home is a gift from God. I can only imagine how unsettled Adam and Eve felt after being evicted from their garden. Every Bible story after that is in some way part of God's plan to bring his people back home. Jesus addressed our yearning for home when he said, **"My Father's house has many rooms; if that were not so, would I have told you that I am going there to prepare a place for you?"** (John 14:2).

Jesus left his Father's house and took up residence in a flimsy tabernacle of flesh just like ours. He had no permanent place to lay his head. His base of operation was here and there. After he did what he came to do, he returned to his mansion above. We can follow him home.

Growing pains
Mike Novotny

One of the early Christian church's biggest struggles was growth. After Jesus' small band of merry men and women exploded into a megachurch of five thousand-plus people in the early chapters of Acts, we read, **"In those days when the number of disciples was increasing, the Hellenistic Jews among them complained against the Hebraic Jews because their widows were being overlooked in the daily distribution of food"** (Acts 6:1). Like a childless couple who just had twins, the growth of the Christian family caused some complications. The widows' tummies were rumbling, and their mouths were grumbling. How would the apostles address the issue without neglecting their call to preach the gospel? (You'll find out in tomorrow's devotion!)

For today, I want you to see that growth makes messes. When a family, business, or church grows, it gets messy. People get overlooked and feel undervalued. The old ways that used to work stop working. Leaders are called to step back and figure out new solutions.

Do you know anyone who is experiencing such growth pains? Maybe your friend is a first-time parent struggling to get everything done at home. Maybe your church family is adding a second service that threatens the intimacy of your fellowship. These are hard situations. But God will give you wisdom if you ask him so that people can be served and leaders can be saved.

Growth is wonderful and messy. May the Holy Spirit bless you as you step back to see the problem and step up to solve it.

Set limits
Mike Novotny

Have you come to accept the fact that you are not God? Here's a quick test of your answer—Do you feel guilty about saying no to people or opportunities because you believe you are not omnipotent (all-powerful) nor omnipresent (able to be everywhere at once)? If not, well done, fellow human!

The apostles accepted their humanity. When the early church faced some growing pains and new ministry needed to be done, they said, **"It would not be right for us to neglect the ministry of the word of God in order to wait on tables. Brothers and sisters, choose seven men from among you who are known to be full of the Spirit and wisdom. We will turn this responsibility over to them and will give our attention to prayer and the ministry of the word"** (Acts 6:2-4).

Peter & Co. knew they couldn't spend tons of time in prayer, give their attention to robustly preaching the Word, *and* personally care for these widows. They were followers of Jesus, but they were not Jesus. Others needed to step up so they could preach the gospel and preach it well.

Please learn from their example. You are not selfish or sinful if you limit yourself to doing a few things well. Pray that God would raise up others to meet the needs you see around you. And sleep well knowing you are doing what you can with the limited time God has given you.

The name of Jesus
Matt Trotter

The pastor read Matthew 1:23: **"'The virgin will conceive and give birth to a son, and they will call him Immanuel' (which means 'God with us')."** A sweet voice whispered in my ear, "Daddy, if Immanuel means 'God is with us,' what does Jesus mean?"

Hmm, maybe I should know this. "I'm not sure. Let's google it."

Turns out Jesus is generally thought to mean "the Lord saves" or "salvation."

Maybe you grew up in a church that taught such news. Maybe I missed it in new member classes. OK, I probably missed it, but consider these: **"At the name of** [*The Lord Saves*] **every knee should bow"** (Philippians 2:10). **"They were on their way up to Jerusalem, with** [*Salvation*] **leading the way"** (Mark 10:32).

Can you imagine the legal scholars of Jesus' day and the challenge that acknowledging the meaning of Jesus' name would have presented? Upset over Jesus' compassion, would they whine: "*Salvation* is healing on the Sabbath!"? Upset about his hanging out with people of low social status, can you just hear them talking amongst themselves: "*The Lord Saves* is again with tax collectors and prostitutes!" You have to imagine it, because generally these men who were opposed to Jesus' ministry referred to him as a teacher, a fellow, "this" man, and more.

What's our challenge? Maybe as loud as possible . . . better yet, as softly as necessary, when you find a willing ear, ask, "What do you think of the name of Jesus?"

Lost and found
Nathan Nass

Being lost is not a good feeling. My family and I once hiked to the top of a mountain. It was great, until we started back down. Suddenly the trail split into a bunch of little paths. We didn't know where to go. We chose a path, but soon we realized we weren't on any path at all. Worse yet, there was no cell coverage. No GPS. Just us in a dense forest. Lost. Let me tell you, being lost is not a good feeling!

I bet you know that. Maybe not hiking down a mountain, but I bet you've been hiking through life and gotten lost in all the little paths leading in all different directions. Being lost is not a good feeling—feeling like there's no hope, feeling like no matter where you turn it's going to get worse. Do you feel lost?

Then listen to these words from Jesus: **"The Son of Man came to seek and to save the lost"** (Luke 19:10). The message of the Bible isn't, "You need to get your life back on track." It's, "Jesus came to seek and to save you."

No matter where you're at in your life, you're not alone. Jesus is calling out to you in the Bible: "I love you! I've forgiven you! I have plans for you! I've prepared a place for you in heaven!" You are not lost, not when Jesus has you. You are found. Found and loved forever.

JUNE

Let us not become weary in doing good, for at the proper time we will reap a harvest if we do not give up.

Galations 6:9

Evidence of life
Mike Novotny

Have you heard of a "born again Christian"? Do you know what *born again* means? After studying the appearances of that phrase in God's Word—twice from Jesus and once from Peter—I can think of six connections between being born physically and being born again spiritually, which I will unpack for you in our upcoming devotions. The first—evidence of life.

When you were born, there was evidence of life. Heartbeat. Brain waves. Breathing lungs. If you have been born again (when you became a Christian), there is evidence of spiritual life, namely, repentance and faith. Your heart beats with repentance (no true Christian can live in sin) and looks to Jesus for salvation (no true Christian looks to themselves to be saved). This is why Jesus summarized Christianity by saying, **"Repent and believe the good news!"** (Mark 1:15). Everyone who repents and believes has evidence that they are a born-again member of God's family.

But please don't confuse strength with life. A baby is not strong, but it's still alive. And you might not be strong in your faith or as mature as other Christians, but you're alive. Some of us doubt our place in God's family because we feel weak or struggle with the same sin year after year, but that doesn't deny the evidence of true faith. I hope your faith gets bigger and stronger, but even God's littlest kids have life.

Do you regret your sin? Do you believe Jesus died for you too? Then take heart! You have been born again!

Embrace the process
Mike Novotny

What's the process that makes a baby? If you don't know, you should probably ask the apostle Peter and a Pharisee named Nicodemus. In their conversations about being born again, they use phrases like "perishable seed," a reference to male sperm, and "a mother's womb," where a fertilized egg grows. Sperm plus egg is the proven process that leads to physical birth, a stunning sequence of evidence that we wouldn't believe unless we had seen it.

God's Word plus a human heart is the process that can lead to another stunning result—being born again. Peter writes, **"You have been born again . . . through the living and enduring word of God"** (1 Peter 1:23). When the living Word of God hits our hearts, miracles can happen. Repentance can replace stubbornness. Faith in Jesus can drive out self-righteousness.

So embrace the process! If a couple wanted a baby, they wouldn't just pray. They would . . . you know . . . embrace the process. Similarly, if you want someone to be born again, embrace the process. Don't *just* pray that your kid or your friend becomes a believer. Find a way to share the Word with them: "Hey, I heard this sermon and thought of you." "I know you're not super into church, but I'd love for you to come with me and give church a second chance."

It's amazing what seed and egg can create. Even more amazing is what the Word can do when it gets to your heart.

A family of love
Mike Novotny

When I was in college, we played against a soccer team *way* up in Duluth, Minnesota. One year we took the four-hour bus ride from my college town to Duluth only to get demolished in front of zero of our fans. It was too far from home for them to travel. Actually, there was one fan. I didn't see him until the game had already started. It was my dad. He had driven five hours from Green Bay to Duluth and was about to drive five hours back after watching me play an hour and a half of soccer. That's a lot of driving to see some not-so-good soccer. Why did my dad do it? Because I was born into a family of love.

If you have been born again, you were too. You may or may not have rock star parents like mine, but every Christian has a Father in heaven who is bursting with love for all his children. Your life may be as unimpressive as my performance that day in Duluth, but your Father still shows up to see you, support you, and be with you. And Jesus has promised that he will never leave you nor forsake you. The Holy Spirit has made your body his temple, the place where he lives to guide you through life.

How sweet it is to be born again! **"See what great love the Father has lavished on us, that we should be called children of God! And that is what we are!"** (1 John 3:1).

Grow up
Mike Novotny

When you were born, you had a clear purpose—to grow up. If you are 35 and still sipping on a bottle of warm milk while watching *Cocomelon*, you should probably talk to someone, because the purpose of your birth was not just to be born but rather to grow, mature, and become independent.

The same is true with being born again. When the Word of God changed your heart and brought you into God's family, you were also given a clear purpose. Not just to sit around and wait for heaven but to grow up in your faith. Peter writes, **"Like newborn babies, crave pure spiritual milk, so that by it you may grow up in your salvation"** (1 Peter 2:2).

Growing up as a child of God means an increasing awareness and gratitude for Jesus' forgiveness (we never grow out of the gospel!), a better ability to do the right thing even when our parents (or pastor) aren't watching, and a stronger grasp of God's Word, which saves us from the bad influences of this world.

Want to know God's purpose for your life? We all do. But we don't have to guess or wait for a whisper. Grab the Bible with the passion of a hungry baby, and you will find plenty of ways to grow up in your salvation.

Lots of spiritual resources
Mike Novotny

When you were born, you likely had lots of resources to help you grow—diapers, food, a roof over your head, and more cute onesies than you were capable of wearing. Add to that people to feed, rock, hold, and teach you. How many resources did you have at your disposal during those essential years?

Being born again is the same. Your Father has given you resources to help you pursue your purpose. Peter writes, **"Like newborn babies, crave pure spiritual milk, so that by it you may grow up in your salvation"** (1 Peter 2:2). Want to grow? Then crave the "pure spiritual milk" of the Bible.

One of the best parts about being a 21st-century born-again believer is that we live in one of the most resource-rich generations in history. We have Bibles, Christian books, YouTube videos, sermon podcasts, worship music on the radio, and so much more. It would take you years just to explore all the resources that Time of Grace has created to help you! If you are craving God's Word, you can get it free of charge.

Growing up as a child of God is a challenge. Thankfully, our Father wants to help. Not only did he send Jesus to save you. Not only did his Spirit give you new life. But God has filled your life with spiritual resources so you can get spiritually bigger and stronger than ever before.

Your inheritance
Mike Novotny

According to the Bureau of Labor Statistics, 30-40 percent of Americans receive an inheritance. For one-third of you, some riches (a chunk of money, the family cabin) are on the way.

But don't get down if that's not you, because 100 percent of born-again believers are even richer. Earlier in his letter, Peter wrote, "[God] **has given us new birth into a living hope through the resurrection of Jesus Christ from the dead, and into an inheritance that can never perish, spoil or fade. This inheritance is kept in heaven for you**" (1 Peter 1:3,4).

Because of Jesus, there is a place prepared for you, a spot where there is no suffering or wondering, no regretting or repenting, no holding your breath, no hoping things work out, no missing him or her, no missing out. It's a place where your face would hurt from the laughter (if it was possible to hurt in heaven); a life where everything is right, and nothing will ever go wrong; the moment when you know you'll never have to worry again or apologize again or try and fail again; a place where you see the face of God. Those born into an earthly inheritance will spend their money all too quickly. But the born again will enjoy their inheritance forever.

Child of God, if life has got you down, reread Peter's words and remember the inheritance that nothing and no one can touch, the riches kept in heaven for you!

Just traveling through
Katrina Harrmann

I went into my garden the other day, humming and feeling happy. When I went to fill the birdbath, I stepped back in dismay and dropped the hose. There was a dead bird floating in the water.

This tripped me up. It was a rip in an otherwise picture-perfect afternoon. Do you ever encounter rips like this? They are little snags that shock you until you remember . . . there's something very wrong here! This place isn't our home! We are destined for something SO much better!

Life tends to work like that sometimes. We get lulled into a sense of complacency. Life is good! Things are going great! Let's dig in, put down roots, get comfortable, and gather earthly treasures! We let our guard down. We get lazy. And then . . .

Maybe it's something as simple as a dead bird that startles us. Or worse—a horrible car crash on the side of the road. Sometimes it's much graver such as a terminal diagnosis or the death of a child. Whatever it is that jars us, it reminds us that Satan is on the prowl like a lion, leaving his messy tracks everywhere (1 Peter 5:8,9).

But God had a plan, fulfilled through his Son, who died to save us. And he urges us NOT to get complacent but remain on guard and battle ready!

We are traveling through this place on the way to something *much* better—something PERFECT. Heaven is our home! And what a perfect home it will be!

10
Daron Lindemann

Have you ever received a 10 in an event scored by judges? It means you can't get any better. God uses the number 10 in the Bible 242 times to tell us that if we believe in him, life can't get any better.

He gave Moses 10 Commandments. In the first chapter of the Bible, the words *God said* appear 10 times! God is saying, "This world is my creation. It is so good; I can't make it any better!"

God delivered his people from slavery in Egypt with 10 plagues. His rescue mission was so successful that it couldn't have gotten any better. Do you know what the 10th plague was? Since God's people were spared from this plague of death, they celebrated the Passover, where everyone who believed in God celebrated a special meal featuring lamb.

Guess what day of the month God told them to eat this sacrificial lamb and use its blood to mark their homes as belonging to him—saving them from slavery and death? **"On the tenth day of this month each man is to take a lamb for his family"** (Exodus 12:3).

Those Passover lambs pictured the complete rescue and salvation for all sinners through Jesus Christ.

The Bible book of Revelation uses the number 10 to emphasize the absolute authority and victory of Jesus Christ over our enemies—for a completely unending period of time.

Can all these 10s from God move you to give him a 10th of your income?

Life from God can't get any better! Live it to the max!

Healthy fear of God
Matt Ewart

I was extremely intimidated by the older students when I started high school. They were so big that it seemed like they could walk into a liquor store and not get carded. I was initially so afraid of them that I did my best to avoid them.

Have you ever felt that way about God? Have you ever been filled with fear when you think about his power and his presence? And has your fear of him made you want to avoid him?

There are about two hundred places in the Bible that talk about the "fear of God." To fear God means that you are so aware of his power and his presence that it profoundly changes the way you think, feel, and live. But a healthy fear of God doesn't make you want to hide from him.

In high school, I eventually learned that the guys I had been most afraid of were the best possible teammates to have on the football field. I remember the protection they provided to advance me (and the ball) forward.

God sent his Son not to condemn you but to rescue you. He wrapped his infinite power in love for you. A healthy fear of God means you live with the awareness that his proximity is what keeps you safe.

"So do not fear, for I am with you; do not be dismayed, for I am your God. I will strengthen you and help you; I will uphold you with my righteous right hand" (Isaiah 41:10).

One dark spot
Jason Nelson

The speaker used a memorable object lesson. He showed us a large white poster with one black dot right in the middle. He asked us what we saw on the poster, and we responded in unison, "A dark spot." Then he politely busted us for not noticing all the white space.

Broken people tend to focus on the brokenness of others. And we love to talk about it. We come home and gripe about rude drivers who had the gall to give us a dirty look, and we don't mention the very pleasant person who helped us check out our groceries. Our children overhear us and become jaded as well. Negativity gets passed from one generation to the next. What if we made a habit of sharing with each other all the good we see each day?

Sin is the dark spot on our natures. God dealt with it by looking away and looking to Jesus. We run to him.

Just as I am and waiting not
To rid my soul of one dark blot,
To thee, whose blood can cleanse each spot,
O Lamb of God, I come.

(Charlotte Elliot, 1835)

God sees us as we are and as he intends for us to be. **"Though your sins are like scarlet, they shall be as white as snow; though they are red as crimson, they shall be like wool"** (Isaiah 1:18).

All I need, in thee to find, O Lamb of God, I come.

People matter
Mike Novotny

I'm amazed that the book of Acts has more than two chapters. Imagine you are the apostle Peter or Mary Magdalene. When Acts 1 ends, you are part of a cozy Christian community of around 120 people. But by the end of Acts 2, your church is 30 times bigger! Not 30 people bigger, but 30 times bigger! Dr. Luke records, **"Those who accepted his message were baptized, and about three thousand were added to their number that day"** (Acts 2:41). Yet the book of Acts doesn't end there. Peter and Mary and the masses of new Christians kept going, kept preaching, kept sharing the good news of salvation in Jesus' name.

I'm not sure if you attend church or how big the church you attend is, but I do know this—our story isn't over. You and I may be saved. Our churches may have more than enough to do. But we cannot lock the doors and put a period on Jesus' story just yet. Because people matter. Your cousin who has lost touch with Jesus matters. Your brother who says he doesn't need church matters. Your friend who is living for here and now, for sin and herself, matters.

The same God who patiently waited for your repentance and faith is patiently waiting for theirs. He is holding back judgment day to give us another chapter, another chance to preach the good news to all creation. Let's take the baton that the apostles passed on and **"make disciples of all nations"** (Matthew 28:19).

The company you keep
Matt Trotter

This morning when I returned from the gym, my daughter asked me how my swimming had gone. I said, "Fast. I was next to a guy who was faster, and that helped me swim faster. Just like when you hang out with smart people, you get smarter. You are the company you keep!"

A Bible passage we associate with that idea is this: **"Do not be misled: 'Bad company corrupts good character'"** (1 Corinthians 15:33). But the Bible footnote is remarkable: "From the Greek poet Menander." That means that inspired Scripture borrowed from common culture to challenge the people of Corinth to hold fast to the resurrection of Christ.

Think about that. The apostle Paul challenged Christians in Corinth to keep the faith they had been taught, and as a curb for behavior he used a quote from a Greek playwright! Could you and I be so adept with culture today to present those around us with lyrics from a Shakespearean drama? What about a foremost present lyricist like Ms. Taylor Swift? Maybe not.

But it's a tension to hold. Be careful about the company you keep and the media you read or listen to, but be on guard not to isolate yourself from culture when loving people. Paul knew he was to be all things to all people for the sake of Christ. The challenge is to be aware of those you serve and what drives their culture so the gospel can get through.

The smell of the sheep
Jason Nelson

Pope Francis said, "The shepherd should smell like the sheep." This is a brilliant and godly admonition for any leader in any endeavor. Be among the people. Get on their level. Let their smell rub off on you. If you can understand them and relate to them, they will follow you.

What do sheep smell like? I know what pigs smell like because I worked for a pig farmer as a teenager. I couldn't get that smell off of me. I found out no girl would date a guy with his pig boots on. Similarly, I know what cows and chickens smell like. Stinky too, but distinct from each other. I have no idea what sheep smell like, but I'm sure every good shepherd knows the smell of sheep.

Jesus is our Good Shepherd. He **"became human and lived among us"** (John 1:14 GW). We follow the Lamb of God because we have complete confidence that he understands us at ground level and wants what is best for us. He made himself approachable through his humility, compassion, and empathy. He calls to us: **"Come to me, all who are tired from carrying heavy loads, and I will give you rest"** (Matthew 11:28 GW). He took the heavy load of human sinfulness on himself. He showed us that people will flock to a Shepherd who has no ulterior motives or hidden agendas but who will sacrifice himself for the sheep.

I'll tell you later . . .
Nathan Nass

There's a little phrase that God likes to use. It's this: "I'll tell you later."

Think of Abraham in the Bible. You can read his story in Genesis 12–25. God called Abraham to move his household to a distant country. Abraham said, "Where?" God said, "I'll tell you later." God told Abraham that he and his wife, Sarah, would have a son in their old age. Abraham said, "When?" God said, "I'll tell you later." God told Abraham that his family would be a blessing to the whole world. Abraham said, "How?" God said, "I'll tell you later." Again and again, God made promises to Abraham, but he didn't give Abraham all the information. He said, "I'll tell you later."

Why did God do that? So that Abraham's life depended on faith. At the heart of Abraham's story is this verse: **"Abram believed the Lord, and he credited it to him as righteousness"** (Genesis 15:6). Through every "I'll tell you later," Abraham learned to believe in God, even though he couldn't see him or his promises. He put his faith in the Word of God.

God says that same phrase to you and me, doesn't he? "I'll tell you later." God promises an end to all pain and tears. How? "I'll tell you later." God has prepared a home for us in heaven. When? "I'll tell you later." Can we trust him? Of course we can! One day, we'll see that God always keeps his promises.

Struggle to be still
Katrina Harrmann

Being still is harder than it sounds.

Don't believe me? Try asking a toddler to sit still. Better yet, try it yourself!

I've started doing this recently in my garden. I'm trying to relax a bit more so that I'm more aware of what God is doing in my life. So I make myself sit still and try to count four animals in my yard before I let myself get up. They can't just be four birds (too easy!) or four flies (that would only take a second!). They have to be slightly unique, like a dragonfly or a chipmunk or (if I time it right) a hummingbird. Before long, I've relaxed and begun to pray. By the time I really get rolling, it's been several minutes, and I'm refreshed after my conversation with God.

Why is it so hard to be still? We're wired for movement. We were created to dance and move and run, and stillness feels like inaction—laziness.

But Christ himself urges us to be still.

When we're still, we remember who to be grateful to (God) and what to be grateful for (everything we have!).

Best of all, stillness brings us to a place where we can acknowledge our dependence on our great Father and be mindful of everything he has done for us—and continues to do for us—every day!

"The Lord will fight for you; you need only to be still" (Exodus 14:14).

Who's in my house?
Karen Spiegelberg

My front door is a revolving one. Well, not literally, but I'm flexible in welcoming anyone to our home, whether out-of-town guests, friends in need, or the many foster kids who came in the night needing a safe place. I remember in one such case, waking up in the morning and thinking, "Who's in my house?" It's now a question that pops into my head each day as I embrace any possible new houseguest.

Recently, as a church service began, I wondered if God asks the same question. Surely it pleases the Lord to see his children worshiping together in his house. He desires our worship, although he doesn't need it. *We* desperately need it. Some will say that we don't have to be in the house of the Lord physically to worship him. True, but let's face it—if left on our own with that thought process, there likely would be precious little worship. A congregation that gathers regularly encourages and builds each other up. Then, with the help of the Holy Spirit and the preached Word, believers are strengthened to go out and be salt and light in a very dreary world.

King David glorified the concept of gathering for worship. He penned his delight for it when he wrote, **"I rejoiced with those who said to me, 'Let us go to the house of the Lord'"** (Psalm 122:1).

Let us praise the Lord through our corporate worship and affirmatively answer his call: "Who's in my house?"

I'm a lot like my dog
Linda Buxa

My husband and I took our black lab, Jack, with us on a recent vacation. Though Jack loved the activity and attention, he was also a hot mess. Even though he was with his people (he got to see two-thirds of the kids!), Jack wasn't comfortable because he wasn't home, which is his favorite place. Plus, without the ability to reason, he didn't know we wouldn't leave him behind, no matter how much we promised.

I bet you know where this is going, but if you don't, let me be clear: I'm a lot like Jack—and maybe you are too. I'm surrounded by blessings—family, friends, my dog, church, volunteering, work, vacations—and yet I'm wistful because I'm not Home (with a capital *H*). Even though this world is a beautiful gift from God, it's not my forever home, and I am not comfortable.

Even with the ability to reason and no matter how often I hear, **"The Lord himself goes before you and will be with you; he will never leave you nor forsake you. Do not be afraid; do not be discouraged"** (Deuteronomy 31:8), I get afraid and discouraged and forget he is always with me. I forget that Jesus is preparing my place right now and will come back for me.

That's why I'm thankful that God sent the Holy Spirit, who Jesus promised **"will teach you all things and will remind you of everything I have said to you"** (John 14:26).

Thankfully the Holy Spirit will teach this old dog new tricks.

Confusing things Christians say
Mike Novotny

One day when I was in Argentina, I ran into a teeny problem at an ice cream shop. The menu was in kilograms. I don't speak metric, so I wasn't sure how many kilograms equaled a pint of ice cream, so I chose the half kilo. And that's when the employee grabbed a bucket—a bucket!—and started scooping . . . and scooping . . . and scooping! Finally, he took one of those tiny gelato spoons and—bloop!—stuck it in my bucket. The moral of my story? It's hard to know what to do when you don't know what something means.

That's true in church too. There are moments that feel "metric" to us, words we use that aren't totally foreign but are a bit fuzzy. "You must be *born again*." "How's your *walk with God*?" "Do you know God's *calling* for your life?"

Your Father wants you to understand his Word so you can apply it in your life and enjoy it in your heart. As Paul wrote, **"Otherwise when you are praising God in the Spirit, how can someone else . . . say 'Amen' to your thanksgiving, since they do not know what you are saying?"** (1 Corinthians 14:16).

Nothing is sweeter than hearing about God's grace and getting it. That's why I want to urge you to slow down, ask questions if you don't get it, and humble yourself for the sake of understanding. You who humble yourselves will be exalted, exalted in knowing—truly knowing—the Word that a loving God is speaking to you.

The death of unhealthy fears
Matt Ewart

Every day you arrange your life around your greatest fears—even if your greatest fears are not legitimate.

One of my children went through a phase when they were unwilling to go upstairs in our house unless they were accompanied by someone else. What was upstairs that was so scary? Nothing. It was all in their imagination. But for a while, we had to arrange our lives around that fear.

What if you are arranging your life around a fear that need not be feared? Most adults are not afraid to go upstairs, but we are afraid of being inadequate. We are afraid of being unworthy. We are afraid of enemies who threaten our way of life. The world around us doesn't just supply these fears. The world also lists all the reasons why we should be afraid.

But when your greatest fear is God, something incredible happens. To fear God is to arrange your life around his presence and his promises. Because of Jesus, your iniquities and inadequacies have been clothed in righteousness. Because God is for you, no enemy can stand against you. Because of Christ's resurrection, your Way, Truth, and Life can never be taken from you.

To fear God is to put to death every unhealthy fear. What unhealthy fear do you want him to put to death today?

"Fear God and keep his commandments, for this is the duty of all mankind" (Ecclesiastes 12:13).

The extra mile
Jon Enter

Does God care about your emotional health, or does he command you to be a doormat to those who willfully stomp all over you? The first answer is yes, and the second is no. So why did Jesus say this? **"I tell you, do not resist an evil person. If anyone slaps you on the right cheek, turn to them the other cheek also. If anyone forces you to go one mile, go with them two miles"** (Matthew 5:39,41).

Jesus was talking about something his Jewish listeners despised. It was Roman law that a soldier could force any conquered civilian to carry his heavy soldier's pack a mile. If the civilian didn't or couldn't, the soldier brutalized them.

Jesus told them and us today to "go with them two miles." Why? Bullies like to bully when their victims feel victimized. If we don't give bullies the satisfaction of our pain, they move on. When we show them kindness, it can change their perspective on us and others. This is what we pray for in the Lord's Prayer, that God would forgive us our sins as we forgive those who sin against us.

Those who bully often have hurt they don't know how to express. Pray for them. Treat them with kindness. Go out of your way (even an extra mile) to show them the love of Christ as Jesus has shown to you.

Love-doubt
Jason Nelson

Shortly after his resurrection, the all-knowing Son of God asked Peter a very direct question three times. In rapid succession for emphasis and reassurance, Jesus pressed, **"Simon son of John, do you love me?"** A pensive Peter didn't hesitate: **"Lord . . . you know that I love you"** (John 21:17).

There was a lot going on in this exchange. Love was questioned and reaffirmed. There wasn't much wordplay between them. Neither was coy about it. Peter had a sad reason to wonder whether his relationship with Jesus was mortally wounded. His denial in the run-up to Jesus' death seemed to show that Peter's love for Jesus was in doubt—even though Jesus' love for Peter never wavered.

At our most human level, traumatic events also cause us to question the love of others and seek reaffirmation of it.

"Honey, you know I'm not the man I used to be. Do you still love me?"

"What a dumb question! Would I have stayed with you for 47 years if I didn't love you?"

Sometimes love-doubt needs to be dismissed with unglamorous reminders that love has been durable. It helps to have short memories and quickly forget about things that cast doubt about love. It also helps to take the long view and cherish how love has endured for better and for worse over time. And it helps to say it: "You know I love you and always will." Just like God's love for us, ours can be durable forever.

Are you called by God?

Mike Novotny

When I typed the words *call/called/calling* into a Bible search engine, I learned there are over 750 Bible verses on the subject that focus on two "calls" that every Christian has in common.

You have a call to a gospel-given identity: **"To all in Rome who are loved by God and called to be his holy people"** (Romans 1:7). If you ever doubt who you are at your very core, remember what God calls you. He calls you loved and holy and so much more! (Read 1 Peter 2:9,10 if you didn't smile when you looked in the mirror this morning.)

At other times your call is to obedience: **"For God did not call us to be impure, but to live a holy life"** (1 Thessalonians 4:7). If you are searching for purpose, don't pray and wait for a whisper, because your call is clear. You are called, no matter where you live, what you do, and who you are, to live a holy life.

You don't need to preach Jesus in a jungle. Just be like Jesus wherever you are. Be a patient driver after church. Be humble enough to listen and communicate well when you disagree with a family member. Show up to work on time, do your job faithfully, and be someone your boss can trust. That's your calling. This is the holy life that God has called you to.

Are you called by God? Every Christian is. Called *holy* by the blood of Jesus and called to live a holy life for the name of Christ.

Can't stop giving
Linda Buxa

After the Israelites escaped slavery in Egypt, it came time for them to build a portable worship space (they called it a tabernacle). So when the people who had been put in charge of construction and decorating asked their fellow citizens for donations of supplies and money, the people were beyond generous.

After all, the whole impetus for the exodus—fancy word for exit—from Egypt was because Pharaoh wouldn't let them go into the desert to worship God. They were so overjoyed to donate to the project that the artisans doing the work said, **"'The people are bringing more than enough for doing the work the LORD commanded to be done.' Then Moses gave an order and they sent word throughout the camp: 'No man or woman is to make anything else as an offering for the sanctuary.' And so the people were restrained from bringing more, because what they already had was more than enough to do all the work"** (Exodus 36:5-7).

Whoa! These former slaves were so excited to be set free that they could not stop giving. For them, giving was a joy. And that's how believers today give too—freely because they've been set free. It's not a stingy reluctance. It's a celebration that God gave Jesus freely to rescue us too, to give us an exodus from slavery to sin to freedom in Jesus.

Let's pray today that we all have the same attitude of generosity when it comes to our time, prayers, money, love, and acts of service.

Still a Christian!

Mike Novotny

The other day I realized that God has blessed me with one particular blessing for over 15,000 straight days, namely, the blessing of his keeping. **"The LORD bless you and keep you"** (Numbers 6:24). The Holy Spirit called me to faith in Jesus when I was little, and then he has kept me with Jesus for more than four decades. I haven't always been healthy, but God has kept me a Christian. I haven't always been wealthy, but God has kept me a Christian. I haven't always been comfortable, but I have always had faith in Christ. One of my greatest spiritual blessings is God's keeping.

You too? Maybe when you get out that gratitude journal or say your prayers at night, you could add this one to your thank-you list—Still a Christian! I read that post from someone who doesn't believe the Bible, but it didn't persuade me. I'm still a Christian! The devil wanted to lead me away from the church, the Bible, and the gospel, but God called me, preserved me, and kept me in the one true faith. I'm still a Christian! Despite countless demons, endless temptations, and my own sinful nature, the Lord has been kind enough to protect me from my soul's greatest danger. Still a Christian!

Friend, you may not have everything you want in life, but if you (still) have faith, you are blessed. Thank God today for the blessing of his keeping!

Afraid to be far
Matt Ewart

When I was 19, I had an opportunity to spend an entire summer in Alaska. I would be staying with a friend and his family, and our summer employment was all lined up. It was an easy decision for me. I said yes and made all the arrangements to go.

While that summer brought so many memories, the one that sticks most in my mind was saying goodbye to my parents. One of them (who shall go unnamed) was showing more tears than normal.

Today as a dad whose kids are getting close to adulthood, I understand those tears. It used to be that my kids were afraid to be far from me. But then came playdates. Then school. Then sleepovers. Then summer camps. And soon there will be college, and then . . . no more fear.

My goal as a parent is to love my kids so much right now that they won't be afraid to be away from me in the future. It's a bittersweet goal. I now understand the tears from my parents.

Spiritually speaking, we should never outgrow our fear of being far from our Father in heaven. The more you grow as a person, the more you become aware of how his strength is made perfect in your weaknesses.

"Therefore, whoever takes the lowly position of this child is the greatest in the kingdom of heaven" (Matthew 18:4).

Coming soon
Clark Schultz

I love going to the movies. It's not the popcorn or re-clining seats that I love but the moment the lights dim. The big screen reads, "Coming Soon" or, "The Following Is a Preview." For the next 30-90 seconds, I'm taken to a place of wonder, excitement, and heart-pumping action. It's not the real movie, just a snippet of what's to come.

In the following Bible verse, the prophet Joel gives his listeners a snippet of what is to come: **"And afterward, I will pour out my Spirit"** (Joel 2:28). After what? The Israelites had not followed God's commands or believed his promises, and they were selfish. God was going to send a devastating swarm of locusts. But when the Israelites turned back to the Lord and repented, the merciful God gave them this reassuring promise of the Holy Spirit.

Locusts may not be swarming in our backyards, but we do have "stuff" swarming around in our heads that keeps our focus away from God and his will for us. Instead of loving him and our neighbors as ourselves, we bow down to the idol of self.

But Joel's words ring true for us today. Like a cool glass of water on a hot day, the Holy Spirit is poured out on us at our baptisms. We are children of God. The words "given and poured out for you" in the Lord's Supper assure us that because Jesus lived and died in our place, all our sins are forgiven. When we turn to God in repentance, he restores us.

The Holy Spirit's gift
Clark Schultz

Yesterday's devotion was about the preview Joel gave the Israelites of the Holy Spirit being poured out on God's people. But those same words preview the Holy Spirit's presence at Pentecost well before it happened as recorded in the New Testament book of Acts. **"I will pour out my Spirit on all people. Your sons and daughters will prophesy, your old men will dream dreams, your young men will see visions"** (Joel 2:28).

God chose the time after Jesus' death and resurrection to begin the main mission work of the early church. The disciples were scared, perplexed, and unsure of what was to come. That's when God sent the Holy Spirit on Pentecost (see Acts 2:1-13). The disciples spoke in many languages! They were now bold spokespeople for Jesus through the gift of the Holy Spirit.

Today that miracle continues through foreign and home mission work being done by God's faithful servants. Men and women are given gifts and training to translate the gospel into many languages so all may hear it. This isn't a preview of the Holy Spirit. The Holy Spirit is here now as you read this. The Holy Spirit has gifted you too. Just as the rock-solid truth of Jesus has passed down all the way to you. Who will you tell about your Savior? Where will the Holy Spirit's blessing take those words next?

When fears compete
Matt Ewart

I learned how to use the subway during a family vacation to New York City. All you do is hold up your payment app to the subway kiosk, and it will unlock the turnstile so you can walk through.

One day I successfully swiped my payment app four times, allowing my wife and three children to walk through the turnstile. But then my payment app decided to quit. I was stuck, and two competing fears overwhelmed me.

I was afraid to leave my wife and kids alone in a New York City subway. At the same time, I was afraid of what would happen to me if I jumped over the turnstile. (I envisioned the security footage going viral.) I confess that I did in fact jump over the turnstile to be with them.

What fears are competing in your life? Sometimes it's easy to see which turnstiles we should jump over, but it often happens that the wrong fear wins out. What I have seen in my own life and in many others is that we often tend to hold on to the familiar, unhealthy fears that separate us from God.

Thank God for his love. Jesus was not afraid to jump the turnstile—even entering death—to be with us and rescue us. Ask him for the wisdom and courage to say no to the unhealthy fears that have a grip on you today.

"For the joy set before him he endured the cross, scorning its shame, and sat down at the right hand of the throne of God" (Hebrews 12:2).

Everybody's riddle
Daron Lindemann

How about some riddles?

I have branches but no fruit, trunk, or leaves. What am I? Answer: A bank.

What question can you never answer yes to? Answer: Are you asleep yet?

Why don't I do the good things I'd like to do . . . and why do I keep doing the bad things I don't want to do?

Answer: This is everybody's struggle. Paul wrote it like a riddle in the Bible book of Romans, pondering his struggle as a Christian to live a spiritually decent, God-pleasing life.

Guilt, shame, or fear of getting in trouble isn't enough to keep us from sin. We know it's wrong, we know it'll make us feel good for a minute but guilty for a week, and we know . . . but we sin anyway. Why?

Here's Paul's solution to the riddle: **"What a wretched man I am! Who will rescue me from this body that is subject to death? Thanks be to God, who delivers me through Jesus Christ our Lord!"** (Romans 7:24,25).

The saving solution is not good intentions, better discipline, or second chances. The solution is a rescue: the powerful death and resurrection of Jesus Christ.

You were already rescued from sin's curse and control at the cross and in the tomb of Jesus Christ!

Hey, that doesn't make you flawless by any means. But you are forgiven because there's something more powerful than the riddle. The rescue.

Justify your existence?

Liz Schroeder

I felt closest in my relationship with God during the time when I could not justify my existence. I was in the hospital with a confounding illness that was misdiagnosed as everything from viral meningitis to lung cancer. As a mom of five, I couldn't make dinner or read a bedtime story. As a wife, I couldn't be a supportive companion for my husband. As a volunteer, I couldn't welcome visitors to church. I was just Liz: weak, spinal-tapped, and covered in hideous hives.

It was during this bleak season that God reassured me through his Word and through the visitors who ministered to me in the hospital. His message: "Sweet daughter, my love for you was never based on your performance but on who I AM."

Although I had memorized this Bible verse back in fifth grade—**"For all have sinned and fall short of the glory of God, and all are justified freely by his grace through the redemption that came by Christ Jesus"** (Romans 3:23,24)—there was a part of me that felt I had to do something to merit God's favor. I had no trouble believing I had fallen short, but the concept of being justified freely by his grace didn't hit home.

Through the saving work of Christ, when God sees me, he sees Jesus. My sin has been wiped clean, and all of his Son's perfect deeds are credited to me.

Through Jesus, my existence has already been justified, and so has yours. Thank You, Lord!

JULY

You are a chosen people, a royal priesthood,
a holy nation, God's special possession,
that you may declare the praises of him who called
you out of darkness into his wonderful light.

1 Peter 2:9

Cross it out
Matt Ewart

I know someone who loves to make extra-spicy salsa. (It's someone at my church.) I also know someone who likes to eat extra-spicy salsa. (That's me.) We get along great.

One day as this person was giving me some jars of salsa, they shared other things too. Along with the jars of salsa, I was delighted to find some homemade jam.

But when I got home and looked at the jars of jam, I had to laugh. This person had reused some jar lids that had previously been used for salsa. I could clearly see the words *HOT SALSA* crossed off with a marker and the words *BLUEBERRY JAM* written beneath them.

I laughed because I wish life worked like that. I wish I could just cross out the things I want to change and write something new. But I don't have a marker big enough for that. And even if I did, my attempt to relabel something wouldn't change what's beneath.

But the cross of Jesus is big enough to both relabel our circumstances and change what's beneath. Because death has been defeated, we can look at TRIALS and consider them PURE JOY.

And because of what Jesus did, my identity as SINNER has been changed to SAINT.

"But you were washed, you were sanctified, you were justified in the name of the Lord Jesus Christ and by the Spirit of our God" (1 Corinthians 6:11).

Challenge accepted
Liz Schroeder

My accountability partner recently gave me a challenge. The challenge was to start every one of my prayers with praise.

Why praise? Because starting with praise reframes all the other things I pray about: my worries, my shame, my petitions, and my gratitude.

While Paul was in prison(!), he issued a challenge to the church in Philippi: **"Rejoice in the Lord always,"** and then a little louder for those in the back, **"I will say it again: Rejoice!"** (Philippians 4:4).

I'm no Greek scholar, but I am a word nerd with an English degree and Google, so let me tell you what I found out about the word *rejoice*. It is in the present active imperative, second person plural, and means to be "favorably disposed to God's grace." In other words, "Y'all better rejoice and keep on rejoicing because you're going to see the grace of God everywhere you look."

I was skeptical that starting every prayer with praise would make a difference. I also worried that my needs wouldn't be met and that it would feel forced or inauthentic.

But I accepted the challenge. Even when my heart is heavy, I start with praise. It changes my focus from what I want changed in my life to the God who never changes. My gaze shifts from self to Savior, and I am beginning to see his grace in unexpected places.

Not to be dramatic, but it's changing everything. Are you up to the challenge?

Cast it away
Ann Jahns

I'm an expert worrier. I've had over 50 years to perfect my craft. One of the hardest verses in Scripture for me to live is 1 Peter 5:7: **"Cast all your anxiety on** [God] **because he cares for you."**

I started thinking about the word *cast* in that verse. In the original Greek, it's *epiripto*—a verb of forceful action. It's not a gentle handing off or setting aside. It's more of a hurling something away with purpose. Picture a weary cowboy heaving a weighty pack onto the broad back of his horse, which will now easily carry it for him. That horse was built to bear that burden.

God asks for our burdens. He wants the mess we throw his way because he loves us. He even invites it: **"Come to me, all you who are weary and burdened, and I will give you rest"** (Matthew 11:28).

Are you aching over a fallout with a loved one? Cast it on God. Are you battling a persistent sin? Cast it on God. Are you shattered from a diagnosis? Cast it on God. Cast it all onto him in prayer—from the smallest, nagging pebble of doubt to the largest, crushing boulder of fear.

I invite you to bring your worries to God right now: *Lord, today I cast _____ onto your powerful shoulders. I can't handle this on my own. I cast it onto you because I know that you love me, have a plan for me, and will give me the deep and abiding rest only you can give. Amen.*

Attitude of gratitude
Katrina Harrmann

Have you ever gotten a thank-you card? Doesn't it warm your heart and make you feel like the gift you gave was completely worth the expense?

Have you ever NOT gotten a thank-you for something you gave? Me too. If I'm being honest, it seriously made me rethink my generous gift!

Take a moment to read the story of Jesus healing ten lepers on the way to Jerusalem (Luke 17:11-19). There's a very important nugget in it. Out of the ten lepers, only one turned back (once he'd been healed) and thanked Jesus.

Jesus got one thank-you note out of ten. ONE. For a *life-changing* gift.

I believe this story teaches us that saying thank you—showing gratitude—is a *huge* part of the process when it comes to answered prayers.

Do you return to God when he answers your prayers and say thank you? Oof. I think we *all* tend to fall short, don't we? We often pray for days or weeks for something we really want. Then when we get it, we skip on our merry way without a backward glance at the healer.

Take time today to thank God for answered prayers. And as we celebrate Independence Day in the U.S., remember to pray for your country and its leaders. God answers those prayers too.

Just as you enjoy getting a well-deserved thank-you note, your heavenly Father loves to receive your gratitude and praise! And boy is he ever worthy of it!

"Give thanks to the Lord, for he is good; his love endures forever" (Psalm 107:1).

Look up to Jesus
Jon Enter

Do you have a family member or friend who messes up perpetually, who just can't get it together? You and I, on the other hand . . . puff out our chests a little bit . . . know better and live better, right?

But the person who goes to strip clubs, who clicks through porn, who cheats on their spouse, who's quick to lie, who drinks too much, who disrespects their parents, who despises another . . . that person is no different from you or me. You may or may not do something on that list, but if you don't, you have your own sinful vices.

Sinning less than other people won't get you to heaven. **"Therefore no one will be declared righteous in God's sight by the works of the law."** Following and trying to fulfill God's law can't save you. Being a better version of yourself won't save you. It's never enough. **"Rather, through the law we become conscious of our sin"** (Romans 3:20).

Don't look down on others because they sin differently from you. Look up to Jesus! Look up to the One who was placed on a cross to heal your very life. Look up to the One who knows just how hard life can be, just how difficult it is to get up each day to face new problems and new pains. Look up to the One who walked this earth out of love for his Father and for you—his purpose was to save you. Look up to Jesus!

Lying lips
Andrea Delwiche

"I call on the LORD in my distress, and he answers me. Save me, LORD, from lying lips and from deceitful tongues" (Psalm 120:1,2).

I read these words, and two applications come to mind.

The first is what seems to be most intended by the text. This psalmist asks the Lord to protect him from those who defame him personally or agitate against his overtures of peace and goodwill. We've probably all felt the wounds of someone's lying lips that left us feeling helpless and sputtering, the fire of our good intentions stamped out and left to smolder. *"What can I say, Lord? What can I do to combat these lies? Vindicate me! Preserve me and my good reputation!"*

Perhaps there is an additional way to pray this psalm: *"Lord, save me from (my own) lying lips and deceitful tongue."*

I am wounded and corrupted by my own deceit that tries to paint a glossy veneer over my own habits. I twist a few words, and suddenly I've created a fantastical reality that avoids pinpointing my own culpability for hurting others and not *actually* living for God.

What to do? Ask God to deliver us from the sins of others. Ask him to show a way forward to resolution and forgiveness. The Holy Spirit works continually, revealing our own deceptions that prevent cleansing light from shining on our internal messes. God's arms are open. He embraces us as we are. We are always forgiven. Each moment is a new beginning.

Learning to wait
Nathan Nass

God likes to make people wait. Have you noticed that? When you pray, you usually don't receive an answer right away. When you make plans, they often don't work out on your timetable. God likes to make people wait. As Moses and the Israelites traveled to the Promised Land of Canaan, God set up an interesting system. When the cloud of his presence was over the tabernacle, the people had to wait. When the cloud set out from over the tabernacle, they could go. **"Sometimes the cloud stayed only from evening till morning, and when it lifted in the morning, they set out. Whether by day or by night, whenever the cloud lifted, they set out. Whether the cloud stayed over the tabernacle for two days or a month or a year, the Israelites would remain in camp and not set out; but when it lifted, they would set out"** (Numbers 9:21,22).

How would you have handled that? It sounds like a lot of waiting! What was God teaching his people? To depend completely on him. To trust completely in his plan and in his timing and in his will. That's why God likes to make people wait.

Believers waited thousands of years for the Savior—Jesus!—to come. Christians have waited two thousand years for Jesus to come again. All that waiting gives God's people a wonderful opportunity: to learn to depend on God, to learn to trust in God's promises. God likes to make people wait.

Give thanks to the Lord, for "it" is good

Jan Gompper

What if you woke up and all you had was what you were thankful for yesterday? Gulp! Depending on the day, I might find my storehouse empty. If you're like me, your prayer list is often more request oriented than thanks focused.

God doesn't *need* our thanks. Yet he directs us to be thankful or to have gratitude throughout Scripture.

Author Amy Morin cites the following scientifically proven benefits of expressing gratitude: It opens the door to relationships. It improves physical and psychological health. It improves sleep. It enhances empathy and reduces aggression. It improves self-esteem.*

The God we worship has commanded us to do something that would ultimately benefit us! So how does this list translate to us as Christians?

Giving God thanks strengthens our relationship with him, reminding us of our reliance on him for everything.

Expressing gratitude to God gives us peace. When we focus on how good God is, we worry less and feel less stressed.

When we are less stressed, we sleep more soundly.

Thanking God for *our* blessings inspires us to want to be a blessing to others.

Giving thanks to God reminds us of how cherished and loved by him we are.

"Give thanks to the Lord, for he [and it] **is good"** (Psalm 136:1).

* Amy Morin, "7 Scientifically Proven Benefits of Gratitude," *Psychology Today*, April 3, 2015, https://www.psychologytoday.com /us/blog/what-mentally-strong-people-dont-do/201504/7 -scientifically-proven-benefits-of-gratitude.

Not guilty!
Paul Mattek

Guilt tormented me. I'd hear in church about Jesus taking away my guilt, but I'd still feel guilty. The more I tried not to feel guilty, the more I remembered the bad I'd done. I'd wonder, "Do I have a weak faith? If I believe, doesn't Jesus promise to take away my guilt?" Years of guilt-induced faith questioning went by, to the point that I let that guilt influence my identity and actions. If I was going to feel guilty anyway, why not just have fun doing bad stuff? So I did.

I wasn't giving God enough credit. He does more than deal with guilty feelings. He kills their cause—sin. He transforms our very identity and gives us a "not guilty" certificate to prove it. I love where the apostle Paul confidently says, **"God made him who had no sin to be sin for us, so that in him we might become the righteousness of God"** (2 Corinthians 5:21). Jesus earned our righteousness (made us right with God) by never sinning, voluntarily being killed as though he was the guiltiest sinner, and then rising from death like he just had a restful nap so he could hand his righteousness to us.

When I finally grasped this truth (thank you, Holy Spirit!), it was like blinders fell off my eyes, mind, and soul. Maybe that's what the guilt-ridden Saul, a.k.a. the apostle Paul, felt in Acts 9 (read it if you haven't!). Our memories might bring up the bad things we've done, but thanks to Jesus, God won't. His righteousness is now our identity.

God is nearer than you think
Dave Scharf

On September 11, 2001, terrorists attacked and brought down the twin towers of the World Trade Center in New York City. Those old enough to remember can likely tell you the place where they were when they heard the news. It was shockingly evil, even for our world. When God is mentioned in documentaries about that day, mourners often question why God was so far away. We might wonder it too in the more "minor" tragedies of our lives that feel major. But is God really so far away?

Moses asked, **"What other nation is so great as to have their gods near them the way the Lord our God is near us whenever we pray to him?"** (Deuteronomy 4:7). God is near. Your God came here to save us. Your life is now one filled with the assurance of heaven. Christ's life is your life . . . his death is your death . . . his resurrection is your resurrection. Who else can say that of their god?

God came so near that the virgin Mary felt his warm breath on her face. Lepers felt his touch. Children were held in the arms of the Almighty. Joseph of Arimathea wiped the blood off the King of kings. The disciple Thomas touched Jesus' wounds. God touched you with water and the Word in your baptism. His body and blood touch your lips for your forgiveness in the Lord's Supper. He listens to you when you pray. What God comes so near? Only Jesus.

What's doctrine?

Mike Novotny

Doctrine seems like a dirty word. When I recently typed "doctrine" into an internet search bar, Google responded with related words like *indoctrination, brainwashing,* and *propaganda.* Not exactly the words we most want in our lives!

But before you wash my mouth out with soap, let's slow down and define what doctrine is. Doctrine simply refers to a set of beliefs held by a group. If you and your friends believe that racism is wrong, then you have a specific doctrine. If you believe in racial equality so much that you try to persuade racists to change their ways, you, technically, are trying to "indoctrinate" them, that is, to get your "doctrine into" them.

The issue then isn't if you have doctrine but which doctrine you have. What exactly do you believe and why? When it comes to Jesus, heaven, religion, sexuality, abortion, or anything else, how did you come to your convictions? Did you absorb the opinion of your friends? Copycat your parents' beliefs? Trust it just because the pastor said it?

God encourages us, **"Watch your life and doctrine closely"** (1 Timothy 4:16). That's what I want to help you do in the days to come. Let's check out what the Word has to say about good doctrine, false doctrine, and how you can make sure that your doctrine is God's doctrine.

Sound doctrine
Mike Novotny

Nothing matters more than sound doctrine. Paul told Titus, "[The pastor] **must hold firmly to the trustworthy message as it has been taught, so that he can encourage others by sound doctrine and refute those who oppose it**" (Titus 1:9). That's not just essential for pastors. It's vital for all Christian people, including you.

"Sound" doctrine is a set of beliefs that come from God himself and, therefore, are good for your soul. You don't believe them because of your feelings or your friends or your family. No, you "hold firmly" to them, because a trustworthy God can always be trusted. When you can back up your beliefs with the Bible, you know what you believe is good for your soul, because it comes from the God who knows what is best for your soul.

The result? Encouragement. Those beliefs will give you courage to stand strong when the world strays from God's truth and courage to run to Jesus when you have strayed into sin. Those same beliefs will be your source of encouragement for others, the truth you text to an anxious friend before her job interview or the hope you give to a dying father lying in a hospice bed.

I love sound doctrine. It comes from God's heart and not my own. That's why you can trust it. That's why you can encourage others with it.

Watch closely!
Mike Novotny

I was trying to buy some camping gear for a family vacation, and I found a website with unbelievable prices. There was the fancy sleeping bag I wanted at less than half the price of anywhere else, so I added it to my cart, typed in my debit card, and bought it before they sold out. Then I kept finding crazy deals—camping mats, camping stoves, and camping everything at insane rates. Add to cart! Add to cart! But before I sealed the deal with my last click, my wife said, "Hold up. I think this website might be fake." I leaned into my laptop and, for the first time, paid attention to the details. The typos. The grammatical errors. The misplaced logo. Weeks later, 16 unexpected charges from Singapore showed up on my card. I had been scammed.

What happened? How did I miss the clues right there in front of me? Simple. I stopped watching closely because someone told me exactly what I wanted to hear.

No wonder Paul wrote, **"The time will come when people will not put up with sound doctrine. Instead, to suit their own desires, they will gather around them a great number of teachers to say what their itching ears want to hear"** (2 Timothy 4:3). There are plenty of teachers who will offer you an exciting and convenient path to God ("No repentance required! Be you! Do you! And get God too!").

Don't make the mistake I made. **"Watch your . . . doctrine closely"** (1 Timothy 4:16).

Something more
Mike Novotny

At the seminary that I attended, there is a Greek phrase in big letters over the doors of the chapel where future pastors gather for worship: κηρύξατε τὸ εὐαγγέλιον. That first word means "Preach!" It's a message that comes with authority and not merely personal opinion, like messengers sent from the king to notify the citizens of the kingdom. The last phrase means "the gospel." The good news. The declaration that our God did a very good thing for very bad people, sending his Son to save sinners for eternal life.

Some people cringe over words like *preach* and *doctrine*. Not me. We need forgiveness that is more than a human invention or a friend's opinion. No, we need a message that comes with authority and power, one that originated at the throne of the God who will judge the living and the dead. Only something that big could calm our troubled hearts and assure us that we will, without a doubt, see the face of God.

"Preach the gospel," Jesus commanded to his church (Mark 16:15). Give them good doctrine, a message of love from the God of power, grace declared with authority.

Please don't get suckered into the shallow doctrine of 21st-century America, which idolizes human emotion and opinion and "my truth." Your soul needs something more. Listen to gospel preaching. Submit to the Bible's authority. The result is that the good news of Jesus will get the final word over your soul. And his truth will set you free.

Psalm 144 is for *you*
Linda Buxa

"Praise be to the Lᴏʀᴅ my Rock, who trains my hands for war, my fingers for battle. He is my loving God and my fortress, my stronghold and my deliverer, my shield, in whom I take refuge. . . . Lᴏʀᴅ, what are human beings that you care for them, mere mortals that you think of them? Reach down your hand from on high; deliver me and rescue me from the mighty waters. . . . Blessed is the people whose God is the Lᴏʀᴅ" (Psalm 144:1-3,7,15).

Though King David wrote this poem two thousand years ago, I can't help but think it was written for me—and you. We all need the reminder that the same God who prepared and trained David is our God too. He fights for us in every battle we face. He is faithful, even when we are not. He is love, absolutely and completely. He is our shield, protecting us when we have to fight. He is our fortress, sheltering us when we need to rest.

What are you that he cares for you? You are fearfully and wonderfully made. And because he loves you, Jesus became human to wage war against Satan for you. All because you—little you in the scheme of the whole vast universe—are so very worth fighting for. Blessed are you, because God is *your* Lord!

P.S. I encourage you to read all of Psalm 144. There just wasn't enough space today to comment on it all.

How you compare
Matt Ewart

After a person has been on this earth for about 12 years, a simple yet startling realization begins to take root in their mind: "I am my own person."

Along with this realization comes a question that will take at least another 12 years to begin to answer: "What kind of person am I?"

The way we tend to find an answer is by comparing ourselves to the people around us. We try to determine whom we are like. We pay attention to who likes us. We yearn to find a group of people that is like us.

But look at what God did in the beginning. When God set out to design humankind, he didn't identify us in how we compare to other people. And he certainly didn't identify us in how we compare to animals. Here's what he said in Genesis 1:26: **"Let us make mankind in our image, in our likeness."**

In the beginning, the only way to determine our identity was in comparison to God. The one we were most like was God himself.

What might surprise you is that this is still true today. Though we lost God's likeness because of sin, it has been restored to us. Jesus became the likeness of sinful mankind so that God's likeness would be restored to us by faith in Jesus.

So when you begin to wonder what kind of person you are, don't look around you. Just look at Jesus.

The best reunion
Ann Jahns

Does your family love reunions? Are you the family that gathers at the same place each year, sporting brightly colored matching T-shirts and bonding over food and games and crafts? Or maybe if your family does have a reunion, you conveniently have another obligation that day that you simply can't get out of. Because of past hurts, purposefully spending time with your family is far too painful.

Regardless of your personal family situation, I hope you remember that you are part of a larger family: God's family. Through your faith in Jesus, purchased and won by his sacrifice on a cross, his blood now flows through your veins. You may not be able to choose your earthly family, but your Father God has chosen you for his eternal one: **"For he chose us in him before the creation of the world to be holy and blameless in his sight. In love he predestined us for adoption to sonship through Jesus Christ"** (Ephesians 1:4,5).

And what a glorious family reunion awaits us in heaven! Can you picture it? The apostle John describes it in the stunning vision God gave him of heaven: **"There before me was a great multitude that no one could count, from every nation, tribe, people and language. . . . They cried out in a loud voice: 'Salvation belongs to our God, who sits on the throne, and to the Lamb'"** (Revelation 7:9,10).

What a family reunion that will be. Whom can you invite to God's eternal family reunion?

God's Word is a treasure
Clark Schultz

While traveling, in addition to waking everyone else up in the hotel, our boys love to fight over elevator buttons, key fobs to open doors, and the chance to rummage through all the drawers and closets for treasure.

While pillaging room 523 in Cleveland, the boys discovered a Bible and asked, "Dad, someone left their Bible here. Who would do that?" This led to a discussion of who Gideon is and the practice of hotels leaving a Bible in every room.

Then while taking a trip to the Rock & Roll Hall of Fame, another Bible observation was made. The King of Rock's Bible was behind glass for all to see. One of my sons said, "Dad, how can anyone read it if it's behind glass?" Great point.

Quick! Tell me right now where your Bible is? Do you know?

First, I commend you for taking the time to pick up this devotional. However, it is not this devotional that will save you. It's only Jesus, found in the treasure of God's Word.

There is an old phrase by Charles Spurgeon that goes like this: "A Bible that's falling apart usually belongs to someone who isn't."

Continue to feed your faith on these devotions, and instead of using the Bible as a drink coaster, continue to explore it like a child looking for treasure. **"Devote yourself to the public reading of Scripture"** (1 Timothy 4:13).

Offering your whole life
Dave Scharf

Whom do you want to please in life? I would guess it is someone you are grateful to or for. The same is true in our relationship with our heavenly Father. Romans 12:1 says, **"Therefore, I urge you, brothers and sisters, in view of God's mercy, to offer your bodies as a living sacrifice, holy and pleasing to God—this is your true and proper worship."**

Paul describes an Old Testament burnt offering. Imagine you are an Israelite. You pick out your best sheep, the priest examines it, and then you slit the lamb's throat. The priest catches its lifeblood in a bowl and sprinkles it on all sides of God's altar as the sheep is burnt until it's nothing more than ash. You just made a burnt offering. But you didn't have to do it. There is no payment for sin in this offering, just thanks. It symbolizes your complete devotion to God.

Some might ask, "Why?" Go back to the altar. This time go to the altar of the cross and see the sacrifice being offered there. Jesus covers your sin and says, "We're at peace. There is no cost for you to pay." That's mercy. Jesus, the Lamb of God, sweeps all the dead sheep off the altar of God to make room for you to be a living sacrifice until the day he calls you home. That's mercy. Now in view of that mercy, what do you want to do? Offer your whole life.

Our self-sufficient God
Katrina Harrmann

When my family hikes into the woods, we take along 200 lbs. of "stuff." It's *necessary* stuff, like food, shelter, a stove, and water, but it's stuff, nonetheless. Whenever we strap on our 50-lb packs and lumber into the woods like cumbersome turtles with our homes on our backs, it reminds me of how needy we are as humans. And as we start to run out of supplies on the last day, I confess to feeling a bit nervous!

We were not created to be self-sufficient. Not in the least. That's more and more obvious these days when just about anything you could ask for can be delivered to your doorstep within 24 hours at the touch of a button.

We are needy. God is not. God doesn't have to worry about running out of anything that he lacks, because he lacks nothing! **"Ah, Sovereign Lord, you have made the heavens and the earth by your great power and outstretched arm. Nothing is too hard for you"** (Jeremiah 32:17).

We are the exact opposite. We were designed to need God. And only he can meet all our needs—including the most important need: salvation through Christ Jesus. I don't know about you, but the idea of a self-sufficient God gives me *great* comfort. He will always be enough. And he always gives us what we need!

A walking companion
Andrea Delwiche

Psalm 121 is one of the traveling songs of Israel. These psalms were walking companions, providing stability, meaning, rhythm, and heart's ease for the traveler. For travelers back then and for us today, what we learn by heart offers to go everywhere with us to keep us steady. Scripture can provide the rhythm for our walking—both in our literal daily walk and our life journey. Sit with these words and create a picture of them in your mind.

"I lift up my eyes to the hills. From where does my help come? My help comes from the Lord, who made heaven and earth. He will not let your foot be moved; he who keeps you will not slumber. Behold, he who keeps Israel will neither slumber nor sleep. The Lord is your keeper; the Lord is your shade on your right hand. The sun shall not strike you by day, nor the moon by night. The Lord will keep you from all evil; he will keep your life. The Lord will keep your going out and your coming in from this time forth and forevermore" (verses 1–8 ESV).

Good techniques for memorization include carrying a passage in your pocket to read throughout the day. You can write the passage on a wide rubber band and wear it. Be sure to connect the Scripture to your life in a prayerful way.

Jesus himself taught, **"Out of the abundance of the heart the mouth speaks"** (Matthew 12:34 ESV). How could memorizing even this one psalm bring you peace?

God's piggyback ride
Nathan Nass

For a short window of time, a child gets a special treat: piggyback rides! Remember those? Every kid loves piggyback rides. From their parents' shoulders, they get to see the world from on high, feel extra safe, and rest their little legs. Nothing makes a child feel as special as when they get a piggyback ride from their mom or dad.

But you don't get piggyback rides for very long. Soon you grow too big for your parents to carry you. For the rest of your life, you have to navigate life on your own two feet. Aren't there days when you wish you could go back? When you wish you could rest on Mom's or Dad's shoulders again?

Then listen to God's invitation: **"Let the beloved of the Lord rest secure in him, for he shields him all day long, and the one the Lord loves rests between his shoulders"** (Deuteronomy 33:12). Those words were spoken to the tribe of Benjamin in ancient Israel. They lived in the mountains, as if they were resting securely on someone's shoulders. But those mountains didn't provide their security. The Lord did!

Just like he does for you. You are never too big to ride on God's shoulders. He's strong enough to carry you, even with all your baggage and sins and worries and fears. Jesus gives forgiveness and strength. God your Father loves to swing you up on his shoulders and carry you. "The one the Lord loves rests between his shoulders." It's God's lifelong piggyback ride.

No exceptions
Liz Schroeder

My inner lawyer doesn't have my best interest at heart. When I'm tempted to go against the will of God, my inner lawyer is quick to soothe me: *"Sure, God said to be self-controlled and alert, but after the day you had, you deserve to let loose and tune out your responsibilities. You're the exception to the law,"* he croons.

Like a two-faced mythical beast, that same lawyer turns his argument around after I've sinned. *"Look at what you've done,"* he tsks, pushing my nose into my mess like a cruel master to a dog. *"Who could ever forgive you? This 'merciful God' you claim to worship certainly has his limits; it's not like this is your first offense. 'God so loved the world'?"* he sneers. *"Surely you're the exception."*

If my inner lawyer sounds like yours, it's because he's been using the same tactics since the Garden of Eden. His croon-and-tsk combo worked so well on Adam and Eve that he tried it in the wilderness on our Savior. But this time his strategy didn't work. When the tempter twisted Scripture to entice Jesus to sin, Jesus wielded the Word of God to combat the tempter.

Whether your inner lawyer argues that you're the exception to the law or to the gospel, wield this: **"For everyone has sinned; we all fall short of God's glorious standard. Yet God, in his grace, freely makes us right in his sight. He did this through Christ Jesus when he freed us from the penalty for our sins"** (Romans 3:23,24 NLT). No exceptions.

No filter with the gospel!
Dave Scharf

Have you ever noticed that little children have no filter? If you have a big pimple on your face, they are going to point it out! My wife once asked one of our daughters how she looked in a dress, and my daughter said, "The dress makes you look young, but your face makes you look old." ☺

But that lack of filter is a wonderful quality for sharing the gospel. Think of how loudly young children pray in a restaurant while their parents mumble. When children sing in church, they belt out their praises! Children are not ashamed to proclaim the gospel. Why? Because it's true and important! They genuinely care about other people and want them in heaven. How quickly we lose that quality and start thinking about how proclaiming the soul-saving gospel might affect the way people think of us.

The apostle Paul tells us to stop being so grown up and get back to our childlike ways! He says, **"I am not ashamed of the gospel, because it is the power of God that brings salvation to everyone who believes"** (Romans 1:16). Remember that this good news changed your life. Remember that someone was unashamed to tell you about Jesus' love for you on the cross. Remember what you want for every person you meet: for this person to be in heaven with you. Remember that this message is God's power to change hearts. There's no need for a filter with the gospel!

Quietly present
Clark Schultz

Who is your best friend? Why? Do you have too many to count? If you hit a rough patch or need to make a serious decision, who do you ring, text, or snap to give you the wise counsel you need?

To me, one characteristic of a good friend is that they keep their mouths shut when it matters. When visiting someone with a hurting heart, I've been guilty of being "that friend"—the one who spews out all the 50-plus years of knowledge I have, fires a few Bible passages at them, and gives them a diatribe of wisdom. Wrong approach. A true friend is one who is there with you quietly in the moment.

When my brother was killed tragically in a snowmobile accident at a young age, my world was rocked. Some people didn't know what to say or what to do. Due to the stages of grief I was going through, folks who were "that friend" with all the words made me want to punch them in the face. But the most memorable moment for me was when a group of my friends came over and we all just sat in silence. No words, just their presence was soothing to my hurting heart.

Jesus, our best Friend, invites us to come to him in those moments as well. He says, **"Come to me all you who are weary and burdened"** (Matthew 11:28). Whether you see him or not, Jesus is with you in the silence too. He is there; you are never alone.

Love one another
Andrea Delwiche

Today is a new day. Will it be defined by your unbelievable love for others? Think of the words Jesus spoke just after he had washed his disciples' feet and before he was betrayed to suffer and die: **"A new command I give you: Love one another. As I have loved you, so you must love one another. By this everyone will know that you are my disciples, if you love one another"** (John 13:34,35).

In Psalm 122, written centuries earlier, we hear about a demonstration of this same divine love principle: **"For the sake of my family and friends, I will say, 'Peace be within you.' For the sake of the house of the LORD our God, I will seek your prosperity"** (verses 8,9). The psalmist vowed to seek peace and prosperity for others, and so do we. This isn't easy. If it were, perhaps Jesus wouldn't have felt the need to make love the defining distinctive of being his follower.

There is a Christian saying that goes something like this: "My sister or brother is never my enemy." Picture the vast diversity within your family, community, country of origin, and the Christian church scattered across the globe. For whom do you need to pray, setting aside personal differences or preferences to uphold Jesus' command to love and the biblical principle to pray for the peace of others?

We can ask God to guide us, praying this ancient prayer: *Lord, make me an instrument of your peace. Where there is hatred, let me sow love. Amen.*

Learning from sand cranes
Jan Gompper

One of my favorite things about living in Florida is watching the sand cranes. It's rare to see one walking by itself. They instinctively travel in pairs or groups of three to protect themselves from predators, power lines, or oncoming traffic. They also forage and feed together. It's common to see cars slow to a stop while a group of sand cranes slowly meanders across the street.

We can learn from sand cranes.

Most Americans have grown up thinking that independence and self-sufficiency are keys to survival. Even some Christians have the belief that all anyone needs is God to navigate life.

Neither is true. Not long after Adam took his first breath, God realized that **"it is not good for the man to be alone"** (Genesis 2:18). Though Adam had a direct one-on-one relationship with his Creator, God had also designed him with a *need* for relationship, not only with him but also with other human beings.

Knowing that God wired us for human relationship, one would think that Christians and Christian churches would make fostering relationships a high priority. Sadly, this is not always the case.

The early church in Acts 2:42-47 understood and practiced relational Christianity. They worshiped and prayed together. They looked out for one another's physical needs. They ate in each other's homes and enjoyed one another's company. They knew that spiritual predators were all around them, so they stuck together.

We can learn a lot from them . . . and sand cranes.

He drank the cup!
Jon Enter

In a garden called Gethsemane, Jesus prayed earnestly for the Father to take the "cup" from him. What's so bad about a cup? That depends on what's in the cup! So what was in the cup Jesus was praying about? The rebellion of Adam. The drunkenness of Noah. The lies of Abraham. The deceit of Jacob. The adultery of David. The greed of Matthew. The denial of Peter. The betrayal of Judas. The murder of Paul. All of it was in the cup. And more. The sins of my past and yours. They were in the cup! Those times we've given in to the devil's temptations. They were in there. All the guilt, all the godless acts, all the lies, all the lust, all that we've done.

Jesus remained perfectly pure and perfectly in tune with his Father's will. He prayed, **"Abba, Father, . . . everything is possible for you. Take this cup from me. Yet not what I will, but what you will"** (Mark 14:36). Jesus finished that prayer and drank the cup of God's wrath by dying on a cross for our sins.

Do you know what this means? When you fall into temptation, you still have a way out! Confess your sins to the Lord. When you're suffering the effects from falling prey to the devil, turn to Jesus. Turn to his power to remove temptation's lock on your heart. Turn to Jesus and be free!

Jesus needs to show up!
Linda Buxa

I recently started watching a TV series based on the biblical story of Jesus, but it also includes fictional stories and conversations. In every episode, I see the pain of the demon possessed, the outcast, the worried, the sick, the dying. Each time I see their struggles, I say, "I can't wait for Jesus to show up!" See, I know these Bible stories and how they end, so I get antsy for Jesus to come and set things right.

I feel the same way about real life. I see people who are struggling because they are estranged from family, lonely, been hurt by the church, been abandoned by a spouse, or are battling mental illness, and I think, "I can't wait for Jesus to show up!" I want him to make all things right.

And then I realize I know two truths. One, after Jesus conquered death and went back to prepare a place for us, he promised he would be with us to the very end of the age. So that means he is already here. He hasn't left us. He still cares about each of us and our problems and hurts.

Two, he promised he would show up again to take us to that place where all things are new, where there is no more crying or sickness or heartache or pain. And he gives us this promise to cling to: **"I am coming soon. Hold on to what you have, so that no one will take your crown"** (Revelation 3:11).

The fog of war
Liz Schroeder

Friends of ours use the term "the fog of war" to describe their season of raising grade school and high school children. Maybe you can relate. Driving one kid to practice, another to a game, and buying a gift for yet another birthday party—all while discipling their hearts, managing your work and home, and squeezing in an occasional date night so you don't forget the person you married.

Or maybe your fog of war looks a bit different. Taking your spouse to doctor visit after doctor visit, wrestling with insurance claims, wasting hours on hold with customer service—all while trying to preserve your spouse's dignity and your identity.

Whatever your fog looks like, the Bible tells us, **"For our struggle is not against flesh and blood, but against the rulers, against the authorities, against the powers of this dark world and against the spiritual forces of evil in the heavenly realms"** (Ephesians 6:12).

Though it might seem like you're fighting an administration, a boss, a spouse, or a rebellious teenager, it is a spiritual battle. And you can't bring an earthly weapon to a spiritual battle. Your strategy and charisma aren't going to cut it; you need the full armor of God.

"Therefore put on the full armor of God, so that when the day of evil comes, you may be able to stand your ground, and after you have done everything, to stand" (Ephesians 6:13).

The day is coming when the fog will be lifted, and we will stand with our Lord, victorious. Hang in there, soldier.

Strong in weakness
Paul Mattek

"Simon, Simon, Satan has asked to sift all of you as wheat" (Luke 22:31). That Bible passage terrified me at one point in my life when my faith was dry as a bone and nothing seemed to restore it. But at that point, the more I tried, the further my faith went numb and an indescribable terror overtook me.

Satan was sifting me like wheat, and there wasn't anything I could do to stop it. So I fell on my face and submitted to the inevitable. "OK, Lord, if this was what was supposed to be, then I guess I'm a Judas or one of the multitude of horrible kings of Israel and Judah who had your prophetic words spoken to them and didn't listen. You probably knew this about me from the moment I was born." I sat with that for a while and closed my eyes. I didn't want a friend to talk me out of these thoughts. I didn't want to do anything.

But God tapped my memory with the next verse: **"But I have prayed for you"** (verse 32). And then he tapped again with John 17:20-26, where Jesus prays for all believers.

God reminded me that I don't stand a chance when it's me versus the devil. He reminded me that I can't do anything on my own. I need him. He took on the devil and won.

And it was then that I finally knew what another verse meant: **"When I am weak, then I am strong"** (2 Corinthians 12:10).

AUGUST

Confess your sins to each other and pray for each other so that you may be healed. The prayer of a righteous person is powerful and effective.

James 5:16

More than a big fish
Mike Novotny

Don't get distracted by the big fish, because the book of Jonah is really about a big God. If you know anything about this four-chapter book tucked near the end of the Old Testament, it's probably about the giant fish that swallowed ol' Jonah, but the fish is only mentioned three times. Jonah himself is mentioned 18 times, but even he is not the star of this story. That honor belongs to the God who is mentioned 40 times in this 48-verse book!

To be more specific, the book of Jonah is about God's love for all people. From the violent, wicked, and abusive Assyrians to the self-righteous, pouty, holier-than-thou Jonah, God shows his shocking love for all kinds of people before the book is done. We see hints of that love in the very first verses: **"The word of the LORD came to Jonah son of Amittai: 'Go to the great city of Nineveh'"** (Jonah 1:1,2). The Lord told a Torah-loving Jew from a small town near Nazareth to take a mission trip to a metropolitan, Gentile, pagan city. Why? Because God, as John later pointed out, loves the world (John 3:16).

If you struggle with loving "those people" or believing that God loves you, keep reading the book of Jonah. And don't get distracted by the big fish! This book is about the even bigger love that God has for the world.

God loves *all* people
Mike Novotny

Why would Jonah run? **"The word of the Lord came to Jonah son of Amittai: 'Go to the great city of Nineveh and preach against it, because its wickedness has come up before me.' But Jonah ran away from the Lord"** (Jonah 1:1-3). Running from the Lord who is everywhere all the time is about as dumb as Adam and Eve trying to hide from the God who is always behind every tree. Why did Jonah do it?

You might assume he was afraid. After all, Nineveh was known for decapitating, impaling, and peeling the skin off of its enemies. Would you want to march up and down its streets all alone, preaching fire and brimstone? Spoiler alert!—Jonah didn't run out of fear of being flayed. He ran out of fear that God would forgive. This prophet knew enough about God's character that if, by some miracle, the people of Nineveh would repent, the Lord would certainly relent. He would save them by grace. That thought—"those people" saved—was so abhorrent that Jonah sprinted in the opposite direction of God's call.

Is there anyone you know whom you wouldn't want to be saved? As we journey deeper into the book of Jonah, wrestle with these questions: Who don't you pray for? Who wouldn't you share the gospel with? And why? I pray that this book, saturated with God's love for the world (and you!), inspires you to love the world too.

Follow Jesus' example
Mike Novotny

Why did God bother with Jonah, the runaway, rebellious, self-righteous prophet? When Jonah **"ran away from the Lord"** (Jonah 1:3), why didn't God just let him run? Or let him drown in the storm? Why didn't God tell the angels to find a new prophet? Simple. Because God loves "those people."

I had to wrestle with that fact earlier this year. Recently, I had a request to do an interview with a Christian group whose social media pages rubbed me the wrong way. Post after post was about "those people" who are the real problem with America. Article after article was about "those people" whose sins are destroying this nation. It felt so pharisaical that I wanted to keep my distance from such folks.

But one day it hit me. Am I doing what Jesus did? When a tax collector invited Jesus over for dinner and his rule-breaking buddies were at the table, what did Jesus do? He went. He ate. He spoke the truth, and he spoke it in love. And when a Pharisee invited Jesus over for dinner and his rule-keeping but incredibly judgmental buddies were at the table, what did Jesus do? He went there too! He ate there too! He spoke the truth, and he spoke it in love there too!

Jesus embodied what the book of Jonah is all about, namely, God's love for all people. May we, full of grace and truth, be the next example of showing and sharing that love with the world.

Rock-bottom prayers
Mike Novotny

Have you ever hit rock bottom? Like when people are telling you what you said at the party but you can't remember a word of it? Or when you are Googling "divorce lawyers in my area" for the very first time? Or when you think for the first time about why you do what you do and wonder how many of your "good works" have been fueled by bad motives?

Here's the tricky part: When you hit rock bottom, it's hard to reach out to the Most High God. As much as you need God, sometimes you don't run to him, because you feel so far from God. You wonder if he wants anything to do with you. You wonder if he's even listening. You're disgusted with yourself, so wouldn't a holy God who hates sin be even more disgusted? Why bother to ask him for help?

If that's you, here's what I want to tell you: God responds to rock-bottom prayers. Even if it's your fault that you're there, God responds to rock-bottom prayers. Even when you're that low, God will respond from on high. Here's the proof: **"From inside the fish Jonah prayed to the Lord his God"** (Jonah 2:1). Jonah, the rebellious, runaway prophet, prayed . . . and God answered!

There is no place, no matter how low, that is too far from the ears of God. Call out to him! Cry out for mercy! The God who loves the world, including those who've hit rock bottom, has promised to listen.

Turn to the Psalms
Mike Novotny

Unless you are an Old Testament scholar, you probably didn't know Jonah quoted so much Scripture. While inside a big fish, Jonah prayed, **"You hurled me into the depths, into the very heart of the seas, and the currents swirled about me; all your waves and breakers swept over me. I said, 'I have been banished from your sight; yet I will look again toward your holy temple.' The engulfing waters threatened me, the deep surrounded me; seaweed was wrapped around my head. To the roots of the mountains I sank down; the earth beneath barred me in forever. But you, LORD my God, brought my life up from the pit. When my life was ebbing away, I remembered you, LORD, and my prayer rose to you, to your holy temple"** (Jonah 2:3-7).

Almost every line of that prayer is a snippet from the Psalms—Psalms 30, 42, 5, 103, 18, and 107, proof that when you're in a dark place (pun intended), it's good to know your Bible. When life gets hard, there's no better place to turn than the Psalms.

Some Christians love to start their day with a chapter of Proverbs, since it's filled with wisdom to prepare you for the day ahead. I suggest you end your day with a chapter of Psalms, a book filled with the God who saves, who is our refuge, who hears our prayers, and who lifts us up, providing peace no matter what happened during our day. Be like Jonah today and spend some time in the saving words of the Psalms.

Joyful worship
Mike Novotny

How can you resist a sin that feels so good? How can you fight your critical nature or stay sober when everyone else isn't or love that tough-to-love person in your family? How can you give more money away or be courageous enough to stand up to your friends when they gossip? In other words, how can you follow God with a joyful, willing heart?

Jonah knows. **"Those who cling to worthless idols turn away from God's love for them. But I, with shouts of grateful praise, will sacrifice to you. What I have vowed I will make good. I will say, 'Salvation comes from the Lord'"** (Jonah 2:8,9). Why repent? Why obey?

First, so you don't "turn away from God's love." God loves the world, but you can turn away from that love if you "cling to" anything besides God. Is any sin worth throwing away his eternal love? Is any temporary thing worth more than being with God forever?

Second, because the Lord saved you. Jonah is shouting (not mumbling), is grateful (not grumbling), is ready to sacrifice to God. Why? Because "salvation comes from the Lord." That's the spiritual game changer! You made a mess, but God made you clean. You did the crime, but the cross did the time. You broke it, but your Father bought it. You were dead, but God made you alive. That salvation will change your heart and compel you to joyful worship.

Fix your eyes on the cost of sin and the cross of Jesus, and you will joyfully worship God too.

By God's grace
Mike Novotny

Can you think of someone who will never become a Christian? Someone so set in their ways and their sins that there is no chance they will repent and believe in the true God? Before you answer, check out what happened in Jonah chapter 3:

"Then the word of the Lord came to Jonah a second time: 'Go to the great city of Nineveh and proclaim to it the message I give you.' Jonah began by going a day's journey into the city, proclaiming, 'Forty more days and Nineveh will be overthrown'" (verses 1,2,4). Jonah walked into this ancient metropolis, famous for its wickedness, and turned over God's sand timer of judgment. "Forty days and you're dead!"

You would think that the next verse would say, "Then the men of Nineveh arrested, tortured, and murdered the prophet who dared to defy them." But that's not what the next verse says. Here's what it says: **"The Ninevites believed God"** (verse 5).

No. Way. Nineveh?! There wasn't a chance that people so bad could do something so good! But apparently they did. The Holy Spirit can do more than we ask or imagine. Just ask Jonah!

There is no promise that everyone you love will be saved, but there is the potential. Don't stop praying. Don't stop loving. Maybe one day something will change, and God will grant them a change of heart. It happened back then, and by God's grace, it can still happen today.

What's repentance?
Mike Novotny

What is repentance? Is it something you feel? think? something you do? We can learn a lot by looking at the repentance described in the book of Jonah:

"The Ninevites believed God. A fast was proclaimed, and all of them, from the greatest to the least, put on sackcloth. When Jonah's warning reached the king of Nineveh, he rose from his throne, took off his royal robes, covered himself with sackcloth and sat down in the dust. This is the proclamation he issued in Nineveh: . . . 'Let everyone call urgently on God. Let them give up their evil ways and their violence. Who knows? God may yet relent and with compassion turn from his fierce anger so that we will not perish'" (Jonah 3:5-9).

In this crash course on repentance, we learn a few key truths. First, repentant people are sorry for sin. They aren't proud of sin. They can't plan to live in sin. Next, repentant people show they are sorry. In this case, it was fasting and sackcloth. In other passages, this is called the fruit of repentance, the visible proof that we are sorry for our sins. Finally, repentant people call on God's compassion. They know they deserve his anger, justice, and wrath, so they call on God's compassion, mercy, and grace. They look to his love to save them from their sins.

You may not be wearing sackcloth today, but a repentant heart is sorry for sin, focused on Jesus' forgiveness, and willing to make necessary changes. May God give all of us humble, repentant hearts.

God's abounding love
Mike Novotny

If you have trouble forgiving yourself or believing that God isn't mad at you after you messed up in a big way, look at how God treated the wicked people of Nineveh after they repented. **"When God saw what they did and how they turned from their evil ways, he relented and did not bring on them the destruction he had threatened"** (Jonah 3:10). Despite their countless sins, God immediately showed them mercy.

By nature, we tend to think of our relationship with God as a scale that balances good and bad choices. If we do more good things than bad things, God smiles. If we do more bad things than good things, God scowls. So if you've done too many bad things, you better pile up some good things before God brings destruction down on your head.

But that isn't true, and this story is the proof. God relented before these sinners had time to put in much effort. Their hearts turned from sin and turned to him, and—boom!—God showed compassion, a preview of how Jesus would later treat the thief on the cross.

The Lord treats you the same way. You might think you have to earn back God's love, but you don't. You might assume you need some time to balance the scales and be worthy of his affection, but you don't. Because God is God—abounding in love and full of grace—you can run back to him in repentance any time, on any day, and find his arms wide open.

Isn't grace amazing?

Angry at God
Mike Novotny

A few months ago, I reached out to a Christian counselor and asked, "What makes people get mad at God?" His answer? "Expectations." People have an idea about how God should act, and when God doesn't act like he "should," people get mad. I think he's right. For example, you might get mad at God when he allows more pain in your life than he "should."

Or like the prophet Jonah, you might get mad that God is so quick to forgive. After God's mercy on the wicked people of Nineveh, we read, **"But to Jonah this seemed very wrong, and he became angry"** (Jonah 4:1). Jonah was red in the face furious because he felt it was wrong for God to forgive "those people" who had no right to grace after committing such horrific wrongs.

Imagine someone who hurt you deeply showing up at church and sitting three rows in front of you. Imagine, even if they are sorry for their sin, how you would feel as the pastor says, "God loves you. God forgives you for everything. Because of Jesus, God isn't thinking about your sin. He likes you!" If you see the one who wounded you nodding, wiping away a tear, and smiling at grace, would you grimace?

The final chapter of Jonah forces us to think deeply about God's grace toward those who have sinned against us. If they repent, do you want God to rescue them? Do you want them in heaven with you? Will it seem very wrong if they are right with God?

God's character
Mike Novotny

Do you know the most-quoted verse in the entire Old Testament, the one that shows up over 20 times throughout the Law, the Prophets, and the Psalms? Jonah did. In fact, he memorized it.

In the midst of his tantrum over God's love for the world, Jonah said, **"I knew that you are a gracious and compassionate God, slow to anger and abounding in love"** (Jonah 4:2). Those four descriptions of God come from a famous interaction between God and Moses in Exodus 34, where the Lord reveals what he's really like. Gracious—not punishing those who repent. Compassionate—blessing those who deserve to be cursed. Slow to anger—God takes a deep breath before his justice comes. Abounding in love—more acts of love than hairs on your head. God reveals the beautiful balance between his grace for his people and his justice upon those who do not repent.

My mom used to repeat this before I went out with friends: "No drinking, no smoking, no sex, no drugs." My dad still repeats, "You don't know how good you got it." I repeat to my daughters, "You know God loves you, right?" And Jews would repeat, **"The Lord, the Lord, the compassionate and gracious God, slow to anger, and abounding in love"** (Exodus 34:6).

Got a few minutes today? Read—better yet, memorize—Exodus 34:6,7 and get to know the character of our God.

The heart of God
Mike Novotny

Imagine a spectrum of morality with the worst people on one end and the most-loving people on the other end. Moral monsters here; Mother Teresas there. From Hitler to child abusers to violent criminals to desperate addicts to the arrogant, the average, the kind, the generous, the good examples, the people you want to babysit your babies, and the people you want to be like. Can you picture a lineup of humanity according to morality?

Who has a chance of going to heaven? And who is in danger of the torment of hell? According to God, everyone and everyone. No one, according to Jesus, is so good they deserve to be with God. And no one, according to Jesus, is so bad they can't make it to God, can't be saved.

That is what made Jonah mad. After seeing the wicked men of Nineveh spared, he whined, **"I knew that you are a gracious and compassionate God, slow to anger and abounding in love, a God who relents from sending calamity. Now, Lord, take away my life, for it is better for me to die than to live"** (Jonah 4:2,3).

True Christianity is unbearable to some people, because salvation is not by works. Sin—every size and shape of it—is worse than you think, so bad that even the best life can't pay its debt. Grace—abounding in God's heart and poured out on the cross—is better than you believe, so good that even the worst sinners can be saved. Grasp that, and you'll get the heart of God.

At the heart of our emotions
Mike Novotny

The reason that the prophet Jonah was mad enough to run from God is that Jonah was infatuated with Jonah. Skim the final chapter of this Old Testament book, and you'll find plenty of "I" and "me" and "my" on Jonah's lips. To expose his self-centeredness, look what God did: **"Then the Lord God provided a leafy plant and made it grow up over Jonah to give shade for his head to ease his discomfort, and Jonah was very happy about the plant. But at dawn the next day God provided a worm, which chewed the plant so that it withered. When the sun rose, God provided a scorching east wind, and the sun blazed on Jonah's head so that he grew faint. He wanted to die"** (Jonah 4:6-8).

Jonah was so angry about his sunburn that he wanted to die. But when God saved thousands of others from burning in hell, Jonah didn't care. Scratch that. Jonah claimed that God's grace had gone too far!

Take note of your strongest emotions today. What makes you angry? What triggers you to excessive reactions? Probe your emotions, and figure out what's at the heart of it. You, like Jonah, may be too interested in yourself and not interested enough in others. Drag that sin to Jesus. If there's anything we learn from the book of Jonah, it is that our God truly does love and forgive sinners like us.

The essence of our faith
Mike Novotny

Ready for a cliff-hanger? Here's how the book of Jonah ends: **"But the Lord said, 'You have been concerned about this plant, though you did not tend it or make it grow. It sprang up overnight and died overnight. And should I not have concern for the great city of Nineveh, in which there are more than a hundred and twenty thousand people who cannot tell their right hand from their left—and also many animals?'"** (Jonah 4:10,11). God said, "Jonah, you care about a little vine and some extra shade. Shouldn't I care about a big city and saving souls?"

That question hangs, unanswered, at the end of Jonah. How will Jonah answer? How will we? Will we have the humility to celebrate God's love for "those people"?

This story is not about a big fish but about the biggest issues of faith. It's about a God who really does love the world: violent Assyrians, self-righteous Jews, me, and you. It's about a God who calls people to repent, to be sorry for their sins, to show they are sorry for their sins. It's about a God who saves, who rescues pouty people who think they're good and wicked men who know they've been bad. It's about a God who would love the world so much that he would send his one and only Son that whoever believes in him—whoever!—would not perish but have eternal life.

Never mind the fish. Jonah is about the essence of our faith.

The flesh is weak
Jon Enter

When Jesus was tempted in Gethsemane not to drink the cup of God's judgment, his disciples were sleeping nearby. Jesus rose from prayer focused on completing the plan of salvation. He warned his disciples not to grow weary but to stay awake. They didn't. These words of Jesus are so often misunderstood. **"'Simon' he said to Peter, 'are you asleep? Couldn't you keep watch for one hour? Watch and pray so that you will not fall into temptation. The spirit is willing, but the flesh is weak'"** (Mark 14:37,38).

Many Christians hear those words and think they were spoken in disgust and anger. To hear Jesus say those words in that tone is a guilty conscience talking. Jesus had just left prayer in which he resolved himself to follow fully the Father's will of suffering alone and winning our salvation. Immediately, he was reminded why his death was needed. When Jesus said, "The spirit is willing, but the flesh is weak," he emphasized the first phrase. The disciples wanted to be faithful, but they couldn't.

Our spirit is willing and wanting to resist the devil, but our flesh is weak. So Jesus gives himself as our strength to resist temptation and be healed when we fail. That's why Jesus told the disciples and us what to do. "Watch and pray." Watch—be on your guard against the devil, knowing he will never stop tempting you. Then pray—rely on Jesus' forgiveness when you fail, knowing you are spiritually healed.

Our infinite God
Katrina Harrmann

Recently, I was looking at something I had made with my kids. "That was two years ago already," I commented to my husband. He looked at me: "Sweetie, that was like *five* years ago!" No way! We looked it up in the photo albums. Sure enough, it had been five years!

Looking at photo albums gives me a sense of time warp. Weren't my kids just five years old *yesterday*? Didn't we *just* take that vacation? And now my oldest is engaged!

Where does the time go?

Our God has control of our days. He is not intimidated or even concerned by the passing of years. He is outside of it, with his eyes on all our years at once—a staggering thought and yet one of immense comfort. Whom better to trust our futures and days with than the One who has a view of it all—from beginning to end?

"With the Lord a day is like a thousand years, and a thousand years are like a day" (2 Peter 3:8). Our infinite God sees time as we never will. What a blessing!

All we are asked to do is to be good stewards of the time God has given to us. So use your days wisely. Seek God's will in your daily walk, and when your own little fabric square of time doesn't make sense or baffles you, trust the God who holds the entire quilt in his hands, because he's fashioned it himself from day one and has a plan for each of our pieces in his masterpiece.

Struggling to pray?

Matt Ewart

"In Christ you have been brought to fullness" (Colossians 2:10).

If you are struggling to make prayer a regular part of your life, I could sit down with you over coffee and help you understand why it's a struggle. But before you even have time to put creamer in your coffee and stir it around, I could explain why you don't pray very often with one abrasive sentence—The reason you struggle to pray is because you believe there are better ways to spend your time.

You might believe that there are more productive ways to spend your time. Or you might believe that there are more fulfilling ways to spend your time. Or you might believe that there are more rewarding ways to spend your time.

The reason you don't spend time in prayer is because part of you believes what isn't true—that there are better ways to spend it.

And if I come off as judgmental or accusatory, just know that I'm writing this devotion for myself today. I need to hear this just as much as you do.

What we all need to hear is that Jesus loved us so much that he spent his time here on earth for us. He delighted in us, even as he prioritized the perfect prayer life with his Father.

Because of all he did, there is no more productive, fulfilling, or rewarding way to spend time than to think about God's presence and say, "Our Father in heaven . . ."

Nothing can separate you from God's love
Nathan Nass

Nothing can separate you from God's love. Do you believe that? It's hard. Sometimes we seem to be separated from God's love. Sometimes it seems like no one loves us at all. Sometimes our lives seem to scream out: "You are all alone!" You're not. Nothing can separate you from God's love.

Here's proof: **"I am convinced that neither death nor life, neither angels nor demons, neither the present nor the future, nor any powers, neither height nor depth, nor anything else in all creation, will be able to separate us from the love of God that is in Christ Jesus our Lord"** (Romans 8:38,39).

That's quite a list! Death, life, angels, demons . . . None of those can separate you from God's love! You could make your own list: depression, cancer, heartache, rejection, criticism, pain, old age, loneliness . . . Can any of those things separate you from God's love? No!

Because God's love is undeserved. It's not based on your behavior or your circumstances. It's based on Jesus, who lived, died, and rose for you. When you're good and when you're bad, God loves you. When life is good and when life is bad, God loves you.

Nothing can separate you from God's love. You need to hear that today. No matter what's going on in your life and in your head and in your heart, nothing will be able to separate you from the love of God that is in Christ Jesus.

Waiting for God
Andrea Delwiche

"I look to you, heaven-dwelling God, look up to you for help. Like servants, alert to their master's commands, like a maiden attending her lady, we're watching and waiting, holding our breath, awaiting your word of mercy" (Psalm 123:1-4 MSG).

Do you and I consider enough that we are God's creatures? Do we remember that our daily lives and breath are sustained by him? Think of a dog waiting with expectant eyes for a bite of food. Picture birds pecking around a bird feeder in the winter when seeds are scarce and buried under snow. We are like them, blessed to wait upon someone else for our daily bread. Our "heaven-dwelling God" answers our seeking eyes, hearts (and stomachs).

Jesus' own prayer teaches us to ask God to give us what we need for today. How would it change our scurrying lifestyles if we remembered that we are sustained by God's providence? He doesn't require us to neglect relationships, our own personal well-being, or our soul-tie with him to elbow our way through life.

This psalmist is also looking for physical protection. What if we relied more on God's protection and less on mustering our own resources for physical safety?

More of Jesus' words come to mind: **"Can any one of you by worrying add a single hour to your life?"** (Matthew 6:27). Better to use our time to meditate on God's promises than to chew on our problems. What does it look like for you and me to practice waiting for God—eyes lifted to heaven and palms outstretched in prayer?

Jesus is our everything
Clark Schultz

Want to find out who your true friends are? Make a mistake. I have noticed over the years that everyone loves you when you are on top of the mountain. I have also noticed the list of people dwindles greatly when you are kicked to the curb.

I have good friends, and I have best friends. The friends who've stood by me when my heart was broken are the same friends who stood by me when I watched my bride walk down the aisle. In both instances, they were there, not running the other way.

Recently, I took a police academy course. One of the police officers told the class, "When folks are running from the danger, we (the police) run to it to protect others." That made me realize who my best Friend is— Jesus. **"Cast all your anxiety on [Jesus] because he cares for you"** (1 Peter 5:7).

When others have turned their backs on me, he has not. When my sins have made a mess of life, Jesus reminds me that he took the full burden of my sins and yours to the cross with him. Will my life with Jesus be roses and grape Kool-Aid? No, in fact there will be ups and downs. The constant has and will always be my Friend and yours, Jesus. Some may say, "Is that all, just having Jesus as your friend?" That is not all; it is everything.

Serious sin, serious forgiveness
Dave Scharf

Have you lost the sense of seriousness about your sin? Have you been through the routine so many times that you've lost the realization of what sin does between you and God? It separates you. King David held on to his sins for nearly a year. This is what King David said it did to him: **"When I kept silent, my bones wasted away through my groaning all day long. Then I acknowledged my sin to you and did not cover up my iniquity. I said, 'I will confess my transgressions to the Lord.' And you forgave the guilt of my sin"** (Psalm 32:3,5). Are you holding on to a sin? Is it weighing heavily on you?

"Then I acknowledged my sin to you . . ." Admit that there is a clear standard. God's law is clear. " . . . and did not cover up my iniquity." Don't excuse your sin or shift the blame. Admit that you are the cause of your sin. "I said, 'I will confess my transgressions to the Lord.'" Notice this is not self-pity that hates the consequences of sin. Nor is this self-flagellation, hating yourself instead of your sin. This is sorrow for wronging your God. "And you forgave the guilt of my sin." Immediately, Jesus wraps you up in his arms and says, "I have loved you to hell and back on the cross. I will always love you. I could never love you more. You are forgiven." Take sin seriously, but just as seriously, rejoice in your forgiveness!

I am my brother's keeper
Ann Jahns

In 2023 the U.S. Surgeon General released a report. In the introduction, he talks about crossing the country and listening to Americans of all ages and backgrounds confess that they feel "isolated, invisible, and insignificant."*

People are lonely like never before. Despite our 24/7 digital connection, we are hungering for actual human connection. We want to know someone sees us—and cares.

In Genesis, Cain's jealousy of his brother Abel eroded his heart. Cain murdered Abel and attempted to hide it from an all-knowing God. **"Then the Lord said to Cain, 'Where is your brother Abel?' 'I don't know,' he replied. 'Am I my brother's keeper?'"** (Genesis 4:9).

According to Jesus, Cain *was* his brother's keeper. So are we. After listing the most important commandment—loving God with all of our hearts—Jesus established the second most important commandment: **"Love your neighbor as yourself"** (Mark 12:31).

Our love of God and of our neighbor go hand in hand. I am called to the privilege of being my brother's keeper. And my sister's. And my neighbor's. And my coworker's.

How can we show God's love to our neighbor? We can check in and ask questions. "God brought you to my mind today. How can I pray for you?"

We can provide human connection and love. We can then let that love point our neighbor to Jesus.

* Dr. Vivek H. Murthy, "Our Epidemic of Loneliness and Isolation," https://www.hhs.gov/sites/default/files/surgeon-general-social -connection-advisory.pdf, 4.

Your guilt is gone
Paul Mattek

Confession time. Before I even reached puberty, I snuck my "girlfriend" into an empty church and kissed her. It was exhilarating for about 3.2 seconds . . . before guilt set in. This was not something the pastor would approve of. I knew because he was my dad. I deliberately did something forbidden. I told no one. For years, I hid it.

Perhaps you're hiding something too. Perhaps you see God as angry or your parents as disapproving, devoid of forgiveness and love. Perhaps you're used to a church culture where when you confess, no one forgives . . . unless you prove you are oh-so-very sorry first. Perhaps the thought of having to earn someone's forgiveness is too crushing, so you hide it.

You're not alone. David, a king of Israel, hid too. He committed an adulterous sin and then tried to cover it up with murder. It didn't work. His hidden guilt literally rotted his bones. But God reached out. In a gripping dialogue found in 2 Samuel 12, God sent a prophet named Nathan to draw David out of hiding with a pointed parable that confronted David with two very important truths: No sin is ever hidden from God, and guilt ends with God.

Psalm 32:5 recounts David's confession: **"Then I acknowledged my sin to you and did not cover up my iniquity. I said, 'I will confess my transgressions to the Lᴏʀᴅ.' And you forgave the guilt of my sin."** God knew David's sin and was more than ready to declare him not guilty!

Confess your sins to him. In Jesus, your guilt is gone too.

Let brotherly love continue
Jan Gompper

I recently had a conversation with a woman at church who had lost her husband in a tragic car accident. Through her tears, she told me she had been a member of our congregation for five years and that it wasn't until her husband died that anyone reached out to her. It grieved me to hear this, as I considered our church to be one of the friendliest I've ever attended.

While most churches offer warm smiles, handshakes, and even a free donut on Sunday mornings, it takes more than these to feel connected. The larger a church becomes the more isolated new people can feel. This doesn't mean we should avoid church growth, but perhaps we can do a better job of tuning in our radar to those most vulnerable.

Of course, getting connected is a two-way street. If people only show up on Sundays and don't get involved in church groups or activities, they will likely still feel isolated. Some people, however, just need a direct nudge, and it's not just up to church leaders to do the nudging.

Perhaps we start by inviting someone we don't know out for brunch after church, or we make an extra place at our holiday dinner table for that single or widowed person. How about asking a newcomer to go with us to a church or non-church event?

In whatever way possible, **"let brotherly love continue. Do not neglect to show hospitality to strangers, for thereby some have entertained angels unawares"** (Hebrews 13:1,2 ESV).

Do something or do nothing?
Matt Ewart

There are times when God calls on you to act. For example, he wants you to use your gifts in service to others. He wants you to be prepared to give a reason for the hope you have. He wants you to **"fight the good fight"** (1 Timothy 6:12).

But there are also times when God calls on you to do nothing. He wants you to be still and know that he is God. He wants you to know that there are some battles he fights for you—you need only be still. He wants you to watch what his mighty right arm can do.

So how do you know when to do something and when to do nothing? I would answer that by asking another question: Who is in control?

The apostle Peter thought nobody was in control when Jesus was about to be arrested, so he took matters into his own hands. He drew his sword and **"struck the servant of the high priest, cutting off his right ear"** (Luke 22:50).

In reality, when you read the account of Jesus' arrest, it is clear that Jesus was in control the entire time. He was asking the questions. He was guiding the outcome. So when Peter fought for control, he was resisting the One in control.

If Jesus was in control even in the darkest hour possible, he is in control of your circumstances too. Let that truth guide you to trust him, whether that means you do something or do nothing.

The main thing
Jon Enter

In Matthew 12, the Pharisees accused Jesus' disciples of breaking Sabbath law when they pulled heads of grain from a field and ate them. Jesus called his disciples innocent because they broke the rules, or traditions, of the Pharisees, not God's law. What made the Pharisees' tradition wrong was that they demanded the Jews *must* observe their tradition in order to follow God properly. Jesus disagreed.

There are traditions in Christian churches too. Traditions are good if they draw a believer's focus to Jesus, but traditions become wrong when they are demanded as the only way to worship and honor Jesus. Over one hundred years ago, churches and families split over whether to continue Lutheran worship in German or switch to English. Debates raged over the traditional version of the Lord's Prayer or the version without *thy*. Is it right for the pastor to wear a gown or not? Is music best on organ, piano, or with a worship band? Should there be worship screens or not? These questions have divided Jesus-loving Christians, leading to some awful words and accusations. When we turn something of worship into the main thing of worship, we fail.

"Worship the Lord your God, and serve him only" (Matthew 4:10). Worship is about Jesus. It's about realigning our hearts and lives to his will, not ours. The devil wins when he divides our hearts against each other over tradition or pushes our hearts from worship because of our preferences. How have you made worship about you?

The everlasting arms
Nathan Nass

It seems like everything is falling apart, doesn't it? When you look at the world . . . When you look at your own life . . . Who is holding all this together? Doesn't it seem like everything is falling apart?

It's not. It can't. Oh sure, bad things can happen and will happen. But everything isn't falling apart. It can't. Know why? **"The eternal God is your refuge, and underneath are the everlasting arms"** (Deuteronomy 33:27). The world isn't held together by chance or luck or some unknown force. The world—and your life—are held together by the everlasting arms of God. He is our refuge!

Even in death. Those words from the Bible are some of the last words of Moses, the great prophet who led God's people out of Egypt to the Promised Land. Even in death, Moses had confidence in the Lord. When human strength gives out, when there's nothing left that you can do, it's okay! Life doesn't depend on your strength. "The eternal God is your refuge, and underneath are the everlasting arms."

Jesus adds one more incredible detail to that picture. The arms that hold your life together have nail holes in them. Why? Because Jesus gave his life for you. To forgive all your sins. To win eternal life for you. The everlasting arms that hold the world together were once stretched out on a cross to save you. So no matter how life looks today, trust this: "underneath are the everlasting arms."

Muttering day and night
Linda Buxa

People who talk to themselves are usually considered a little crazy, right? (Although some say you aren't crazy unless you answer yourself.) But Psalm 1 has a different idea. It says people who talk to themselves are blessed. See for yourself: **"Blessed is the one . . . whose delight is in the law of the LORD, and who meditates on his law day and night. That person is like a tree planted by streams of water, which yields its fruit in season and whose leaf does not wither—whatever they do prospers"** (verses 1-3).

The day I learned that in Hebrew *meditate* means "to mutter" or "speak quietly," I muttered this psalm to myself. It changed so much. See, it's easy for my mind to get distracted as I'm looking at the words or skimming them. Muttering helps me slow down and read each word. The bonus is that the Bible promises blessings on the one who meditates day and night—and I like God's blessings.

It also makes me think about how we could mutter Scripture to ourselves all day.

When we're frustrated with people, we can mutter that love keeps no record of wrongs. When we're feeling alone, we can tell ourselves that God is always with us. When we are worried about our government, we can mutter that God is in charge. When we wonder about our purpose, we can remember that God sets the times and places where we live and that we are here to use our gifts for his glory.

What will you mutter today?

Your third strand
Liz Schroeder

On a hike through the foothills of the Sonoran Desert, I saw that a 20-foot saguaro cactus had keeled over. Nearby, a cluster of three saguaros stood tall. One had lost a limb, but they were otherwise thriving. This got me thinking about relationships, and Ecclesiastes 4:12 (NLT) came to mind.

"A person standing alone can be attacked and defeated." Your enemy cackles with glee when you self-isolate, which is fertile ground for pride, temptation, and loneliness. You're easy pickings.

"But two can stand back-to-back and conquer." When you're hiking through life with a Christian confidant, you can go farther than when you go alone. Seek out someone who will encourage you toward holiness, not mere happiness. A prayer warrior and fellow soldier helps protect you from a sneak attack.

"Three are even better, for a triple-braided cord is not easily broken." As for the third strand, think honestly about your most important relationships: spouse, friend, roommate, sister, son. What is your third strand right now, the thing at the center of your relationship? Is it Netflix? A bottle of wine? A gym membership? Or is it growing in the grace of the Lord?

God doesn't tell you to put him at the center because he's desperate for attention. He tells you to put him at the center because he is the only being in the universe who can withstand the weight of your worship. Your spouse and kids can't. Your friends can't. Don't put that kind of weight on them. Instead, lean on Jesus and stand tall.

More than a name
Andrea Delwiche

"Our help is in the name of the Lᴏʀᴅ, the Maker of heaven and earth" (Psalm 124:8).

God's name is more than a name. It saves. God's name reveals his nature, power, reputation, and much more. Jesus spoke his name to a hostile crowd in the Garden of Gethsemane, and they fell backward to the ground.

We can't fully explain this mystery. But we can increase our understanding by spending time in holy wonder, contemplating a few examples.

"Save me, O God, by your name" (Psalm 54:1).

"Peter said, 'Silver or gold I do not have, but what I do have I give you. In the name of Jesus Christ of Nazareth, walk'" (Acts 3:6).

"God exalted him to the highest place and gave him the name that is above every name, that at the name of Jesus every knee should bow, in heaven and on earth and under the earth, and every tongue acknowledge that Jesus Christ is Lord, to the glory of God the Father" (Philippians 2:9-11).

"And this is his command: to believe in the name of his Son, Jesus Christ, and to love one another as he commanded us" (1 John 3:23).

How does God's power and goodness resonate today when we speak his name? Spend some time praying with and meditating on the name of Jesus. Ask the Spirit to lead you to a deeper understanding of all that is possible when you call on and believe in God's name.

You are not an orphan
Ann Jahns

Years ago I attended the funeral for the mom of a dear friend. Her mom had died unexpectedly, and my friend was still mourning the loss of her dad a few years prior. As my friend and I clung to each other in front of the casket, she whispered in my ear, "I am now an orphan." She was hurting because the two people who had loved her most in the world were now gone. She knew she wouldn't see them again until she too was taken to heaven.

As Jesus spent his final days with his disciples before his death, he spoke to them with an urgency that impending goodbyes bring. As he talked about leaving them to return to heaven, their hearts were heavy. They didn't understand why Jesus needed to leave. You can almost hear the hurt and confusion in Peter's voice: **"Lord, where are you going? . . . Why can't I follow you now?"** (John 13:36,37).

But Jesus wasn't leaving his friends to flounder alone. He gave them this assurance: **"I will not leave you as orphans; I will come to you. . . . You are in me, and I am in you"** (John 14:18,20). Jesus promised to send the Holy Spirit to empower them, to help them do the work he had prepared them to do.

You see, we are never truly orphans, even when our earthly parents pass away. Jesus lives in us. God, our heavenly Father, is our forever Father. And nothing—not even death—can separate us from his glorious presence.

SEPTEMBER

We live by faith, not by sight.

2 Corinthians 5:7

Irresistible habits
Matt Ewart

Wouldn't it be nice if bad habits were easier to resist? And wouldn't it be nice if good habits were irresistible?

A mentor and friend of mine helped me understand why I was experiencing inconsistency when trying to implement new habits. It was not a matter of knowledge—I knew what to do. But knowledge did not make the new path irresistible.

The problem was not my mind but my heart. Specifically, my heart was believing something that made good habits way too resistible. I believed that today doesn't matter.

I had fallen for a lie. The truth is that the only day that I can work with is the today that God gives.

God is giving you another today, not just for your recreation or for your personal growth. He has a purpose for you that's bigger than this world. He has declared that you have a part in his story. His resurrection power is at work in you to transform your life to be like Christ. Through you, his light can shine in dark places.

If you've been wanting to develop new habits, align your heart to the truth of your God-given identity and purpose. That kind of good news is hard to resist.

"I will lead the blind by ways they have not known, along unfamiliar paths I will guide them; I will turn the darkness into light before them and make the rough places smooth. These are the things I will do; I will not forsake them" (Isaiah 42:16).

But to serve
Linda Buxa

One of Jesus' most well-known miracles is the feeding of five thousand people. (That's just men. Women and children were there too.) The people were hungry, but there wasn't enough food to feed everyone. A little boy shared his five loaves of bread and two fish. Jesus thanked God for the food, and the disciples handed it out. Everyone ate—and 12 basketfuls of food were left over.

It's easy to forget the context of this story though.

Jesus had *just* heard his cousin John had been murdered and, understandably, wanted privacy (maybe to grieve, to pray, to ponder his own death). So he took a boat to a secluded place, but the huge crowd walked to find him. When Jesus saw all of them, he didn't tell them to leave. Instead, he had compassion on them, healed them, and fed them.

Can you feel his humanity? The Son of Man was exhausted and grieving, yet he continued serving. Moments like this amaze me about my Lord and leave me speechless about my Savior. See, I usually just think about the big temptations he overcame but forget these "little" temptations too. He overcame the temptation not to serve, not to love. **"For even the Son of Man did not come to be served, but to serve, and to give his life as a ransom for many"** (Mark 10:45).

There's a lesson for us too when we face the temptation not to serve: **"Do not use your freedom to indulge the flesh; rather, serve one another humbly in love"** (Galatians 5:13).

I found what I'm looking for!
Dave Scharf

The band U2 has a song entitled, "I Still Haven't Found What I'm Looking For." You and I can relate. We go through life feeling like something is missing, fearing what will go wrong next. The women at the tomb on the first Easter didn't find what they were looking for either. They were looking for Jesus' body, but **"when they looked up, they saw that the stone . . . had been rolled away"** (Mark 16:4).

Have you ever wondered why the stone was rolled away? The stone was not rolled away so that Jesus could get out but so that the women could peek in! God's message was, "There's nothing to see here!" And that nothing changes everything!

You see, by finding nothing in the tomb, you find everything it is you are looking for in life because Jesus lives to give it. Are you looking for peace from a guilty conscience? Stop trying to get it by your own effort. The living Jesus says, "I give you a peace that passes all understanding." Are you looking for contentment? Stop trying to get it by getting more only to feel less content. The living Jesus says, "You have all you need in me and more." Are you looking for an answer to the grave? Stop looking for it in health programs and diets that only serve to stave off the inevitable. The living Jesus says, "See how my empty grave means yours will be too." I've finally found what I'm looking for! You too?

Our immeasurable God
Katrina Harrmann

Every year on the first day of school, we line our kid-dos up and mark their heights against a wall, marking the passage of time and the growth of our family. I often get choked up looking at it, remembering the little people my kids once were.

As human beings, we're very measurable. We grow "this" tall. We are "this" many years old. We have "this" much patience and X amount of energy. We've been at our jobs X number of years, and those jobs start at a specific time on the clock each day.

One of the things that makes God GOD is that he is immeasurable. He is ageless and timeless. He has been at his "job" countless years. And he has infinite amounts of patience and love. We can't put him into a box with numbers and limits. We can't mark his height against a wall, and his love and patience are infinite. He is beyond all of our measuring and understanding.

"Great is our Lord and mighty in power; his understanding has no limit" (Psalm 147:5).

Wow. Our God is divine and powerful! So the next time you're frazzled because you're running late or don't have enough time in the day or feel like you're not measuring up, go to God and get everything you need to get through your measurable day and life, because he is your immeasurable Father.

Oh my God?

Jan Gompper

Oh my Buddha! My Brahma, did you see that accident? That movie was Allah-awful.

Do these phrases sound strange? Now substitute the name God. Sound a little more familiar?

Most of us likely learned this commandment: **"Thou shalt not take the name of the L**ORD **thy God in vain"** (Exodus 20:7 KJV). More recently it's translated as, **"You shall not** *misuse* **the name of the L**ORD **your God"** (NIV).

Church reformer Martin Luther expounded on the meaning of this commandment: *"We should fear and love God so that we do not curse, swear, use satanic arts, lie, or deceive by His name."**

You might be saying to yourself, "Okay, I get how all those things would be a 'misuse' of God's name. But 'Oh my God!' doesn't mean anything, does it?"

Aye, there's the rub.

I'm partial to the wording in the KJV: "Thou shalt not take the name of the L**ORD** thy God *in vain.*"

Webster's dictionary gives these synonyms for the phrase *in vain: unsuccessful, futile, useless, empty.* So saying God's name *in vain* means uttering it as if it has no value, purpose, or ability to accomplish anything.

So how are we to use God's name? Martin Luther further elaborated that we are to *"call upon it in every trouble, pray, praise, and give thanks."*

Using God's name in these ways is never *in vain.*

* Martin Luther, *Luther's Small Catechism* (St. Louis: Concordia Publishing House, 2019), https://catechism.cph.org/en/10 -commandments.html.

Through the pain
Paul Mattek

My two-year-old loves playing in puddles. She gets joy and contentment splish-splashing her hands and feet.

As adults, our default becomes skepticism and cynicism, not contentment. When we've experienced more pain than is "fair," we grumble, putting the burden of proof on others: "I've been burned before. Convince me otherwise."

Perhaps I can't convince you, but I can ask you to zoom out from your experience and realize what else isn't fair: that God had to give up his Son to brutal treatment and death.

Why? Because of pain—the pain of burying that parent whom you were starting to reconcile with, of having your church community reject you when you dared to bring a painful secret to them, the pain of mental anguish that doesn't let up, and the countless other horrible pains. It was never supposed to be this way.

But through, not around, the pain you'll find God's ultimate why: *you*. The Father, who has already shown how much worth you have by giving up his Son so that you can be with him, perfectly protected, content, and even able to have some splash-splash joy now, is here to guide you through the pain and loss. **"I consider that our present sufferings are not worth comparing with the glory that will be revealed in us"** (Romans 8:18). The pain is passing away; you are not! If you can believe that, you can live with contentment and joy even in the midst of pain and even be the hands that reach out, receive, and revive other pained people.

Where's your heart?

Jon Enter

Nobody has to tell you to honor the things that are important to you. You just do. If you're a sports fan, nobody has to tell you to turn on the game. You just do. When you hold your newborn child in your arms for the first time, nobody has to tell you to smile. You just do.

In Genesis 4, Cain and Abel offered God sacrifices, but only Abel's offering was accepted. In God's eyes, Cain wasn't giving an offering because it didn't come from his heart. Cain was just going through the motions. Jesus said it this way: **"Where your treasure is, there your heart will be also"** (Luke 12:34). In other words, the place where you direct your heart reveals exactly what your treasure is.

During the month, do you give more to God or streaming services? more to God or to eating out? more to God or your cell phone company? It's okay to have a hobby and spend money. It's okay to go to the mall or the movies. Yet if you turn your money over to those things happily but when it comes to turning it over to God, you hold on to it very tightly, then you're saying, "These things are worth it, but God isn't." And that's something God won't tolerate. What will it take for you to give offerings like Abel, with a joyful heart?

Christianity is a relational religion
Mike Novotny

A few weeks ago, I was at a Christian musical festival where I saw a note stuck to the back of a minivan that read, "It's not a religion; it's a relationship." Have you ever heard that comment about Christianity?

It's kind of confusing, if you ask me. Because technically, isn't Christianity the world's largest religion? And doesn't that phrase encourage people to disconnect from church, accountability, and godly spiritual authority? And wasn't Jesus a fairly religious man himself, given his custom of going to the synagogue regularly (Luke 4:16)? On the other hand, didn't Jesus judge the religious Pharisees whom he claimed had no true relationship with the Father? And don't all of us know someone who goes to church but has no real connection to God?

Here's the biblical road between those two extremes, which I hope to explain in the devotions to come— Christianity is a relational religion. As James points out, there is a type of religion that **"God our Father accepts as pure and faultless"** (James 1:27). That religion follows the path of sacrificial love, a path we learn from our relationship with Jesus.

Don't let a sweet-sounding phrase pull you into an unhealthy place. Stay connected to church, pastoral leadership, and a community that provides accountability, *and* remember the God who is your Father and your friend. Because true Christianity is a relational religion.

Staying connected
Mike Novotny

Are you a religious person? I hope so. The word *religion* comes from a Latin word that means "to bind." True religion binds you to certain beliefs and behaviors that are outside of you. Instead of following their hearts/feelings/desires, religious people are bound to something unchanging, objective, and stable. That's why Christians don't get to invent their own list of Ten Commandments. We are, instead, bound to the list that our Lord already made.

Imagine holding a Bible and then having someone wrap a rope around both it and your hand. Thanks to that rope, you and the Bible would stay connected to each other, even if your grip started to slip. That, essentially, is what the Christian religion does. Weekly church services and other spiritual disciplines are the "rope of religion" that keeps you hearing God's commands and promises, even on those weeks when you are rather weak in your faith. Without religion, you might not hear the voice of your God at all.

No wonder the author to the Hebrews wrote, **"Let us hold unswervingly to the hope we profess, for he who promised is faithful. And let us consider how we may spur one another on toward love and good deeds, not giving up meeting together"** (10:23-25). Did you notice the connection between "meeting together" and our "hold" on the Christian hope? That's no coincidence. Because Christianity is a relational religion.

Don't run away!
Mike Novotny

Religion is unappealing to many people because of its rigid, restrictive nature. That's not an inaccurate description, because religion binds you to beliefs and behaviors that you don't get to choose or edit. You don't create your own commandments or design your personal path for salvation. Jesus is Lord and Savior, not you.

But this religion is for your good. I think of the Greek tale of Ulysses and the Sirens. Ulysses and his men were on a journey home after fighting in the Trojan War, but they had to pass by the Sirens, savage monsters who lured sailors toward their death-trap island with an irresistible song. Thankfully, Ulysses had been warned, so he ordered his men to tie him to the mast of his ship with ropes before plugging their own ears with wax.

As the temporarily deaf sailors sailed by, the Sirens sang their enchanting song, which was far more alluring than Ulysses could've imagined. Everything in him wanted to run toward the sound, but the ropes held him down and, in a way, saved him.

The Christian religion saves you too. James, in a chapter that mentions religion multiple times, writes, **"Humbly accept the word planted in you, which can save you"** (James 1:21). God's Word gets the last word over your heart, but that same word ties you to the comfort of the gospel when you feel unworthy, unlovable, and too sinful.

Don't run from religion. Bind yourself to God's Word and God's Word-bound people. That will keep you safe when temptation sings your name.

Partly religious?
Mike Novotny

Be careful with religion. Very, very, very careful with religion. Because people who are partly religious but not religious enough are a great danger to the name of Jesus.

You may recall that a religion is something that binds you to certain beliefs and behaviors. The problem, however, is when a person binds themselves to some but not all of what God has written in his Word. Picture a dad who goes to church and prays but then comes home and dominates his family with his rage. Or a pastor who compassionately counsels a hurting young woman but then crosses a line into inappropriate behavior. The problem in both of those examples is not that the father and the pastor are religious but that they aren't religious enough, not bound to the commands to be patient and pure.

James mentions this: **"Those who consider themselves religious and yet do not keep a tight rein on their tongues deceive themselves, and their religion is worthless"** (James 1:26). God has zero interest in a pick-and-choose version of Christianity. He wants his Word to get the last word over every area of our lives.

Is there any part of God's Book that your life is not bound to? Anything that God has said clearly that you've clearly skipped? Consider these questions carefully at the foot of the cross, where you can find forgiveness for every failure. Because your Father wants you to be *really* religious.

Treasured children of God
Mike Novotny

I love that Christianity is a relational religion. Yes, despite what some people say, the Christian faith is a religion, something that binds you to beliefs and behaviors outside of you. But please don't assume that makes it stiff, rigid, or boring. Because according to the very religious men who wrote the Bible, Christianity is a relational religion.

Listen to John, likely over 90 years old, gush about his religion: **"See what great love the Father has lavished on us, that we should be called children of God! And that is what we are!"** (1 John 3:1). As a father, there are few things I have ever loved in life more than my daughters. My affection for them could fill up oceans, which is why I lavish them with words and actions to prove my love.

The way God feels about you is even better than that. He doesn't just have love for you. John says that he has "great love." And he doesn't just give that great love to you. John says he "lavished" that love on you. Notice the double exclamation points in that single Bible verse. John can't believe that he, despite his sins, is a child of God!

And that is what you are too! Our religion binds us to a nearly unbelievable claim, convincing us of something we would never, ever assume to be true: We are holy, beloved, adored, cherished, treasured children of God.

Man, I love being religious!

God rejoices over you
Mike Novotny

My friend Paul got married last weekend. Paul is the goalkeeper on my soccer team, a tough dude you wouldn't want to mess with (especially in front of his net!). But last weekend as his soon-to-be wife, Allie, walked down their backyard aisle, I had my eyes on Paul. Like so many grooms before him, myself included, Paul was visibly emotional as he looked at his wife.

I love that moment, because Christianity compares it to our relationship with God. Isaiah writes, **"As a bridegroom [a.k.a. groom] rejoices over his bride, so will your God rejoice over you"** (Isaiah 62:5). Since Jesus dressed us in his perfection, we look more stunning to God than a bride does to her husband on their wedding day. I beg you not to miss the emotion in those verbs— God *rejoices* over you! He smiles, laughs, lights up with love visible in his eyes.

We live in a world that judges us by our works, which is why we rarely see that look in other people's eyes. We fall, fail, and fail to stand out from the crowd, causing others to look in the other direction. But the Christian religion binds us to the stunning belief that God is rejoicing over us with that wedding day look.

Can you even believe it?! It seems too good to be true, but the beautiful thing about being religious is that we are bound not to our thoughts and feelings but to the unchanging promises that God has made to us in Jesus. Rejoice today, my friend, because our God is rejoicing over you!

More than an hour on Sunday
Mike Novotny

Recently, my wife and I celebrated 20 years of marriage. To quote the classic film *Dumb and Dumber*, "I like her a lot." Our marriage isn't perfect, but it's really good. If you asked me why, I would tell you that a huge cause of our affection is how religious we are about date night. Every Friday from January through December, Kim and I try to go on a date. Since we both work, have two active kids, and have nearby parents whom we love, our schedules are busy, sometimes leaving us with less time together than we would prefer. But every Friday night gives us a weekly chance to reconnect and re-express our love for each other.

Sound familiar? Christianity commands us to **"not** [give] **up meeting together, as some are in the habit of doing,"** but rather to regularly gather week after week with our fellow believers (Hebrews 10:25). Why? There are many reasons, but perhaps the simplest is so you and God can reconnect at least once a week. Christianity is much more than an hour on Sunday, of course, but like my date night, church gives you a chance to affirm your love for God and for God to express his love for you.

Be religious about your Christian religion, meeting together from January through December. That is one of God's best ways to remind you of the good news that isn't too good to be true.

A work in progress
Nathan Nass

You are a work in progress. Do you realize that? Let me clarify. You are God's work in progress. Here's what Isaiah learned to say to God: **"You, Lord, are our Father. We are the clay, you are the potter; we are all the work of your hand"** (Isaiah 64:8). We are all God's work in progress.

A lot of our anxiety in life comes from a misunderstanding. We think that God is done with us. We think that we're looking at the finished product. We get it in our heads that once we grow up and become adults, God's work in us is over, right?

No! You're God's work in progress. You're not the finished product yet, and you won't be until you get to heaven. What you see in your life today is just one chapter on the way to eternity.

God is still forming you, like a potter forms clay. Whatever trial you're dealing with today isn't the end of the story. God's refining you and leading you to trust in him. Whatever heartache you're experiencing today isn't going to last forever. God's cutting something away to one day reveal something even better. If it seems like there's got to be something more than what you see, there is!

You're a work in progress, God's work in progress. So say with faith, "You, Lord, are our Father. We are the clay, you are the potter; we are all the work of your hand."

Fulfillment, Simeon style
Paul Mattek

Art invites you to consider something familiar with new eyes. *Song of Simeon*, a picture drawn by artist Jason Jaspersen, opened mine. Tucked into the events surrounding Jesus' birth in Luke 2, an elderly man named Simeon appears and sings prophecies over the baby Jesus and his parents. Starkly rendered in white on a black canvas, Simeon's look pierces you with an array of emotions. Sure, there is joy that he is seeing the fulfillment of God's promises. But there is also pain, longing, realization, and wonder. I've read the story countless times without grasping the moment's enormity, which is displayed in Jaspersen's artwork.

God revealed to Simeon that he wouldn't die until he met Jesus. But those revelations also showed the pain and injustice the devil and his allies would inflict along the way. There would be hard questions and intense pain for Mary and Joseph, pain for hearts hiding deep secrets and doubts, and death for the child himself.

But with all that on his heart, Simeon still sang! Glory! Salvation! He knew that anything less than God's perfect fulfillment of these prophecies would leave us with the ultimate lack of fulfillment—death and eternity without God's love. So Simeon held his baby Messiah, sang praises and blessings, and was filled.

And you? Read the story in Luke 2 and believe that what Simeon beheld has been accomplished. See the wondrous, complex, eternal, and beautiful fulfillment of God's love in Jesus—ready to be held by you too.

That's what love does
Linda Buxa

My daughter and I were talking about ways that I serve people, and she admitted that she wasn't sure she could do that. I admitted that sometimes I prefer to stay home in stretchy pants, but I give up some of my time because "that's what love does."

I thought about that concept as I started looking at ways that other Christians serve.

With an attitude of "that's what love does," they take their dad to multiple doctor's appointments, they care for their medically needy child, and they have hard conversations about things that have eternal implications. Others spend money on charities that serve their communities, some spend time building relationships and loving their neighbors, and some spend time praying continually for family members who don't believe in Jesus.

By serving others, they live out the encouragement to **"follow God's example, therefore, as dearly loved children and walk in the way of love, just as Christ loved us and gave himself up for us as a fragrant offering and sacrifice to God"** (Ephesians 5:1,2).

Mind if we consider two takeaways?

One, take time to consider how you walk in the way of love. What ways do you serve that show others what love does? How can you use your time and gifts to bless others?

Two, as you see others living their lives as fragrant offerings and sacrifices to God, encourage them. Service and sacrifice aren't always easy, and God's dearly loved children could use some of your support as they walk in the way of love.

Ears to hear
Jan Gompper

Political leanings aside, I have a vivid memory of a 2008 presidential debate between John McCain and Barack Obama. What I remember most is how courteous Obama was whenever McCain was speaking. Not only did Obama not interrupt McCain; he also turned and gave McCain his full attention before offering any rebuttal.

We've moved a long way from this example. Perhaps, like me, you don't even like watching political debates anymore because of all the interrupting candidates do, so much so that you can't understand what anyone is saying.

It seems that listening, especially to those whose philosophies differ from our own, has become a lost courtesy—and not just in political arenas. Even in Christian circles, shouts of condemnation can sometimes drown out the cries for help.

All you need to do is read Scripture to find that this isn't a new phenomenon. Solomon warned, **"To answer before listening—that is folly and shame"** (Proverbs 18:13). And James the half brother of Jesus advised, **"Everyone should be quick to listen, slow to speak and slow to become angry"** (James 1:19). It seems even in biblical times, people loved the sound of their own voices.

Will we ever get back to days of more civil discourse? I pray we do. I believe that wise leaders and influencers can help change the tone of rhetoric in our nation. And those of us who profess Christ can especially lead the way as courteous listeners.

"Whoever has ears, let them hear" (Matthew 11:15).

Do for others
Katrina Harrmann

My dad used to play Yahtzee with me when I was a kid. There was something about that game that I just loved . . . rolling the five dice and hoping all the numbers turned up the same. I asked him to play with me, and he always did. He never rolled his eyes and sighed and never said he was too busy. He just put down whatever he was doing and sat at the old dining room table with me and played.

As an adult, I found out, to my surprise, that Yahtzee isn't my dad's favorite game. Not even close! Yet he played that silly game with me time after time, because he knew it brought me joy.

It's rare these days to find people doing things for others, isn't it? It doesn't happen a lot. People tend to do things for themselves—whatever makes them happy or requires the least effort.

This simple game of Yahtzee still reminds me that sometimes it's a great thing to set aside your own preferences and "do" for others. Do you want to spend an evening on the couch, but someone needs a home-cooked meal? Do you want to watch Netflix in peace, but your elderly neighbor is struggling to carry in their groceries or mow their lawn?

Following our heavenly Father's example and "doing" for others can be life-changing for those on the receiving and the giving end.

"Finally, all of you, be like-minded, be sympathetic, love one another, be compassionate and humble" (1 Peter 3:8).

Chasing faithfulness
Matt Ewart

If God's goal is for you to be with him forever in heaven, does it really matter how you live your life here on earth? Jesus taught that it does matter, but not for the reasons you might think. Here's an excerpt from one of his parables that talks about the importance of your life:

"The man who had received five bags of gold brought the other five. 'Master,' he said, 'you entrusted me with five bags of gold. See, I have gained five more.' His master replied, 'Well done, good and faithful servant!'" (Matthew 25:20,21).

The idea contained in this parable is not that you should spend your life chasing success. The king didn't say, "Well done, good and successful servant!"

He commended the servant's faithfulness, not his success. The servant did the best he could with what he was given, and that delighted the king.

It is so easy to get caught up in success, thinking every achievement proves you're a somebody.

It's also easy to get caught up in failure, thinking every mistake proves that you're a nobody.

For a moment, consider what it means that God's opinion of you has nothing to do with your successes or failures. He has already judged you in Christ. Your successes and failures went into his tomb, and something even better walked out three days later. You have life and hope.

So don't chase success. Don't let failure ruin you. Seek to be faithful with what God has entrusted to you.

I beg your pardon
Liz Schroeder

"Then Manoah prayed to the LORD: 'Pardon your servant, Lord. I beg you to let the man of God you sent to us come again to teach us how to bring up the boy who is to be born'" (Judges 13:8).

A little context: Manoah and his wife were unable to have kids. An angel of the Lord appeared to his wife and told her she would have a son (Samson). The angel also told her that Samson was supposed to follow a strict order of living where he would not drink any wine or eat anything unclean, among other restrictions. When Manoah's wife told him all that had happened, he wanted to get some clarification, so he prayed.

This all took place about three thousand years ago, but the time was not so different from now: **"In those days Israel had no king; everyone did as they saw fit"** (Judges 21:25).

In these days, everyone does as they see fit. If you are on the exciting roller coaster of parenting, Manoah's prayer is more than appropriate: "Lord, please teach me how to bring up this child!" Raising kids takes more wisdom, patience, and stamina than any human possesses. On top of that, if you are raising a child to follow Christ, you will face even more challenges. In these days, it seems like it is celebrated to let a kid be anything he or she wants to be—except a follower of Christ.

Parenting will bring you to your knees, so you might as well start there.

Jesus gets us
Clark Schultz

Batman has Robin. Shaggy has Scooby. Jordan had Pippen. A friend is one who gets you and your quirks, gets your odd sense of humor, and can relate to what you are going through. A good friend is the person who can sympathize and empathize with you.

The Dynamic Duo gets each other because they can relate to fighting crime. The Mystery Machine crew is always in search of a mystery while some are in search of the kitchen. And debate who's the GOAT in hoops if you want, but when the chips were down, one Bull picked the other up. Who does that for you?

Your heart was broken by an affair. Who is your hero to cry with? You're struggling with addiction. Who is the one who drives you to rehab? You just lowered a casket into the ground. Who is the friend who picks you up when all seems lost?

Having a true friend is wonderful, but remember that Jesus is your best Friend. He too felt pain; the nails of the cross pierced his flesh. Jesus was tempted by Satan like we are every day. Jesus felt the hurt of friends leaving him and ultimately the sting of death. He not only sympathizes with us, but his heart goes out to us because he truly gets us. He's not just a friend who says, "Man, this stinks. I wish I could know what you're going through." No, he's the only one who can, does, and delivers when he says, **"I will give you rest"** (Matthew 11:28).

Don't touch it
Clark Schultz

While on a six-hour car trip, this conversation actually took place:

Five-year old: "Mom, my lip hurts when I touch it."

Mom: "Well, then don't touch your lip."

Five-year-old: "Okay."

While it made a few miles of Chicago traffic humorous, it also made me think of a time that wasn't as lighthearted.

In the Garden of Eden, Eve was talking to the serpent. Bad idea.

Satan: **"Did God really say, 'You must not eat from any tree in the garden'?"**

Eve: **"God did say, 'You must not eat fruit from the tree that is in the middle of the garden, and you must not touch it'"** (Genesis 3:1,3).

Eve's answer to Satan is similar to the car-ride scenario: "Don't touch it." Her answer seems harmless and makes sense. But God hadn't said that. He had commanded Adam and Eve simply not to eat from the tree.

Was Eve trying to help God out or was it to help herself out of a temptation? Like Eve, we may feel we are helping God out by blurring the lines of right and wrong. We often change the pages of Scripture to fit our own agendas or lifestyles. Adding to or subtracting from God's Word never ends well. What a blessing that Jesus came in human flesh to journey through life for you and me. What was undone by a tree in the garden was recovered by Jesus on a tree in the shape a cross.

Satan, you've lost!
Ann Jahns

What's your biggest fear? Mine is spiders. Despite what a wise kindergartner once told me—that spiders are "very useful animals"—I'm not having it. I've heard too many death-by-spider stories. Every morning as I peel back the shower curtain, I also keep my eyes peeled for any furry, furtive movement.

Here's a possible fear you might have—the devil. Yes?

Too many people don't believe in the devil. One of the biggest mistakes we can make is underestimating his power and his unrelenting desire to destroy our faith. That's exactly what he wants us to do. Jesus calls the devil **"a murderer from the beginning, not holding to the truth, for there is no truth in him. . . . He is a liar and the father of lies"** (John 8:44).

The devil knows how to exploit all our human frailties, leveraging everything from the tiniest lies he plants in our minds to full-blown, life-shattering temptations to try to separate us from God.

But 1 John 3:8 tells us plainly why Jesus came to earth: **"The reason the Son of God appeared was to destroy the devil's work."** And destroy it he did in glorious, decisive fashion on Easter as he descended into hell to announce to Satan: "You've lost. They are mine! You will never take them away from me."

Should we be wary of the devil? Yes. But thanks to Jesus, we don't fear him.

Like fighting a toddler
Matt Ewart

Picture a toddler—a little boy just beyond the baby stage who is toddling around with chubby cheeks that jiggle with every step.

Now that I've gotten you to smile, imagine that this toddler is very angry at you with tantrum-level anger. He starts hitting you with his chubby little fists, pattering against your leg over and over.

Here's a silly question: How many times would he have to hit you for you to defend yourself and fight back?

Now that the smile has left your face, I'm hoping that your answer is the same as mine. You would never have to fight back. He's a toddler. If anything, you might restrain him so he doesn't hurt himself by trying to hurt you.

Chances are small (but not zero) that you'll be attacked by a toddler today. Chances are much higher that someone closer to your age will hurt you in some way. They might say something offensive. They might take something that's yours. They might humiliate you. Maybe it has already happened.

Because of what Jesus gave you, the threat level in these situations is similar to that of a toddler who's swinging his little fists at you. He can't hurt you. Nobody can devalue your self-worth that is tied to Christ. Nobody can dim Christ's light that shines through you. And nobody can rob the home that's awaiting you in heaven.

"Who shall separate us from the love of Christ?" (Romans 8:35).

Nobody. Especially not a toddler.

Direction, action, Person
Mike Novotny

Before words like *sanctification* or *discipleship* described the Christian life, "walking with God" was the Bible's preferred metaphor. **"Enoch walked faithfully with God"** (Genesis 5:22). **"Noah . . . walked faithfully with God"** (Genesis 6:9). **"The Lord appeared to [Abraham] and said, 'I am God Almighty; walk before me faithfully'"** (Genesis 17:1). **"And what does the Lord require of you? To act justly and to love mercy and to walk humbly with your God"** (Micah 6:8). When Jesus, who was God walking on our earth, wanted people to become believers, he most commonly invited, "Follow me," which is another way of saying, "Walk with God."

Why would walking be the number-one way to describe our spiritual lives? I can think of three reasons, which I'm excited to explain to you in the devotions to come. For now, here's a quick summary to get your gears turning: To walk with *God*, you have to be moving in God's direction. To *walk* with God, you have to be taking steps or personal action. To walk *with* God, you are blessed to be accompanied by a certain Person.

Read those last three sentences again. They matter more than almost anything else in your life. Direction, action, Person. That's what it means to walk with God.

Walking with *God*
Mike Novotny

This might seem insultingly obvious, but "walking with God" implies walking with *God*. It means choosing the path that God is on, joining him on the narrow and rarely traveled road of righteousness. In a world that runs after short-term pleasure, Jesus urges us to **"seek first"** the things that last forever by walking with God (Matthew 6:33). I won't lie. It's not the easiest direction to choose. But I can promise you that this direction leads to a glorious destination.

One summer my family hiked the Hidden Lake Trail at Glacier National Park. It wasn't an easy path, which climbed a few hundred feet over a couple of miles and was still snow-covered in certain spots despite being late June. But when we got to the end of the trail, none of us regretted the path we had chosen. Beautiful Bearhat Mountain towered above Hidden Lake with its deep glacial blue water. We were wowed and tried to capture God's glory with our man-made devices.

I imagine your Christian life, like mine, has not been easy all the time. Trusting God when you have cancer. Denying a desire within you. Loving someone who is nearly impossible to love. But please remember that the Christian direction leads to the best destination, a heaven that will make Hidden Lake look lame, a place that St. Paul called **"surpassingly great"** (2 Corinthians 12:7).

Keep walking with *God*. You are one day and one step closer to your glorious destination!

Take a step!
Mike Novotny

"Walking with God" implies *walking* with God. Seems obvious, right? It means moving when God is moving, taking action when God calls you to obedience. This is why Paul urges, **"Let us keep in step with the Spirit"** (Galatians 5:25).

I picture the Holy Spirit like my wife. Kim is a fast-walking woman who was raised by her mother, Candi, an equally fast-walking woman. You can only imagine what it is like to be my kids on a family vacation with their long-legged, marathon-runner dad and their on-the-move mom! We push them pretty hard so they can see more of the world than those who are sitting around.

God's Spirit pushes the pace too, and he wants you to keep in step. When temptation comes, he's moving fast into obedience, holiness, and trust. Can you picture him? When you're annoyed with someone, he immediately steps toward a deep breath, toward patience, toward not snapping in anger. When you are thinking about a past sin, he leaps toward grace, toward the cross, toward remembering the God who remembers your sins no more. He loves you too much to let you sit down in sin and shame. That's why he wants you to keep in step.

The next time you are tempted, picture the Spirit stepping ahead, looking back in love, and encouraging you to keep up. Then take a step! Because there's nothing better than *walking* with God.

With you every step of the way
Mike Novotny

This might seem as insultingly obvious as my last two devotions, but "walking with God" implies walking *with* God. It means that your entire life is not a lonely journey *to* God but instead is a lengthy journey *with* God. God is with you every step of the way to encourage you, listen to you, and carry you when necessary.

King David loved that aspect of his walk. In his most famous song, he wrote, **"Even though I walk through the darkest valley, I will fear no evil, for you are with me"** (Psalm 23:4). The road of life can take you through some pretty dark valleys, but you don't have to be afraid, because you are walking *with* God.

Are you grieving today? rubbing aching joints? praying for your headache to go away? stressed by family drama? frustrated by your continual struggle with sin or the lack of struggle by a loved one living in sin? Do you see no solution to the brokenness of our culture or of your own family tree? If so, don't be afraid. Your faith is not a walk to God. It's a walk *with God*. And your Father won't let you take a single step without being right by your side.

"Those who hope in the Lord will renew their strength. They will soar on wings like eagles; they will run and not grow weary, they will walk and not be faint" (Isaiah 40:31).

Carrying you home
Mike Novotny

I once planned a family hike to a beautiful waterfall in Yellowstone National Park, but before we got to the water, our youngest daughter hit a wall. We were miles from our destination when she ran out of gas, so I crouched down and said, "If you don't walk faster, a grizzly will get you."

Just kidding. I crouched down and invited, "Hop on." As I walked toward our destination with my beloved on my back, I could feel her joy increase. She was overwhelmed by a distance she didn't think she could walk, so the ride was a delightful surprise. When I finally set her down 1,554 steps later (we counted ☺), she was a different kid.

Jesus does something similar but so much better. He knows that heaven is equally beautiful and unreachable for our little human legs, which is why he carries us. Not for 1,554 steps or for a few miles but from start to finish. Peter wrote, **"Christ also suffered once for sins, the righteous for the unrighteous, to bring you to God"** (1 Peter 3:18).

There is such joy in those words! How do you get to God? By walking fast enough? By grinding out enough spiritual steps of obedience? No. Just Jesus. Jesus suffered to bring you to God. The cross carries you all the way to the Father's presence. Your "walk with God" is not an overwhelming, keep-up-or-a-grizzly-hell-awaits-you walk. No, it's a joyful journey with the God who will carry you home.

What a walk!

OCTOBER

"Salvation is found in no one else, for there is no other name under heaven given to mankind by which we must be saved."

Acts 4:12

Jesus is like my mother-in-law
Mike Novotny

Over the past 25 years, I have come to know my mother-in-law as a devout, hardworking, reliable, and generous child of God. Also (she gave me permission to tell you this), I have learned that she is a walking spoiler alert! If she sees a great movie before you do, watch out! She has a hard time keeping the good news to herself.

Jesus is a lot like that. Instead of making us live with the suspense and the fear (Will I be good enough to go to heaven? Will modern culture sweep away true Christian faith?), Jesus tells us how the story of human history ends.

Will Christianity die? **"I will build my church, and the gates of Hades will not overcome it"** (Matthew 16:18).

Will evil win? **"And the devil, who deceived them, was thrown into the lake of burning sulfur, where the beast and the false prophet had been thrown"** (Revelation 20:10).

Will you be good enough to be with God? **"[God] has reconciled you by Christ's physical body through death to present you holy in his sight, without blemish and free from accusation"** (Colossians 1:22).

There is hard work to do, a good fight to be fought, and a faithful race to be run, but take a deep breath today and let Jesus spoil the ending of our story—God and his people will win!

5 things I love about Jesus

Mike Novotny

In Revelation 19, we get a glorious glimpse of Jesus and of five things I love most about him. John reports: **"I saw heaven standing open and there before me was a white horse, whose rider is called Faithful and True. . . . His eyes are like blazing fire, and on his head are many crowns. . . . He is dressed in a robe dipped in blood. . . . He treads the winepress of the fury of the wrath of God Almighty. On his robe and on his thigh he has this name written:** KING OF KINGS AND LORD OF LORDS" (verses 11-16).

First, he is faithful/true. What Jesus says, he does. If he said he loves and forgives you, he loves and forgives you. Second, he is all-knowing ("his eyes are like blazing fire"). All the evidence is before his eyes, which means he judges with justice. Third, he is authoritative. The embroidery on his robe and the ink on his thigh reads, "KING OF KINGS AND LORD OF LORDS," which means no one can depose, out rule, or outvote him. Fourth, Jesus is holy, carrying out God's wrath against sin, smashing sinners like crushed grapes in a winepress (so don't you dare stand before Jesus holding on to sin!). Finally, Jesus is loving. His robe is dipped in the blood he shed on the cross to take away our sins so we wouldn't be sinners in the hands of an angry God but children in the arms of a forgiving Father.

What a Jesus! What a Savior!

Knocked out by Jesus
Mike Novotny

Apparently, the end of the world will be a lot like the day Mike Tyson fought Marvis Frazier. In 1986 a young Mike Tyson fought the son of boxing legend Joe Frazier, and ABC's *Wide World of Sports* was eager to see if Marvis could knock out Iron Mike. But then the bell rang . . . and Marvis didn't win. In fact, I'm not sure he even threw a real punch. Tyson's meaty uppercut smashed into Frazier's face and knocked him unconscious. Referee Joe Cortez started to count to ten but decided it was over at five. The official bout lasted 30 seconds, the fastest knockout of Mike Tyson's career.

That's what will happen with Jesus. You might think the end of the world, when every evil force gathers to fight against Jesus, will be a nail-biting event, but you'd be wrong. Revelation 19 doesn't give us a blow-by-blow recap of that battle but instead simply says: **"But the beast was captured, and with it the false prophet who had performed the signs on its behalf. . . . The two of them were thrown alive into the fiery lake of burning sulfur. The rest were killed with the sword coming out of the mouth of the rider on the horse"** (verses 20,21). Oh. That's it? Our fiercest enemies will be KO'd by Jesus just like that.

The devil may be a powerful foe, stronger than you, but he is not stronger than Jesus. Cling to Christ, and your biggest spiritual enemies will be knocked out sooner than you think.

Our eager Savior
Mike Novotny

I recently realized that the Bible is the biggest spoiler of any book ever. Instead of making us live the tension of good vs. evil, our Father spoiled the ending of our story on the very first page where our problems began. You might be familiar with the fall into sin, when Adam and Eve doubted God and ate the forbidden fruit (Genesis 3:1-7). But did you notice how long it took God to tell us how our battle vs. evil would end? God didn't wait 2,000 pages until the book of Revelation or 1,500 pages until the birth of Jesus. In fact, he didn't even wait a day!

On the same page where sin entered the world, God promised a Savior. Just verses after the fall, God looked Satan in the eye and said, **"He will crush your head"** (Genesis 3:15). The One Adam and Eve knew as "he" and the One the Old Testament saints called the Messiah is the One we know as Jesus. He came into the world, resisted evil, and crushed the devil by dying on a cross.

The world is so messed up (the headlines, the heartaches), and we are so messed up (our struggles, our sins), but we know how the story ends. We don't have to hold our breath. We don't have to worry where things are going. We know who sits on the glorious throne and who is crushed and thrown into a lake of fire. Don't worry for a single second. In the end, Jesus (and his people) win!

Am I in the wrong place?
Linda Buxa

Mark Gubin is a photographer whose home and studio are directly on the flight path to runway 19 at Milwaukee's Mitchell Airport. In 1978 he was bored and decided to have some fun. He took white paint and painted WELCOME TO CLEVELAND in block letters on his roof. Since then, passengers see the welcome sign, ring the call button, and ask the flight attendant if they are landing in the right place.

This story amuses me, but I'm not amused when I end up where I don't want to go in real life. I like when life is smooth, and I can get frustrated and disheartened when detours change my plans. Then I remember what Proverbs 16:9 says: **"In their hearts humans plan their course, but the Lord establishes their steps."**

I have plans, goals, and wishes, but God knows what I need. Maybe he's protecting me from a decision that won't be healthy for me. Maybe he's allowing me to struggle so I can bless someone with compassion in the future. Maybe he's just telling me to wait because *later* will be better than *right now*.

Proverbs reminds me that my plans are often short-term and shortsighted. Ultimately, God's plan for me includes bringing him glory now and living with him forever eternally. So even while I wrestle with how my path might look now, I know he's far more invested in me seeing the WELCOME HOME painted on the roof of my place when the angels take me to be with him forever.

Raise your right hand
Dave Scharf

"Raise your right hand. Do you swear to the tell the truth, the whole truth, and nothing but the truth?" Why do we raise our right hands when testifying in court? Recently, a tour guide in Boston told me that it dates from the 17th century when there was no standardized method of keeping records. If someone were convicted, the offense was branded on their right hand: "T" for theft, "M" for murder, and so on. It was a way to check the character of the witness who was testifying.

Imagine standing before God in his courtroom. What brands would your hand be given, including for crimes of thought that are just as damning? What letters would reveal your true character? The Bible says, "[Jesus] **forgave us all our sins, having canceled the charge of our legal indebtedness, which stood against us and condemned us; he has taken it away, nailing it to the cross**" (Colossians 2:13,14). That charge that stood against you is the document that records your personal responsibilities for a debt. Do you hear what the Bible says? That piece of paper with your signature on it is nailed to the cross. Instead of "D" being branded on your hand for "debtor," Jesus took the nails in his hands on the cross. Now your hand is "brandless" because of Jesus. He has forgiven all your sins! Raise your right hand and praise him today!

Stand guard
Katrina Harrmann

Once, a huge Cooper's hawk swooped low over my backyard. I have a very tiny backyard, but I also have a tiny chihuahua . . . a snack-size animal for a large, hungry hawk.

I quickly scooped up my dog when I saw that hawk.

And for several weeks afterward, I made sure to accompany our small dog whenever he went out, standing guard over him and glaring angrily at the sky—waving my arms at any large bird that would dare to swoop close.

It's easy to be vigilant when we can SEE the danger physically, isn't it? It's easy to make an effort when the danger is sitting there, staring over the fence line with its sharp beak and razor claws.

But when it's not *physically* there, we quickly forget.

I think our reaction to Satan is often similar.

We can't necessarily see him prowling around our homes and lives *physically*. If we could, imagine how much more on guard we would be! And how much more dedicated to our faith walk!

I'm sure Satan probably prefers it this way. After all, he's so much more crafty and cunning to fight when we can't see him. Often, we completely forget he's there at all!

Instead, let us be vigilant. Let us stand guard constantly and live our lives in a way that does honor to our Father in heaven!

"Be alert and of sober mind. Your enemy the devil prowls around like a roaring lion looking for someone to devour" (1 Peter 5:8).

144,000 in heaven?

Mike Novotny

"Then I looked, and there before me was the Lamb, standing on Mount Zion, and with him 144,000 who had his name and his Father's name written on their foreheads" (Revelation 14:1). What does it mean that John saw 144,000 people with Jesus (the Lamb) in heaven? Is there a capacity limit for heaven? (If so, I'm not sure if I want to share my faith—they might take my spot from me!)

No, like much of Revelation, this is a symbolic number that offers Christians great hope. In Revelation, the number 12 often refers to God's people (there were 12 tribes in Old Testament Israel and 12 apostles in Jesus' New Testament church). And the numbers 10 and 1,000 often represent the complete, full, total of something. Therefore, 144,000 (12 x 12 x 1,000) means the entire church, all true children of God, what some call the holy Christian church.

That makes this verse really good news. Despite the "beasts" we battle here on earth (read Revelation 13), God will bless and keep every last one of his chosen people. There aren't 143,000 in heaven, as if the devil snatched a few from the mighty hand of Jesus. No, all God's people will be saved and kept safe from the evil one. Despite the pushback, the persecution, and the temptation, God will get his faithful followers through it all.

That includes you, child of God. The Lord who began a good work in you will carry it on to completion until the day when you stand with the Lamb in heaven!

No bait and switch here!
Clark Schultz

A recent commercial makes me giggle out loud, and not for the reason you might think. Here's how it goes: A couple is about to take a scenic photo using the timer feature on their phone. There is a beautiful backdrop of mountains. The couple gets in close and begins their pose, but right before the photo is taken, an eagle swoops in and snatches the camera. What ensues is a car chase through rugged terrain, rivers, hills, and rocks to regain control of the camera. If you are caught up in the scene, you may fail to notice the fine print on the bottom that reads, "Professional driver—do not attempt this stunt on your own." It's not even the couple doing the driving. Talk about a bait and switch!

The world is full of bait and switches, but I'm so thankful God's Word isn't. **"But these are written that you may believe that Jesus is the Messiah, the Son of God, and that by believing you may have life in his name"** (John 20:31). Long ago Adam and Eve, the first couple, lost more than a camera in the Garden of Eden. They lost perfection. Enter Jesus, who traveled the rugged terrain of Earth, taking on human form, to win salvation for us.

There's no fine print of work-righteousness to climb the hill of salvation. The final photo to be taken is us enjoying the beautiful backdrop of heaven with our Savior for eternity. Now that's a commercial I can't wait to see.

Sucker punched
Christine Wentzel

Receiving devasting, life-changing news about your health or someone you love can feel like a sucker punch. But you don't need to be beaten to death by it. Reach out to those in your Christian community. They will help you remember what lies ahead for those who believe in Jesus. Allow your Christian family into your pain so they can comfort you in Jesus and lift you up in prayer. Yes, at times it might be awkward; reaching out for help isn't always easy. I must confess my first impulse is to go it alone. But I know that only makes me an easy target for the devil. Being honest with God's people about that tendency to hide from the world is also a good step forward to stay in the protection of God's pasture—a bulwark from the devil, who hates honesty and really hates God's presence.

If you've been hit by a low blow recently, there are those who want to pray for you, eager to talk to the heavenly Father about your pain and remind you of his words to you:

"Do not fear, for I am with you. Do not be overwhelmed, for I am your God. I will strengthen you. Yes, I will help you. I will uphold you with my righteous right hand" (Isaiah 41:10 EHV).

Those punches can't steal your hope and peace in Jesus. You've got God and Christian friends on your side.

Be our guest
Liz Schroeder

As we go into tech week for our daughter's school production of Disney's *Beauty and the Beast*, the song "Be Our Guest" is in heavy rotation. In the bridge, Lumiere the candelabra croons in a thick French accent about how unnerving it is for a servant who isn't doing the job of serving other people.

Lumiere is right on the money! It's discomforting not to be doing something you were designed to do. It's unsettling to be a teacher who's not teaching, a pastor who's not shepherding, an author who's not writing, or an engineer who's not boring the other guests at a dinner party. (Thankfully, my engineer husband has a sense of humor. ☺)

The body of Christ is counting on you to use your gifts for the common good. **"The eye cannot say to the hand, 'I don't need you!' And the head cannot say to the feet, 'I don't need you!' On the contrary, those parts of the body that seem to be weaker are indispensable. Now you are the body of Christ, and each one of you is a part of it"** (1 Corinthians 12:21,22,27).

You are an invaluable part of the body of Christ, so be our guest to sing, invent, compute, nurse, fix, create, and preach. Be our guest to develop your gifts through online courses, hands-on practice, and lots of trial and error. Be our guest to seek out a mentor who will use the gospel to encourage your gifts. We're all servants, so let's get serving!

Shine a light on the bad stuff
Matt Trotter

My friend and I have been talking about our temptations so we can hold each other accountable. Life can keep us down at times, and though we know what we ought to do, we don't always do it. Sometimes we know God's will and choose to sin, and sometimes we just wake up on the wrong side of the bed and can't get the mood right. Toward the back of the Bible are letters from Peter and John, people who knew Jesus. The letters can be tools to change the day, the moment, or the shame that may be upon us. Feeling down, I read about a mindset shift from the apostle John:

"God is light; in him there is no darkness at all. If we claim to have fellowship with him and yet walk in the darkness, we lie and do not live out the truth. But if we walk in the light, as he is in the light, we have fellowship with one another, and the blood of Jesus, his Son, purifies us from all sin" (1 John 1:5-7).

I like this. It reminds me not to wallow in the darkness of my mistakes and guilt. You too can remember God has given us a new life in the light of Jesus, and we can testify to his truth by shining a light on the darkness of sin and shame. Don't deny the power of Jesus by getting stuck in a negative outlook. Darkness is powerless against the light of Jesus.

I (heart) Holy Communion
Mike Novotny

When I was a kid, I wasn't too happy about Holy Communion. My mom, because she's awesome, took me to church every Sunday and, because she's really awesome, took me to McDonald's afterward. That meant after every *Amen*, I could eat processed sausage patties in Jesus' name. But a few Sundays each month, my church celebrated Communion, where people would shuffle up to the altar to chew and sip slowly and then shuffle back to their pews, and—maybe it was just my grade school concept of time—it took forever! Especially when church was full! Didn't these shuffling saints know I was *this close* to sausage?!

But I've changed my mind about Communion. Oh, it still takes time, especially when church is full, but I've come to love it. I love giving Communion to you. I love receiving Communion for me.

Here's why: **"The Lord Jesus, on the night he was betrayed, took bread, and when he had given thanks, he broke it and said, 'This is my body, which is for you; do this in remembrance of me.' In the same way, after supper he took the cup, saying, 'This cup is the new covenant in my blood; do this, whenever you drink it, in remembrance of me'"** (1 Corinthians 11:23-25). Meditate today on the phrases "my body," "for you," "new covenant," "remembrance of me."

If you do, I bet you will come to love Holy Communion as much as I do!

All the single ladies
Jason Nelson

A characteristic of my new community is the number of single ladies who bought homes here. Some are older, and some are young. Some are divorced, and some are widows. They come in different shapes, sizes, and colors. Some work from home, and some go to an office. One of them scares me. But the thing they all have in common is their fierce independence. They can take care of themselves. They are very cautious about letting some guy move in and jeopardize what they have worked hard to establish. I admire them all.

They are a subset in the rich pageant of our society. They present a challenge for the church in reaching out to them. Traditional church talk regarding what men can do and women can do will rub them the wrong way. I doubt that old-school ladies guilds would interest them. But emphasizing their freedom in Christ might. **"They suddenly recognize that God is a living, personal presence, not a piece of chiseled stone. And when God is personally present, a living Spirit, that old, constricting legislation is recognized as obsolete. We're free of it! All of us!"** (2 Corinthians 3:17 MSG).

All of us have been liberated by Jesus. We are independent agents of his love with his Spirit living in us. We are free to become our strongest selves, single or married, male or female. We are free to look out for ourselves and free to obligate ourselves to the welfare of others.

Your brain disagrees
Matt Ewart

It is quite difficult to trick your own brain, especially when it comes to what it thinks about who you are. For example:

You can't go to the gym one time and consider yourself a bodybuilder. Your brain knows better.

You can't write a few sentences and then decide you are an author. Your brain knows better.

You can't call yourself a mechanic because you watched a YouTube video on how to fix your car. Your brain knows better.

What about something much more important? Does your brain ever challenge the idea that you are a loved, forgiven child of God?

Your mind might be quick to point out all the things that are wrong with your life. If God loves you, why are there all these bad things?

Or your mind might be quick to remind you that your life doesn't reflect the identity of a child of God. Your thoughts, words, and actions suggest that you are somebody else. Somebody less holy.

And it's right. But what your mind tends to forget is that you are declared holy because of Jesus' life, not yours. Your mind should recall his perfect righteousness, not your own. So remind your mind that the foundation of your identity was established at Jesus' empty tomb. Then your mind will be in the right place.

"Set your minds on things above, not on earthly things. For you died, and your life is now hidden with Christ in God" (Colossians 3:2,3).

You are a mountain
Andrea Delwiche

Most of the time we picture God as *our* mountain, *our* rock of refuge. In Psalm 125, each one of us is an immovable mountain: **"Those who trust in the Lord,"** the psalmist says, **"are like Mount Zion, which cannot be shaken but endures forever"** (verse 1). Picture it: Family problems, health issues, doubts, and fears rain down, each one capable of causing an avalanche of anxiety and disruption of your peace. All this trouble, yet you see yourself standing firm.

When we have a relationship with the triune God, who is worthy of our trust, we will not be moved. How do we know our God is worthy of trust? The psalm again points the way for us. We can trust God because **"as the mountains surround Jerusalem, so the Lord surrounds his people both now and forevermore"** (verse 2). God is always working for our good.

While God's protection makes us like mighty mountains, our memory of God's protection can be like a crumbling sandcastle. We need to meditate on God's love and faithfulness continually. In Psalm 16, King David shares his habit of meditation: **"I keep my eyes always on the Lord. With him at my right hand, I will not be shaken"** (verse 8).

Spend time in prayer, and consider this picture of yourself as a mountain whose base is God and who is surrounded by a hedge of God's love. Where in the past has God encircled and protected you?

You are never alone. Never forgotten. You are always loved. Always embraced by God.

Why people in heaven are so happy
Mike Novotny

Have you ever gone to a funeral and heard that Uncle So-and-So is now playing golf in heaven? or fishing in heaven? or finally united with his golden retriever in heaven?

I don't know all the details of what eternity will be like, but I do know what the book of Revelation reveals about our forever future. John writes, **"And they sang a new song before the throne. . . . They follow the Lamb wherever he goes. . . . They are blameless"** (14:3-5). These few lines remind us of the big things happening right now in heaven.

First, everyone is exceedingly happy. They aren't pacing in boredom or pouting like heaven is a raw deal; they are singing before the throne of God, bursting with joy and gratitude.

Second, everyone is closely connected to Jesus. Wherever the Lamb goes, his people do too. Being in his presence is all they want, because nothing compares to seeing the face of God and delighting in his unconditional love.

Third, everyone is blameless. Every sin is gone. Every feeling of unworthiness is erased. Everything wrong we've ever done has been left behind, erased by the blood of the Lamb.

Apparently, all the blameless need for eternal blessing is to be with Jesus. The next time you're at a funeral and someone makes a comment about our hobbies in heaven, remember what makes heaven so heavenly—simply being with God.

Running faithfully
Ann Jahns

Are you a runner? My dad, in contrast, was a "jogger." Even calling him that was a bit of a stretch. He moved at such a shuffling pace up and down the road by our house that we jokingly bought him a sweatshirt with an orange triangle and the words "slow-moving vehicle" on the back. Sometimes he was gone so long that we had to look down the road to make sure he was returning.

When I look at the Christian life, it reminds me of my dad's long, sustained jogs—definitely more marathons than sprints. Our Christian race can't be sustained by short, infrequent bursts of spirituality; it requires everyday faithfulness. It involves the discipline of regularly filling ourselves up with God's Word and prayer and fellowship with other Christians.

The writer of the book of Hebrews encourages us, **"Let us run with perseverance the race marked out for us, fixing our eyes on Jesus, the pioneer and perfecter of faith"** (Hebrews 12:1,2). The author knew that our determination alone isn't enough to keep us sustained through this challenging marathon. Only focusing on our Savior will do that. It's only through faith in him, who ran the race perfectly in our place, that we can persevere.

Maybe we can all learn a lesson in perseverance from my dad. He didn't run fast, but he ran faithfully and without fail. With strength only found in God's Word, we too can keep putting one foot in front of the other faithfully with perseverance until the day we finish our race.

Two types of freedom
Andrea Delwiche

Are you desensitized to suffering? It's so easy to scroll through stories, shake our heads, and move on. Absorb these words from Psalm 129: **"They have greatly oppressed me from my youth . . . but they have not gained the victory over me. Plowmen have plowed my back and made their furrows long"** (verses 1-3). What a metaphor of suffering!

But read how the Lord brings relief: **"But the Lord is righteous; he has cut me free from the cords of the wicked"** (verse 4). How do we join with Jesus in cutting people free?

This task radiates through Scripture and in Jesus' own words and actions. We are called as followers of Christ to bring two types of freedom—the good news of freedom from sin and freedom from suffering. In both tasks, we are operating beyond our own capabilities. God alone gives salvation, and no one person can mitigate human suffering. We must work with God and others.

Look to Matthew 25:31-46 and see what Christ asks of us. He asks us to follow his example. There was no person whom he disdained to help. Imagine explaining to Jesus why we turned our backs on others because of fear, hatred, indifference, or busyness.

Listen to God's directive and promise: **"If you do away with the yoke of oppression, with the pointing finger and malicious talk, and if you spend yourselves in behalf of the hungry and satisfy the needs of the oppressed, then your light will rise in the darkness, and your night will become like the noonday"** (Isaiah 58:9,10).

Being recognized
Katrina Harrmann

Several years ago, we switched schools for our kids . . . my son was in fourth grade. Oh boy, was that stressful! I remember going to the fall open house ice cream social and not knowing a single other person there. I could practically see my kiddo wilt at the sight of all those kids who already knew each other, laughing and running and chasing each other on the playground.

And I couldn't "fix" it.

Just when I felt the bottom dropping out of my stomach, a little boy wandered up who had once played summer baseball with my son. And he asked my son if he wanted to throw a football.

The joy on my son's face at being recognized! All it took was one person to do that, and the rest of the day (and year!) were easy by comparison!

There's a big difference between being seen and being recognized.

Walk any major city street, and you can be seen by thousands but still be lonely.

But the minute someone spots you and their eyes light up because they KNOW you? WOW! What a powerful difference that makes!

Our heavenly Father sees AND recognizes us. He looks past the filth of our sin and looks us in the eye and says, "I KNOW you. You are MINE."

WOW! What a difference that makes—an *eternal* difference!

"Do not fear, for I have redeemed you; I have summoned you by name; you are mine" (Isaiah 43:1).

Truth over lies
Dave Scharf

Lying has consequences. There's a story about a father who wanted to teach his son the destructiveness of lying. He took a new board and pounded ten nails into it. He said, "This represents the lies you've told. I want you to fix each of the lies by pulling out the nails." The son did. Afterward, his father asked him, "Could you fix the lies?" The son said, "Well, the nails are gone, but the holes from the nails are still there." He got the point. Trust is destroyed. Feelings are hurt. Lives are changed. Relationships are strained or destroyed. Just think of how lies have affected your life.

What should you do? First John 1:9 says, **"If we confess our sins, he is faithful and just and will forgive us our sins and purify us from all unrighteousness."** The Bible does not say here, "He is faithful and loving," though it certainly could have. Instead, Jesus forgives you because he is "faithful and just." Jesus already paid for your sins on the cross. Therefore, it would be unjust to withhold forgiveness. That would be requiring a double payment since your sins have already been forgiven and paid for. So now what? Confess your sin if you are the one who has lied, knowing that Jesus has forgiven you. And if you are the one who has been lied to? Remember that Jesus paid for that sin. Do what he does with it. Forgive it.

A call for discernment
Jan Gompper

Have you heard someone say, "God spoke to me"—meaning they heard from God through direct revelation outside of reading the Bible?

Abraham, Moses, the prophets, Jesus, Saul/Paul, and John all heard from God directly. But in these instances, God chose to communicate directly in an audible way at crucial junctures in the history of salvation.

Since the salvation story was completed by Jesus and has been fully revealed to us in Scripture, there's no reason for God to give any "new revelations" today.

In a seminar entitled "A Call for Discernment," theologian Justin Peters cautions against claims of directly hearing from God. Peters warns that although the Christian church has won the battle over God's Word being inerrant, we are still fighting the idea that the Word is sufficient.

He elaborates that because many Christians today focus on their *feelings* about God more than on their *knowledge* of God, they desire some sort of experience—a vision or "still small voice." But God doesn't urge us to grow in our feelings but rather to **"be transformed by the *renewal of [our minds]*, that by testing [we] may *discern* what is the will of God, what is good and acceptable and perfect"** (Romans 12:2 ESV).

As Peters puts it: *"If you want to hear from God, read your Bible. If you want to audibly hear from God, read your Bible out loud."**

---

* Justin Peters, "How to Hear God's Voice Today?" youtube.com, May 10, 2015, Video, 44:17, https://www.youtube.com/watch?v=JItLcIFL2F8.

Spend time at the tomb
Linda Buxa

At the Union Oyster House in Boston, you'll find John F. Kennedy's favorite table. At a supper club near my house, there's a money drop that was used by Al Capone and a booth known to be the mobster's table. When I visited the Vatican in college, our tour guide talked about the place where St. Peter is buried.

What is it about being at a place where famous people have been? Why are we so fascinated? Maybe it's because these places remind us that famous people were truly people—real people with real lives who needed to eat with their real friends.

Maybe that's why so many Christians say they spend time at the cross. Not Jesus' literal cross, but going back to the place, the moment, where we hear our real Savior who lived a real life say, "It is finished." At the cross we see that God punished Jesus in our place—and now we have a holy standing before God.

Mind if I suggest that maybe we should spend just as much (if not more) time at the empty tomb? That's where we see that God defeated death. That's where Jesus said Mary's name and turned her grief to joy. That's where we hear that because he's alive, we have eternal life too. Death has no sting, no power, no victory. Jesus wins—and so do we!

"He is not here; he has risen, just as he said. Come and see the place where he lay" (Matthew 28:6).

A better mansion awaits
Clark Schultz

My wife told me to take a hike, a 21-mile hike around Lake Geneva in Wisconsin to be exact. Her family loves to hike. I get tired spelling the word *hike*. Alas, it was a time to be together kid free for a day.

Walking, we saw the Wriggly Estates, Stone Manor, and Edgewood Estates—all beautiful lakefront properties. Even some of the less famous homes took our breath away. Conversations ensued about what a place like that would cost and which was our favorite "mansion." Each conversation ended with something like, "If we win the lottery . . ." or "Someday, maybe . . ."

I'm not sure what mile marker of life you're on, but Jesus tells us that each of us has a mansion already waiting for us: **"In my Father's house are many mansions: if it were not so, I would have told you. I go to prepare a place for you. And if I go and prepare a place for you, I will come again, and receive you unto myself; that where I am, there ye may be also"** (John 14:2,3 KJV). This is his gift to us by grace.

As we hiked around Lake Geneva, we noticed some homes that were run down and not maintained. Our heavenly mansion is not made with earthly materials, so it is **"an inheritance that can never perish, spoil or fade"** (1 Peter 1:4). So fellow hikers, enjoy the walk, take in the sights, and when you see a mansion, know that an even better one awaits.

There's always something . . .
Mike Novotny

There's always something that did, does, or will go wrong, isn't there? Just when you finally fix this, then that happens. Maybe you're killing it at work, but your friends are frustrated that you aren't around like you used to be. So you spend more time with your friends, but then the boss is frustrated you don't do what you used to do. Maybe you're a mom who never feels caught up. Or a dad who can't figure out how to win at work and at home. Or maybe work and home are finally good, but then the doctor tells you something bad. The curse of this earth is that there's always something that can go wrong, did go wrong, or might go wrong tomorrow.

That's why we need a place where there's never something to worry about. Never something to feel bad about. Never something to fix. Never something we wish we had. Never something that went wrong or might go wrong. Never something that keeps us up at night or overwhelms us during the day.

Which is exactly what God promised us at the end of the Bible! **"I saw the Holy City, the new Jerusalem, coming down out of heaven from God, prepared as a bride beautifully dressed for her husband. . . . 'There will be no more death or mourning or crying or pain, for the old order of things has passed away'"** (Revelation 21:2,4).

There will always be something until the day when Jesus returns. Then there will only be something good.

Sons, not slaves
Daron Lindemann

Jesus told a parable about a father and two of his sons (Luke 15). Both sons believed it was by performance that they earned a place in their father's heart and household. **"Make me like one of your hired servants"** (verse 19) was the reinstatement plan of the younger son. He had run away with his father's money but now wanted to return!

"All these years I've been slaving for you and never disobeyed your orders" (verse 29) was the older son's self-justification for pouting. He became upset when his father actually welcomed his little brother home.

The father interrupted the younger son's explanation of his plan, ordered lavish gifts, and called him **"this son of mine"** (verse 24).

To the older son, lost without ever leaving home, the father encouraged, **"Son . . . you are always with me, and everything I have is yours"** (verse 31).

These young men thought they needed to be slaves and servants for their father to accept them. But he loved each of them as his "son." When they wondered, "Can we ever do enough?" he loved them with forgiveness and let them live in faith and freedom.

God's grace does not allow you to find your identity, purpose, or success as a hired servant or coerced slave for your heavenly Father. You still work, but as a privileged son!

Free. Lavished with gifts. Unconditionally loved. Always welcomed.

Who is trying to please you by their performance? Love them the same way.

Perfection made complete
Christine Wentzel

"Son though he was, he learned obedience from what he suffered and, once made perfect, he became the source of eternal salvation for all who obey him" (Hebrews 5:8,9).

Wasn't Jesus already perfect? This was my question during a church service one evening. I leaned in for an answer because I know that Jesus, the Son of God, is perfect, but a casual reading of these verses may seem contradictory.

Here's what I learned: On another evening over two thousand years ago, our Redeemer was in a garden called Gethsemane praying to his Father in heaven. He was in agony over his *final act of perfect obedience* to be the Lamb of God who takes away the sin of the world. Jesus alone lived a life without sin. He took on the sin of the world by giving up his life as a punishment for us.

In that garden just before Jesus' crucifixion, he offered another example of Christian living for his disciples both then and now. The lesson was about what obedience to our Father-God looks like. It's not always easy.

When we walk in obedience, the devil will tempt us to stop. Don't listen! Instead remember the selfless sacrifice Jesus fulfilled on the cross in our place, separated from God the Father because Jesus carried and became our sin. Jesus knew this was coming as he prayed in such sorrow and trouble in the Garden of Gethsemane.

"It is finished!" Jesus said from the cross (John 19:30). Perfection made complete.

The entire Bible in 4 words
Mike Novotny

You can summarize the 700,000+ words of the Bible with four key words.

First, *creation*. **"In the beginning God created the heavens and the earth,"** and it was good (Genesis 1:1). God spoke, and stars, mountains, and people were created, and it was very good. But that paradise only lasted for 2 pages.

Because then came *rebellion*. The devil, a rebellious angel, urged Adam and Eve to follow his example. "Don't!" God had said. But they did. "Follow my truth," God had urged. But they followed their own. And the curse came into the earth like a nuclear bomb. Labor pains, thorns, death, doubting God, and disbelieving his truth became the new normal.

But God responded with *salvation*. God loved those rebels so much that he promised to fix what their sin had broken, to send a Savior to crush the devil and save them and us from what we deserved. And it took a "few" pages (a.k.a. the entire Old Testament), but that salvation came in Jesus. Thank God it did!

But we still ache for more, don't we? For bodies that don't hurt. For relationships that aren't strained. For a world without tornados and floods. That's why the Bible ends with *restoration*. God has promised that one day Jesus will return in glory and there will be a whole new world, a place where our bodies will be made glorious and new, without torn ligaments or anxious thoughts or bad backs, where we will walk with God in perfect happiness.

Creation. Rebellion. Salvation. Restoration. That's the entire Bible in just four words.

An encouraging word
Jan Gompper

If I could have a do-over in my teaching career, I would encourage my students more. I taught college theater for most of my career and often focused too much on how my students could improve, not always giving them the accolades they also needed to hear.

Being an encourager doesn't come naturally. Satan wants nothing more than for us to tear each other down rather than build each other up. Sinful pride, jealousy, and insecurities can prevent us from uttering encouraging words to someone else. If we haven't been the recipient of much encouragement, we may also have a harder time doling it out.

Thankfully, God understands that there might be an "encouragement deficit" in the human condition. That's why he frequently encourages us to encourage others:

- **"But encourage one another daily, as long as it is called 'Today,' so that none of you may be hardened by sin's deceitfulness"** (Hebrews 3:13).
- **"Therefore encourage one another and build each other up"** (1 Thessalonians 5:11).

But God doesn't expect us to go it alone. He sends his Holy Spirit to encourage us in our spiritual journeys and to teach us how to encourage others. Before Jesus ascended to heaven, he told his disciples, **"I will ask the Father, and he will give you another advocate** [encourager] **to help you and be with you forever"** (John 14:16).

"May the God who gives endurance and encouragement give you the same attitude of mind toward each other that Christ Jesus had" (Romans 15:5).

Two key ingredients
Jason Nelson

I spent part of my ministry as a church consultant. I tried to help churches grow. I was invited to churches that wanted to grow because many churches weren't growing. We used a sophisticated process that included community and congregational analyses, questionnaires, and interviews. We provided reports of our findings and made ministry recommendations based on our research. Some churches implemented them with good results.

My son has been a member of a number of churches. He's not a consultant, but he has his own take on what is required to have a growing church. He thinks there are two key ingredients. I would like to pose his observations as questions.

Is the pastor the kind of person people want to be around?
Is the building the kind of place people want to be in?

There is room for lively discussion in responding to his questions. But I think he nailed it. His simple answer to both is . . . lighten up. Be bright! That is a tangible way to be what Jesus told us we are: **"You are the light of the world"** (Matthew 5:14). Who wouldn't want to be around a bright pastor in a bright space with a bright message surrounded by other bright people?

Let's stipulate that it all depends on the power of the gospel and work of the Holy Spirit. Let's dismiss the "yeah buts" of change resisters. And let's accept that there are factors under our control that make a difference.

Hey there, little rowboat
Matt Trotter

When I was becoming a believer in Jesus, I struggled to understand the concept of the moment of being saved. Apparently, I'm not alone, because I learned we Christians can and should be thoughtful about how redemption happens. Is it a choice? acceptance? work? belief? I asked anyone who would listen, "What must I do to be saved?"

So did some people who lived by the sea in Jesus' day, and some of those people were fisherman. The Bible scholars who taught those fishermen whined to Jesus about his claims on the shores of Galilee, and Jesus said, **"Stop grumbling among yourselves. . . . No one can come to me unless the Father who sent me draws them, and I will raise them up at the last day"** (John 6:43,44).

The first 44 times I read that, I skipped right past the verb ("draws") to the victory party ("raise them up at the last day"). Some Bible scholars view that metaphorically: God draws your consciousness to think about him.

But I think this teaching draws a really beautiful fisherman's picture of how we are saved. The Greek word used for "draws" in that instance is also "to draw/drag a boat across sand." I don't know how many times you've tried to draw a boat across sand, but good luck. It's a one-sided tug-of-war between the guy pulling the rope and dead weight.

Point made, Greek language! We are dead weight like a fisherman's boat. No one can come to Jesus unless God drags them. God is dragging you to him now. Believe it.

NOVEMBER

"For where your treasure is,
there your heart will be also."

Matthew 6:21

The generation in between
Ann Jahns

Have you heard the term "sandwich generation"? Are you a card-carrying member? You are if you are "sandwiched" between two generations—your children and your aging parents—and are caring for them both.

The sandwich generation is a place of special blessings . . . and some burdens. It's a place of frantically doing a wellness check on your octogenarian dad because he lives alone and isn't answering his phone. It's a place of keeping your toddler granddaughter overnight so her exhausted parents get a break. It's a place of driving hours to pick up your young adult son on the side of the road because his car broke down. All on the same weekend. And let's face it—you're not that young anymore, and your energy levels aren't what they used to be.

Then Monday comes, and you head back to work, depleted. But this coming weekend, you'd do it all again, because you love them all so much.

Do you ever wonder why God is giving you these special blessings and burdens? Perhaps he gives you these opportunities so you can tap into deep wells of compassion you never knew you had—and through that you fulfill your calling by loving others. **"Let us not become weary in doing good,"** encourages the apostle Paul, **"for at the proper time we will reap a harvest if we do not give up"** (Galatians 6:9).

I know you're weary, friend. But don't give up. God will graciously continue to replenish your well of compassion and will bless you as you bless others.

A positive review for God

Daron Lindemann

The sign at my chiropractor reads, "Give us a positive review on Yelp and Google. Show us, and receive 15% off your next visit."

Businesses thrive on more customers. Positive reviews can help. God wants positive reviews too, but for an additional reason. Your positive review of God is good for you.

Psalm 117 (the shortest chapter of the Bible) says, **"Praise the Lord, all you nations; extol him, all you peoples. For great is his love toward us, and the faithfulness of the Lord endures forever. Praise the Lord."**

The first and last words of the psalm serve as bookends, embracing the main message: "Praise the Lord." When your thoughts begin and end with God . . . when your day begins and ends with God . . . when your priorities begin and end with God . . . then everything else in between will be in its proper place in your life.

Praise means to cheer. A stronger synonym, *extol*, is making exuberant statements about the greatness of something. Why gush about God? Notice that little word *for* in the middle of the psalm. Exuberance about God means you're excited about him and his love more than anything else.

Where is that love of God targeted? "Toward us," not just floating around as positive energy.

Did you know? Not only is Psalm 117 the shortest chapter of the Bible; it is also the middle chapter. The center. The bull's-eye. It's all about this: the great love of God and your positive review of praise.

House of reputations
Katrina Harrmann

When my oldest son was just nine years old, I was helping him study for a social studies test.

As I was quizzing him, I asked, "What two bodies make up the legislature?"

He promptly answered, "The Senate and the House of Reputations."

I got a good laugh. Because, oh my, all those colorful reputations! These days, you can hardly turn on your television or switch on your computer without seeing interesting stories about the antics of our politicians. Their reputations are indeed on full and vivid display.

November makes many people think of politics. Election time gets people riled up as they argue for or against whatever policy or politician they support.

But it's important to remember to keep it in perspective. While God gives us politicians to help lead our nation—from whatever party they may happen to be—HE is the one who holds everything in his hands.

Respect our leaders? Yes. Jesus said, **"Give back to Caesar what is Caesar's"** (Matthew 22:21). And even more, *PRAY* for them! (Oof, this is not always easy, is it?)

But in the end? Rest easy knowing that God is Lord of all. Try to get along peaceably with one another, even with our different opinions on the subject of politics.

"Let everyone be subject to the governing authorities, for there is no authority except that which God has established. The authorities that exist have been established by God" (Romans 13:1).

Accept trouble
Matt Trotter

I collect bikes. My wife and mother both roll their eyes at the pedal-powered fleet. Today I sought to pull my SUV into our garage and not crush my bikes. I missed the bikes and scraped my SUV. I was angry at myself. This made me think of the righteous man Job after his wife encouraged him to blame God. **"He replied, 'You are talking like a foolish woman. Shall we accept good from God, and not trouble?'"** (Job 2:10). Job was right to question his wife. My wife's skepticism of my fleet of bikes is quite different than Mrs. Job, who had lost her whole family and more. Job's question is a good technique to reduce the temperature of our rage.

- When we scrape the paint off our car, should we accept good from God and not trouble?
- When a friend confides his addiction, should we accept good from God and not trouble?
- When a country invades another, should we accept good from God and not trouble?
- When I get a cold from the guy on the airplane, should I accept good from God and not trouble?

Much will come and go in this world, and the pain and trouble will tempt us to anger. Yet as promised to believers in Rome centuries after Job, **"We know that in all things God works for the good of those who love him, who have been called according to his purpose"** (Romans 8:28). Let's not blame but trust in God. No pain matters compared to keeping the faith in the Father, Son, and Holy Spirit.

Scared of Satan?
Mike Novotny

Are you scared of Satan? For all of human history, Satan has been deceiving people into all kinds of sin. If you're a compassionate person, he'll tempt you to be a people pleaser who always says yes, who burns out by ignoring your created limits. If you're a driven person, he'll drive you to forget about others' emotions, opinions, and goals. If you're good with words, he'll make you great at arguing. If you're good with money, he'll fixate your faith on the bottom line. Satan knows what works with you.

Are you scared of Satan? John's Revelation offers us a wake-up call and a way out: **"The dragon** [Satan] **stood in front of the woman who was about to give birth, so that it might devour her child the moment he was born. . . . And her child was snatched up to God and to his throne. The woman fled into the wilderness to a place prepared for her by God"** (12:4-6). The vivid imagery reminds us that we are no match for Satan (infants and postpartum moms aren't the best at battling dragons), yet by God's intervention, the dragon doesn't win.

This symbolic picture reveals to us that God is stronger than Satan. And since God saves and protects his people through the truth of the gospel, you will be okay. Let Satan breathe the fire of his accusations and try to convince you that evil will get the last word. Because of Jesus, he can't devour you. Not today. Not ever.

Amen!

He will watch with us
Jan Gompper

"Then he returned to the disciples and found them asleep. He said to Peter, 'Couldn't you watch with me even one hour?'" (Matthew 26:40 NLT).

Have you ever read this verse and thought, "How terrible of Peter, James, and John! How could they have not honored Jesus' request to watch with him while he went into Gethsemane to pray? I'd have stayed awake!"

Really? I often can't "watch with Jesus" for 15 minutes. While listening to a pastor's message on Sunday, saying my daily prayers, reading a devotion (or even writing one), my focus on Jesus is often pulled in other directions. Too easily daily concerns dart in and out of my brain, robbing me of the quality time I desire to have with my Lord.

And Satan does a victory dance whenever this happens because the last thing he wants me (or you) to do is "watch with Jesus." The more he can distract us from what's most needed in our lives, the more he thinks he can eventually pull us away from Jesus altogether.

But what Satan always forgets is how faithful Jesus is. He not only forgave his sleepy, fearful disciples; he commissioned them, promising that he would always watch with them: **"Be sure of this: I am with you always, even to the end of the age"** (Matthew 28:20 NLT).

And when we struggle to watch with Jesus, or even if we sometimes run from him or betray him, we have this same promise.

From barren to harvest
Andrea Delwiche

Are you in a struggle that makes it hard to imagine sowing seeds of joy? Yes, you have had times of goodness, but now . . . does joy feel impossible? Sometimes it's a struggle to *locate* the seeds of joy, much less prepare the soil and plant them. These are the shadow times. We need someone to witness to us that green leaves and sun-ripened tomatoes (or joy) will come again.

Psalm 126 can provide that service. It begins by recalling a promise fulfilled by God: **"When the Lord restored the fortunes of Zion, we were like those who dreamed. Our mouths were filled with laughter, our tongues with songs of joy. . . . The Lord has done great things for us, and we are filled with joy"** (verses 1-3).

One minute we fly with joy, and the next we crash back down, having forgotten the goodness we so recently celebrated. Our emotions are like dandelion seeds, blown by every breeze.

But here the psalmist holds out a sign of new growth where all seems dead: **"Those who go out with weeping, carrying seed to sow, will return with songs of joy, carrying sheaves with them"** (verse 6). Goodness will emerge from the barren ground. Growth takes time, but with water, nutrients, and sunshine, your harvest will be realized.

Our God is the Lord of the harvest. Growth and greenness out of scorched or parched earth is his specialty.

Ask him to steady your hand as you plant. He will guard your heart and mind to anticipate a harvest of joy.

Everybody's weird but us
Jason Nelson

And I'm not so sure about you. Isn't that what we think sometimes? Especially after a trip to Walmart. I mean, after we get past the polite first impressions of being on our best behavior and get to know each other, we find out we are all weirdos. We all have idiosyncrasies that could alienate others. If you spend enough time with someone, you will realize they are a little off in some way. The question is, will we love them anyway, even if they make us uncomfortable?

I don't think Jesus would shop exclusively at Macy's just to be with a "better class" of people. I think Jesus would be quite comfortable at Walmart or any other gathering place of diverse people because he came to redeem this freak show we call humanity. He once told a prominent Pharisee who invited him for lunch: **"The next time you put on a dinner, don't just invite your friends and family and rich neighbors, the kind of people who will return the favor. Invite some people who never get invited out, the misfits from the wrong side of the tracks. You'll be—and experience—a blessing. They won't be able to return the favor, but the favor will be returned—oh, how it will be returned!—at the resurrection of God's people"** (Luke 14:12-14 MSG).

The invitation to the great banquet of the Lamb of God is extended to all, including weirdos like you and me.

Turning to Jesus
Matt Trotter

I have an idol problem. See if you can guess what it is. Each day I jump out of bed thinking I've got to improve everything right now. I want to fix the world. Here are my top six problems today: 1) everyone needs faith in Jesus, 2) injustice, 3) yesterday, 4) politics, 5) work, 6) snooze button.

Realistically, I can't do much about any of it. So in an effort to improve, I read the Bible, looking for tips and wisdom from books like James and Proverbs, which are excellent sources. But somehow I still wake up edgy about the situations I see and feel, things done and not done.

For an antidote, I can only look to one place. I turn from my problems to look for God's gospel encouragement: **"They tell how you *turned to God* from idols to serve the living and true God, and to wait for his Son from heaven, whom he raised from the dead—Jesus, who rescues us from the coming wrath"** (1 Thessalonians 1:9,10).

Have you figured out what my idol problem is? Every day I wake up . . . angry. The problems are too big for a human to solve. And perhaps by the Creator's design, the problems I perceive won't reduce for the present age.

Tomorrow there will be about six more things that I dream to fix before breakfast. I'd be better off starting my day by turning to Jesus.

So long, earthly body
Liz Schroeder

"Meth and alcohol were my two best friends. I didn't need anyone else." Although Gloria had left that life behind, it had taken a toll on her body. She told our support group that an oral surgeon was going to pull 15 of her teeth that had decayed from drug use and neglect. "What man is going to want me now?" she asked as she grabbed a tissue. "Not that I care," she added without much conviction.

As God would have it, the lesson for that night was on our heavenly bodies. We read Paul's words together: **"The body that is sown is perishable, it is raised imperishable; it is sown in dishonor, it is raised in glory; it is sown in weakness, it is raised in power; it is sown a natural body, it is raised a spiritual body"** (1 Corinthians 15:42-44).

It took zero effort to convince the ladies in the group that their bodies were weak, perishable, and had been dishonored. Even if you haven't abused substances, you feel it too, don't you? When an old sports injury keeps you from exercising, when you can't eat the foods you used to enjoy, or when you research how much it would cost to cover up a tattoo you now regret.

Later that week, I brought Gloria a smoothie and a word of comfort. That's what makes a gospel-centered recovery program so practical and effective. What man will want you now? Jesus. Who is a true friend? Jesus. How will you be raised to life with a glorious body? Only through Jesus.

Conquerors vs. more than conquerors
Karen Spiegelberg

What does it mean to be a conqueror? One definition is, "One who overcomes." I'm sure you can think of things you've overcome or conquered. My most memorable conquest (besides childbirth!) was climbing Pike's Peak in Colorado via the Barr Trail. For a flatlander from Wisconsin, it was no easy feat. The trail starts at 7,500 ft. above sea level. Then for 13 miles, it climbs to over 14,000 ft. The climb sucks the air out of you because of the altitude and elevation change. The view from the top is indescribable though and worth the journey.

What does it mean to be *more than* a conqueror? Human brains can't even process that. In Romans 8:37, the apostle Paul assured the Romans and us that all kinds of things would be thrown at us and challenge our faith. He said, **"In all these things we are more than conquerors through him who loved us."** To be more than a conqueror means that prior to even having a problem or something to overcome, we *can* overcome it through Christ. Before health, work, family, or other struggles come our way, he has already conquered it all, and there is nothing that he can't conquer because of his love and presence within us. We are more than conquerors through him!

When we understand who we are in Christ and what he's done for us, how beautiful it is. More beautiful than any view from the top of a mountain!

Tune up
Matt Ewart

"Since we live by the Spirit, let us keep in step with the Spirit" (Galatians 5:25).

I have an old piano that sits in my house. When I say "old," I don't mean it's an expensive antique. It's just old and worn out. Someday we will have to pay someone to take it from our house.

Another instrument that sits in my house is a guitar that's just as old as the piano. Thankfully it's light enough that I won't have to pay someone to haul it away.

What these two instruments have in common is that they are perfectly in tune. At least they are in tune with each other. A C chord on the guitar will perfectly match up with a C chord on the piano.

The problem with these two instruments is that they are *only* in tune with each other. The piano is several notes flat because it is unable to be tuned. The guitar is tuned down to match the piano.

It's easy to follow that same path in life. Over time, our hearts naturally get "tuned down" to the level of our wants and our desires. And it's easy to miss if we are only in the company of people who are tuned down similarly.

Keep in tune today. Ask the Spirit to enlighten your heart with his truth. It's okay if the world thinks you sound different. God will tune your heart to sing his praise.

When life is suddenly scary
Mike Novotny

One of my friends once went from attending Bible study to facing serious prison time, all in the course of a single day. On Thursday, he was absorbing God's Word, but a day later, he was arrested and facing a scary sentence despite his claims of innocence.

Has life ever gotten suddenly scary for you? Without warning, the landlord raises the rent, the manager cuts back your hours, the medical bill arrives, or the mechanic calls and says, "Are you sitting down?" Out of the blue, you find a lump you never noticed before, something snaps in your knee, or the doctor drops the c-word—*cancer*. On an otherwise sunny day, your parents sit you down and say, "Divorce," your only friend from work tells you she's transferring, or you lose someone you really love. When scary and sudden overlap, it feels like you can't not be afraid.

But those suddenly scary moments are when Jesus is at his best. During a terrifying storm, **"[Jesus] replied, 'You of little faith, why are you so afraid?' Then he got up and rebuked the winds and the waves, and it was completely calm"** (Matthew 8:26). Jesus wants to save you from small faith by giving you powerful proof of how much he can do and how much he cares about you.

Remember who Jesus is—your powerful King, your compassionate Savior, your loving and risen Redeemer—and your faith will have a good reason to be completely calm during the next storm in your life.

Nothing could be more perfect
Dave Scharf

Recently, I attended a worship service that seemed doomed from the start. The pastor introduced the service and pointed to the screen that would guide the service. Just then the screen showed an error message and retracted to show a blank wall. The pastor hadn't noticed, so the organist tried to get his attention from the balcony to no avail. The pastor began speaking, but his microphone crackled more than Rice Krispies, forcing the pastor to switch to the handheld mic to conduct a baptism. The family formed a line around the font, but as the pastor began speaking, the little boy who was soon to be baptized ran away from the font with his father chasing after him. What a mess! Nothing more could have gone wrong. But then . . .

Nothing could have been more perfect. Titus 3:5 says, **"He saved us, not because of righteous things we had done, but because of his mercy. He saved us through the washing of rebirth and renewal by the Holy Spirit."** I watched as the entire family, not just the restless little boy, was baptized. What a beautiful picture of what our Savior does for all of us. He came into this messy, sinful world to save us by his cross. He comes into the mess of our lives to save us through Baptism, that washing of rebirth and renewal by the Holy Spirit. He continues to clean up our messes with his Word and presence. Nothing could be more perfect!

Major objections
Mike Novotny

The faith of countless people has been shaken, even destroyed, by the problem of pain. Here's why: In the Bible, God claims to be (1) all-knowing, (2) all-powerful, and (3) entirely good. If God is entirely good but didn't know about the abuse you endured, you couldn't blame him for not stopping it, but God did know. He is all-knowing. Or if God knew about your learning disability but didn't have the power to cure it, you couldn't be any madder at him than your mother. But God does have the power. He is all-powerful. Or if God knew and had the power but wasn't good, you would get why he'd just sit there and watch you struggle to find meaningful work, but he claims to be entirely good. The combination of those three qualities—all-knowing, all-powerful, entirely good—add up to a major objection to God's existence.

Have you thought about that tension? Have you dealt with it? In the devotions to come, I want to explore some of the most powerful answers that suffering Christians have held on to when pain shakes their faith. But for now, ponder your own answer. If someone asked you how a good God can exist in such a bad world, what would you say? When their souls are crying out, how would you respond to this: **"My God, I cry out by day, but you do not answer, by night, but I find no rest"** (Psalm 22:2)?

How do you personally deal with the problem of pain?

Finding hope
Mike Novotny

There was an old rabbi who traveled in a strange and dangerous country with only his donkey, rooster, and lamp. When he stumbled into a small village, exhausted and desperate for lodging, the villagers denied him room, forcing him to sleep in the nearby forest. The frustrated rabbi settled near a tree, where he lit his lamp to read the Scriptures, but a merciless wind snuffed out the flame. Soon after, wild animals chased his rooster away, and then a group of thieves snatched his donkey. His suffering felt unfair, unjust, pointless.

But the next morning, the rabbi wandered back into the village, where he discovered an answer to his suffering. The previous night, the village had been raided by enemy soldiers who attacked the villagers in their beds, the same soldiers who then marched by the very forest where the rabbi was sleeping. If they had seen the light of his lamp or heard the crow of his rooster or seen the shape of his donkey, he would have died. So the old rabbi sighed, "All that God does is done well."

No matter how painful your life may be or get, the moral of the rabbi's story holds true: **"In all things God works for the good of those who love him"** (Romans 8:28). Whether you see all of God's plan, catch only a glimpse of it, or can't fathom his bigger purpose, God is always using his power and love to work out pain for a greater good.

Believe that, and you will find hope in your suffering.

He gets it
Mike Novotny

I'm not very good at pastoral counseling, but I do know this: Most people are more blessed by deep empathy than by quick answers. Hurting people want a person who gets it, someone who feels with them. Logic and solutions are not bad, but they're not always the best answer to begin with.

If you're hurting today, please remember that Jesus gets it. Perhaps the most famous prophecy about Jesus, Isaiah 53, includes this: **"He was despised and rejected by mankind, a man of suffering, and familiar with pain"** (verse 3). Jesus didn't feel pain once or twice; he was "familiar with" it.

Do you come from a poor family? He gets it. Have you been misunderstood or rejected? He gets it. Have you been betrayed by a friend or hurt by the church? He gets it. Have you seen sickness and darkness up close? He gets it. Have you gone to the funeral of a friend? He gets it. Have you been verbally or physically abused? He gets it.

When you suffer, Jesus looks you in the eyes and says, "I get it. And I'm sorry. This is not how it's supposed to be. This is not how it was in the beginning. This is not how it will be one day. But this is what it is right now. I hate it, but I get it."

Is God working out your pain for a greater purpose? Absolutely. But he is also with you in the darkness, looking you in the eyes with compassion and assuring you, "I get it."

Remember your salvation
Mike Novotny

I was in an Uber as my Middle Eastern driver drove me to my hotel. "What are you here for?" he asked.

"To give a presentation on trusting God even when life hurts."

"I do trust in God like that," he declared. He then told me when Hurricane Harvey flooded his house and threatened not only his stuff but his life, even then he trusted God to do whatever was best.

"How did you get faith like that?" I asked him, curious.

That's when he told me about Afghanistan, about the day during the war when he got shot but lived due to a bulletproof vest.

"It was like someone shoved me to the ground," he said of the bullet that zipped into the vest that saved his life. And once God saved him, this man knew he could trust God.

Once God saves you, you know you can trust him. This was Paul's logic in Romans 8: **"He who did not spare his own Son, but gave him up for us all—how will he not also, along with him, graciously give us all things?"** (verse 32). In not sparing his only Son, God saved you. That's why you can trust him, even when you don't understand him.

I don't claim to understand why you have suffered in the ways you have, but I do know enough about our Savior to trust him. If Jesus died for you, then God must care. He must love you.

Remember your salvation, and you will get through this suffering.

Jesus had a job too
Ann Jahns

Have you ever noticed that we know surprisingly little about Jesus' life before he began his formal ministry around the age of 30?

Because he wasn't born into a wealthy family, we know he worked. The Bible books of Matthew and Mark refer to Jesus as a carpenter, but that word in Greek could also mean a builder, stonemason, or common craftsman. Can you imagine the Lord of the universe, who called all things into existence with his very words, sweating away in the hot sun, working with scratched and callused hands?

But it really doesn't matter exactly what Jesus did for a living, does it? What matters is this: The work Jesus did, he did faithfully and well. He did the job placed in front of him with his whole heart. Through his everyday labor, he supported his family, showed love to others, and honored his Father in heaven. He knew his work mattered.

Our work matters too. Every ungrateful customer we serve, every diaper we change, every spreadsheet we labor over matters. Even if no one seems to notice or care. God does.

The apostle Paul reminds us, **"Whatever you do, work at it with all your heart, as working for the Lord, not for human masters, since you know that you will receive an inheritance from the Lord as a reward. It is the Lord Christ you are serving"** (Colossians 3:23,24).

Jesus had a job too. Just like you. Just like me. Serve God faithfully, and for Jesus' sake, he promises to bless you for a job well done.

You can't just quit God
Jason Nelson

I know some fine Christian people who are in anguish because a child or grandchild isn't going to church. Their loved one may even express doubts or say they no longer believe. This hurts for fear they will be lost eternally. Our concern for their souls can push us to hound them about it or fill their inbox with Grace Moments devotions. But our well-meaning efforts can backfire. For the sake of bringing comfort to so many of us, I am going to overstate my case. It is not our job to hold on to God. It is his job to hold on to us. You see, no one can just quit God. He has given us this assurance: **"I'll never let you down, never walk off and leave you"** (Hebrews 13:5 MSG).

It is very difficult to just walk away from God. There may be times in people's lives when abandoning what they grew up learning about him makes their lives easier. Less internal conflict. Fewer difficult decisions. Not so much guilt. But God insists, "You're not going to just walk away from me. I will do something about it." He will not give up on anyone he has claimed as his own through Baptism or any other conversion to faith in Jesus. I promise you this. Before God quits on anyone, he will orchestrate events in their lives to produce soul searching and wondering if their lives could possibly have any meaning without him.

Resting grace face
Liz Schroeder

Today I met a lady in the checkout lane whose face positively glowed. I struck up a conversation with her and found out that she counsels veterans struggling with mental health. It was easy to see that she loves her job, loves people, and loves her Lord. You could say she has a "resting grace face."

I've been told my face has closed-captioning. Apparently, you don't need to wonder what I'm thinking; just read my face. How about you? Do you have a poker face, or are you an open book?

Proverbs tells us, **"A happy heart makes the face cheerful, but heartache crushes the spirit"** (15:13).

A patient, peaceful countenance stands out in a slow-moving store checkout. A contented heart preaches sermons in a society hell-bent on overconsumption. Your visage makes an invisible God visible. Your face shares the love of Jesus before you even open your mouth!

If God has blessed you with working eyeballs, be on the lookout for people experiencing the second half of this proverb. When you notice a neighbor heavy with heartache or a coworker with a crushed spirit, you can listen, empathize, affirm, and direct them to the source of your joy. You can lead them to Christ. On the cross, the Father turned his face away from the Son because Jesus bore our sins. He turned his face away from Jesus so that he could turn his face toward us.

May the Lord shine his face upon you today, and may your face reflect his grace to everyone God puts in your lane.

Tune your instrument
Katrina Harrmann

Have you ever started your day on the wrong foot? Sometimes it's caused by doing things out of order. The other day, I woke up late. And cranky. And I grabbed my coffee and hopped on social media. First thing. Yikes.

You can guess what kind of mood that put me in. And my day didn't get any better.

What if I had prayed or read some Scripture or a devotion before hopping on my computer? Maybe I would have had a better attitude and a better day!

British missionary Hudson Taylor may have hit the nail on the head when he said, "Do not have your concert first, and then tune your instrument afterwards. Begin the day with the Word of God and prayer, and get first of all into harmony with Him."

Once we align ourselves with our Creator and connect with him, it can help put the rest of our day into alignment.

In Hebrew, there is a word: *Ayekah*. God asked it in the garden of Eden. It means, "Where are you?"

God always knows where we are *physically*. Rather, this word infers something deeper: "How are you? Where is your soul in relation to me?"

Every morning we can ask ourselves that. Are our internal compasses pointing toward God? Once we orient ourselves, we can head in the right direction.

"Since, then, you have been raised with Christ, set your hearts on things above" (Colossians 3:1).

The burden of sin
Christine Wentzel

Have you ever caught yourself feeling the weight of church or personal rules? Traditions with no biblical basis, eating certain foods or not at certain times, or believing that if you just did life the right way God would be pleased?

Thankfully, earning God's favor has nothing to do with you: **"It is by grace you have been saved, through faith—and this is not from yourselves, it is the gift of God—not by works, so that no one can boast"** (Ephesians 2:8,9). Salvation is God's gift to you through Jesus.

The New Testament book of Galatians is a great place to start reading more about this truth. This book is a letter the apostle Paul wrote to Christians in Galatia (modern-day Turkey) to remind them of the freedom they had through the life, death, and resurrection of Jesus. At this time, there were false teachers who said Christians needed to fulfill the Jewish law of circumcision for salvation, and the Galatian Christians were confused and tempted by it. Paul showed them their salvation was all about Jesus, not about what they did. The same is true for you and me.

In our time, there are false teachings to navigate as well, but we can remember, **"It is for freedom that Christ has set us free. Stand firm, then, and do not let yourselves be burdened again by a yoke of slavery"** (Galatians 5:1).

Don't be burdened by your sin. Jesus already carried it away for you. Trust in him!

What exactly is Holy Communion?
Mike Novotny

Christians have long wrestled with what exactly Jesus meant when he said, "This is my body" and "This is my blood." Are Jesus' body and blood somehow present? Or was Jesus saying that the bread and wine symbolically represent his body and blood?

Curious for answers, I searched through the Scriptures. Here's what I found in the texts that teach us about Communion. In Matthew 26, Jesus said, **"This is my body/This is my blood."** In Mark 14, **"This is my body/ This is my blood."** In Luke 22, **"This is my body/This cup is the new covenant in my blood."** And in 1 Corinthians 11, **"This is my body/This cup is the new covenant in my blood."** That's eight instances of the word *is* without any clues that Jesus was speaking in metaphors.

Now, the Bible sometimes does speak symbolically, so I looked up every passage that uses the word *symbol* (there are 13) and every passage that uses the word *represent* (there are 14) and every passage that uses the word *sign* (there are 189), but none of them are about Communion. Ever.

Perhaps this is why St. Augustine, one of the biggest theologians in Christian history, stated, "That bread which you see on the altar, having been sanctified by the word of God, is the body of Christ. That chalice, or rather, what is in that chalice, having been sanctified by the word of God, is the blood of Christ."

A prayer for patience
Jan Gompper

A friend of mine gave me a refrigerator magnet that read: *Lord, grant me patience. . . . but I want it right now!* She was friend enough to remind me humorously that I sometimes have trouble waiting for the Lord's timing.

Truthfully, there is nothing humorous about being impatient. Marshall Segal of desiringGod.org illuminates: "Impatience is a child of our pride and unbelief. It rises out of our frustration that we do not control what happens and when in our lives."*

Remember the Israelites in the wilderness? God had delivered them from slavery in Egypt and provided them with daily bread to sustain them, **"but *the people grew impatient* on the way; they spoke against God and against Moses, and said, 'Why have you brought us up out of Egypt to die in the wilderness? There is no bread! There is no water! And we detest this miserable food!'"** (Numbers 21:4,5).

"Shame on them!" we say. Now think back to our journey through COVID. Did we grumble because of the inconveniences *we* suffered? Or how about our current journey through a world riddled with wars, political tensions, and inflation? Have we, at times, thrown up our hands in despair, thinking *we* will never see better days?

If so, let's revisit the words of King David: **"Be still in the presence of the Lord, and wait patiently for him to act"** (Psalm 37:7 NLT).

Lord, grant me patience . . . to trust *your* timing!

* Marshall Segal, "Impatience Is a War for Control," desiringGod.org, November 12, 2021, https://www.desiringgod.org/articles/impatience -is-a-war-for-control#modal-602-rjekesui.

Sinner or saint?
Clark Schultz

Life is full of contradictions. Think of the person who races to find the closest parking spot to the doors at the gym. Couldn't the workout begin with a few extra steps? Or the person who orders the 20-piece nuggets, the large order of fries, two cherry pies, and . . . a diet soda. I'm not anti-gym or anti-diet soda. But you can see the contradictions.

You know who else is a walking contradiction? You. And me. The apostle Paul tells us in Romans 3:23: **"All have sinned."** Yes, all of us, and we don't need a trainer to show us where our spiritual muscles in giving, loving, and sharing with others are weak. At the same time, Paul says in Romans 3:24 that **"all are justified freely by his grace."** So which is it? Are we saints, or are we sinners? YES! No, I'm not doing an Abbott & Costello bit of "Who's on First?" here, but the life of a Christian can be viewed as a contradiction.

Why does it matter? Perhaps you know a friend caught in sin but ask yourself, "Who am I to say anything to him since I'm just as guilty?" You are, but like him, you are also a sinner who has been set free from the heavy weight of sin. You have been given the greatest gift ever, a guilt-free life full of God's grace.

Use your freedom to speak the truth in love to those who desperately need it.

The real city of gold
Mike Novotny

Back in the 1540s, a Spanish nobleman named Francisco Vázquez de Coronado came to Mexico City and decided that he would be the one to find the legendary Seven Golden Cities. He raised the needed funds, compiled a massive force, and set out to find paradise. After months of travel, Coronado made it to what is now the American Southwest, but instead of finding streets of gold, he discovered the Pueblo people whose homes were made of . . . mud. But a rumor reached his ears that the gold was even further north, which led Coronado hundreds more miles into modern Kansas, where he came upon villages made of . . . straw. After two years of hard travel and zero pieces of precious gold, Coronado headed home.

That adventurer never found what he was looking for, but through Jesus, you will. You will find a place more precious than gold, where every need is met, every desire is satisfied, a place where God is, where nothing bad ever happens (ever!), where the only something you experience is something so, so good. I know life can be bad. I know life sometimes gets worse. But don't worry, because Jesus wins and the new earth is on the way.

"The angel said to me, 'These words are trustworthy and true. The Lord, the God who inspires the prophets, sent his angel to show his servants the things that must soon take place'" (Revelation 22:6).

Spiritual fit check
Clark Schultz

One of the joys of teaching is that the students keep me up to date on all the lingo. A student recently asked me for a "fit check." My seasoned brain began to question: "Does this student know I tend to go to the gym, turn on the treadmill, and sit next to it while I check social media?" *Fit check* (this may be outdated by the time you read this) means, "Tell me what you are wearing and where you buy it."

Currently, I am blessed to be wearing Banana Republic pants, Allbirds shoes, and a quarter zip with our church logo on it. What about you? What about a spiritual fit check? What do you put on when life throws the curveball of health issues, finance problems, or broken relationships your way? The clothes I mentioned above will not do the job to help you and me through tough times. What will? **"Put on the full armor of God"** (Ephesians 6:10-18).

Shield, sword, helmet, breastplate, belt, and shoes. God gives us this fashion free of charge. There was a cost, but Jesus paid that bill so we don't need to face the issues of the world alone. This outfit gets cleaned, updated, and strengthened every time we pick up one of these devotions or cover ourselves with the Word and sacraments. This way when the winds of doubt come, and they will, we can be assured that we're wearing the best and only outfit that protects.

Spiritlink
Linda Buxa

Noland Arbaugh was 21 years old when a diving accident paralyzed him, leaving him with quadriplegia. Eight years later, he is the first person in a clinical trial to receive a brain implant by Neuralink. This Elon Musk company is designing a brain-computer interface that will collect brain signals, analyze them, and then translate those into commands that control external devices. The company wants to give more freedom and independence to those who can't move on their own.

Admittedly, I'm both fascinated and a little weirded out by a brain-computer link.

But then I realized that I'm in the same situation. Before I was baptized, I couldn't do anything on my own. But once I was baptized, I was united to Jesus' death and raised to life—and so are you.

You can read that good news in Romans 6:3-5. And then in Romans 8:10,11, Paul describes that thanks to that connection, we are now implanted with "Spiritlink": **"But if Christ is in you, then even though your body is subject to death because of sin, the Spirit gives life because of righteousness. And if the Spirit of him who raised Jesus from the dead is living in you, he who raised Christ from the dead will also give life to your mortal bodies because of his Spirit who lives in you."**

Because we have the Spirit of the Lord, we have the freedom to do all sorts of things we couldn't do before—love others, exercise patience, be faithful, practice self-control, choose gentleness, be filled with joy and peace.

God and government
Daron Lindemann

Do you feel like the United States government could do a better job? Do you trust the president? Do you wish our nation was more patriotic? Here's what you can do.

Daniel worshiped God, even while taken captive by a foreign country. He was put to work there in the king's cabinet because he **"distinguished himself . . . by his exceptional qualities. He was trustworthy and neither corrupt nor negligent"** (Daniel 6:3,4).

Daniel courageously practiced his faith, even under a government that disagreed with his godly beliefs. He served faithfully in a pagan government.

While doing so, Daniel focused his energy less on changing his government and more on being true to God in his beliefs and behavior. It wasn't always popular. His opponents framed him and got him tossed to the lions for insubordination. But God delivered him.

"No wound was found on him, because he had trusted in his God" (Daniel 6:23). What if Daniel had trusted in government instead of God to save him?

Be careful of trusting in the government to do for you what only God can do. Be careful of trusting in government over God. God is more powerful than lions, kings, and presidents. Serve him fully and faithfully.

God, I pray for our country and that I live in it honorably as I follow you. You are sovereign over all governments. Rule my heart so that I trust you more, shining for you through my beliefs and behavior. Amen.

DECEMBER

Therefore the Lord himself will give you a sign:
The virgin will conceive and give birth to a son,
and will call him Immanuel.

Isaiah 7:14

Best 1,260 days ever

Mike Novotny

The mysterious book of Revelation reveals some of God's greatest promises: **"The dragon [Satan] stood in front of the woman who was about to give birth. . . . The woman fled into the wilderness to a place prepared for her by God, where she might be taken care of for 1,260 days"** (12:4,6). 1,260 days? That's a symbolic way of saying, "God will care for us to the very end."

Here's why—1,260 days is about 42 months (30 days/month), and 42 months is 3.5 years, and 3.5 is half of 7. In the Bible, the number 7 often represents a complete period of history, like God created a 7-day week. Thus 3.5 years or 42 months or 1,260 days is the half of history from Jesus until the end of the world (from his ascension around A.D. 30 to whenever the Last Day arrives). Just like God provided for his people until Jesus came (the first 1,260 days), so he will care for us until Jesus comes again.

The Bible's closing promise is that no matter how dark these last days get, God will care for us. We might be outmatched by the power of Satan, the barrenness of this broken world, or our own unworthiness, but God has a place prepared for us where he takes perfect care of us.

Whether today is your last day or you live until the glorious return of Jesus, please remember what those 1,260 days represent. They are God's promise to get you to the finish line, where the true celebration begins.

Trust God's protection
Andrea Delwiche

Are we preoccupied with self-protection? We worry about financial self-protection and choose political candidates based on who serves our needs. Our obsessive working, careful networking, and even the slate of activities we plan for our children might all be seen as forms of protecting status and opportunities. Yet Scripture also counsels us to work diligently and care for our loved ones. What kind of balancing act is God asking of us?

Here's good counsel from Psalm 127: **"Unless the Lord builds the house, the builders labor in vain. Unless the Lord watches over the city, the guards stand watch in vain. In vain you rise early and stay up late, toiling for food to eat—for he grants sleep to those he loves"** (verses 1,2).

Our plans are nothing if they don't follow God's plan. Whatever we're striving for is chaff in the wind if humble obedience to God and his ways isn't first in our lives. God promises protection.

"Whoever claims to live in him must live as Jesus did" (1 John 2:6). Jesus lived every day of his life trusting in the protection of God his Father. Never once did Jesus justify his actions with arguments of *self*-protection.

How would the world's view of Christianity change if we all started to look and live more like Jesus? Would we have more time to protect *others* if we trusted God to protect *us*?

Meditate and pray with these words from Isaiah 30:15: **"In repentance and rest is your salvation, in quietness and trust is your strength."**

The power of example
Katrina Harrmann

We took our kids sledding several years ago at the dunes near Lake Michigan. These can be quite steep and provide some awesome opportunities for sledding! Our nine-year-old daredevil walked up one of the tallest dunes with his older brother and plunked his sled down. He gained speed pretty fast and went flying through the air in spectacular fashion. His glasses went one way, the sled went a second way, and the small boy flew in a third direction.

I remember shrieking—I was so sure he must have broken something. He was shaken up, but he was okay.

His older brother, age 13, had watched it happen from where both boys had started out, at the top of the dune. After watching it unfold, our older son quietly descended about halfway down the dune before trying his sled out on a calmer slope—one much less likely to send him airborne.

Smart cookie! We learn by example, right?

We see others go through things, and we learn. Examples are powerful, because we see the effects of various actions taken (good and bad) in front of our eyes!

How much more so the powerful examples of our own lives?

The next time you think that leading a quiet life of Christian values isn't doing much at all, think again! Leading by example—even a quiet example—is a powerful witnessing tool!

"In everything set them an example by doing what is good" (Titus 2:7).

Satan's two biggest lies (and how to overcome them)
Mike Novotny

Satan knows that one of two lies will work with you—taking sin too lightly or taking sin too seriously.

Maybe you take sin too lightly. How often do you really feel bad for sinning? You're only human, right? At least you didn't _____, right? Some of us have so much self-compassion that we let go of the perfection.

Or maybe you take sin too seriously. You can't let it go. You can't move on. You can't forgive yourself. You don't deserve to pray (what a hypocrite you would be if you did!). You don't have a chance with God and never will. Joy is something that other people, better people, feel but not a disgusting sinner like you.

Both lies can devour your faith.

Here's the truth that triumphs over them both: **"They triumphed over** [Satan] **by the blood of the Lamb"** (Revelation 12:11). How can your sin not be a big deal if Jesus must bleed for it? How can you claim that your sin isn't serious when you see him suffering? Sin is bad, as bad as the bleeding Son of God.

But how can you be unforgivable if that same blood cleanses you? If the Lamb laid down his life for you, how are you not good with God? If Jesus shouted, "It is finished," how could sin and shame not be finished for you?

Meditate on the blood of the Lamb, and you will have the truth that triumphs over both of Satan's biggest lies.

The dysfunctional family tree
Ann Jahns

All writers know the first few sentences are critical. You need to draw your reader in. (Are you still with me?) Matthew starts his gospel with 17 seemingly dry verses listing Jesus' family tree. This probably wasn't the "hook" his creative writing teacher was looking for.

But guided by the Holy Spirit, God inspired Matthew to write these words for a reason, and what a story they tell! After establishing that Jesus is **"the son of Abraham,"** the descendant of the revered father of the Jewish people (verse 1), Matthew throws in something unexpected.

Unlike typical genealogies of the time, Matthew includes women. Like Tamar (verse 3), who through deceptive and sordid events became pregnant by her father-in-law, Judah. Or Rahab (verse 5), a former prostitute who became a follower of the true God. Or Ruth (verse 5), not a native Israelite but a believer and the grandmother of the great King David.

Each ancestor in Jesus' family tree was sinfully dysfunctional—from the "good" ones, like Abraham, to the "bad" ones, like Rahab. But they also had something else in common: They were made perfect by the blood of their descendant/Savior, Jesus Christ, **"who is called the Messiah"** (verse 16).

I urge you to read Matthew 1:1-17 with fresh eyes. See the miracles in the mundane. Recognize God's grace. Marvel at how God used sinful people to advance his kingdom plan.

If God used people like these in his plan, he uses you too!

Break up the snake
Linda Buxa

Stick with me. There's a lot of backstory . . .

In 1407 B.C., the Israelites were complaining (again!)—and God sent poisonous snakes. The people *quickly* realized the consequences of their absolute disrespect and asked Moses to plead their case—and God sent a solution. Moses made a bronze snake and lifted it on a pole. When the poisonous snakes bit them, people could look at the pole and live.

In 716 B.C. Hezekiah became Israel's king and **"did what was right in the eyes of the Lord"** (2 Kings 18:3). He removed all the items and places associated with idol worship, which included breaking **"into pieces the bronze snake Moses had made, for up to that time the Israelites had been burning incense to it. (It was called Nehushtan.)"** (verse 4).

Instead of worshiping God for the healing of their ancestors, they had been worshiping the snake itself.

So what do we worship in place of God? Are we tempted to focus more on the answer to our prayers than we are on the Answer-er? Maybe it's our cancer-free status, the babies born after years of infertility, the exercise routine that helped with the weight loss, the homes we live in, the income from a job, the doctors who performed the surgery, possibly even the leaders whom God has put in authority over us.

Whatever it is for me and whatever it is for you, today is a good day to reflect on what we worship. If things are in the wrong order, break up the snake.

Which way to pray
Jason Nelson

I recently learned that during my long catastrophic illness, there were differences of opinion on how to pray for me. Thankfully, many people were praying for me. But as time went on and word got out that I had yet another life-threatening complication, there was a debate among folks who cared about me. Do we pray for another healing, or do we ask God to take Jason home? I was at times in the latter camp.

Miracles versus mercy. Sometimes it is a tough call, and only God can make it. Right now, it looks like he was in the let's-heal-this-guy-one-more-time camp. Thank you, Jesus. Many in my generation will pivot from prayers for miracles to live to prayers for a merciful end to it all. It would be a morbid lottery to bet on which of us goes first. But no one will escape that inevitable outcome.

Life and death are God's domain. So, we pray. What did I learn from being the subject of so many prayers? **"I know that through your prayers and God's provision of the Spirit of Jesus Christ what has happened to me will turn out for my deliverance"** (Philippians 1:19). I don't understand why I was delivered and others weren't, why I lived and others didn't. But I have resolved to be as vigorous as I am able and tell people how much I love them.

Yes, I'm ready to die. But not today.

The blessings of being a beginner
Liz Schroeder

It's difficult to start a new language at any age, but it's doubly humbling to learn one later in life. The sponge-like brain of youth has been swapped out for a bowling ball: hard and smooth, and I think there's a hole or two in there.

Because of my work with a global nonprofit, I decided to learn Indonesian. After months of daily usage of the app, I could order eggs for breakfast. How would I like them cooked? Um, yes?

I'm grateful for the experience because it reminds me what it feels like to be a beginner. It's exciting to see progress and how much I have yet to learn.

That's the feeling I get from watching my friend Lucinda grow in her faith. Lucinda will tell you that she is Navajo, a mother, a recovering alcoholic, and a child of God. Our pastor recently gave her a self-study Bible, so Lucinda and I met for coffee to crack open her new treasure.

As we read in the book of Mark about John the Baptizer and the baptism of Jesus, the dawn of realization brightened Lucinda's face. "I'd like to get baptized!" By the grace of God, Lucinda will be baptized next Sunday, just days after celebrating nine months of sobriety.

Jesus tells us in John 14:26, **"But the Advocate, the Holy Spirit, whom the Father will send in my name, will teach you all things."** Better than any app, we have the Holy Spirit to guide us in our baby steps of faith. What a blessing!

Our times, God's hands
Karen Spiegelberg

Ticktock. The hours and minutes ticked away until his alarm clock signaled it was time to get up for work. He had packed his lunch the night before and laid out his clothes, sure of another day ahead. But when the alarm rang, he didn't wake up. The Lord had taken my brother to heaven unexpectedly in the middle of the night.

I thought I was confident in God's promise of his perfect timing, but my brother's sudden death hit me like a ton of bricks. I wanted to question God's timing of taking him, a dad to three young kids and a blessing to our family. I bared my broken heart to God while searching his Word. When I landed on Psalm 31, I was completely taken in by King David's words and reminded of the much greater difficulties that he had encountered. But David knew that he was under the care and perfect timing of our God Almighty. When I hit verses 14 and 15, a peace washed over me: **"But I trust in you, Lord; I say, 'You are my God.' My times are in your hands."** That passage reminded me of God's daily providence while I am still awake in my time of grace.

Ticktock. All of our times are in God's hands. Our pasts are forgiven through the blood of Christ, the present is covered through his provision, and our futures are certain by his promise of eternal life!

Perhaps tithing was easier
Matt Ewart

When God rescued Abraham's descendants from Egypt and made them into a nation, he provided the laws and ceremonies by which they would operate. Among the laws was a command to tithe. The tithe required that each person give back to God ten percent of what they received.

This command enforced a life that kept God first. In fact, God specified that he wanted the first ten percent of what they got, not the leftovers. When they gave back the first portion, it forced them to remember God and rely on him for the rest.

The command to tithe is no longer in effect since it specifically applied to the people of Israel. But before you get too comfortable, Jesus replaced the tithe with an invitation to do even more: **"A new command I give you: Love one another. As I have loved you, so you must love one another"** (John 13:34).

And Paul says in Romans 12:1: **"I urge you . . . in view of God's mercy, to offer your bodies as a living sacrifice."**

Whereas Old Testament tithing enforced a life that kept God first, New Testament giving reflects the truth that God put us first. God gave all of his one and only Son to redeem us from sin and death. His love invites us to reflect a similar love, not just giving because we are commanded to do so but giving freely and giving wholly because this is now part of who we are in Christ.

Turn lemons into lemonade
Christine Wentzel

I sat in a hospital waiting room anxious to take a major heart test. This was the last place I expected to be. Shocked, frightened, and downright mad at God, I sat there stewing in misery. An older woman walked in, and our eyes met with the same knowing look of what we faced. We smiled and mumbled hellos. She asked me how I was. I told her the truth and finished with a resigned, "Whatever . . ." She replied, "We can pray," and we did.

My wise, watchful sister in Christ made lemonade out of our lemons. The taste was sweet and long lasting. She had no idea if I knew my Savior or not, but with faith in her conviction, she took advantage of a God-given opportunity anyway. She had no idea it helped place my fears at the cross of Christ and trust in him. She had no idea she was an inspiring demonstration of a gospel-motivated life.

The apostle Paul encourages us to keep praying, to be alert, and to be thankful. He assures us there will be opportunity to reveal the gospel to others. The situation will be tailor-made. Since that time in the hospital, I've also gone out on a limb of faith and prayed for and with strangers. It's not easy at first but gets better with practice. Help is here!

"But the Advocate, the Holy Spirit, whom the Father will send in my name, will teach you all things and will remind you of everything I have said to you" (John 14:26).

Giving our children to the Lord
Dave Scharf

Hannah from the Bible was barren. All she wanted in life was to have a child. If God were to bless her with a child, she vowed to give him into the Lord's service for his whole life. And the Lord answered. He gave her Samuel, who would become a great prophet in Israel's history. And then the time came for Hannah to take him to serve at the tabernacle.

Hannah said, **"So now I give him to the Lord. For his whole life he will be given over to the Lord"** (1 Samuel 1:28). He was maybe five years old. Can you imagine what it was like for Hannah? And yet, we see in the next chapter that Hannah poured out thanksgiving to God in prayer!

Could you do it? You and I are not in Hannah's situation exactly, but shouldn't we desire to give our children over to the Lord? I think of my own mother, who faithfully read devotions with us, said prayers with us, and lived Jesus for us with her forgiveness. She was intent on giving us to the Lord even after a long day. Yes, I was Mom's child, but it was more important to her that I be God's. For this, you and I will give our eternal thanks to God. If God has blessed you with a child, give that child over to the Lord. Pray with them. Read God's Word with them. Worship with them. Give them to the Lord.

How to prepare for Lord's Supper
Mike Novotny

After studying every Bible passage on the Lord's Supper, I came up with a six-part method to get the most of your next celebration of it: Look back, forward, up, down, in, and around. If you remember to look in those six directions, the Lord's Supper will be the blessing that Jesus intended.

Look back to the cross where Jesus died for you, as you **"do this in remembrance"** of your Savior (Luke 22:19).

Look forward to the feast where Jesus is waiting to eat a better meal with you **"in the kingdom of God"** (Luke 22:16).

Look up to give thanks that our God, unlike the gods of all other religions, has a **"new covenant"** where he forgives you freely (Luke 22:20).

Look down to see the gift, the true body and blood of Christ, which is present with the bread and the wine (Luke 22:19,20).

Look in to repent, ridding your heart of any **"yeast"** (sin) that might spread quickly (1 Corinthians 5:7).

Look around to rejoice, noticing all the people breaking bread with you because they share your beliefs (1 Corinthians 10:17).

Got that? Look back to the cross, forward to the feast, up to give thanks, down to see the gift, in to repent, and around to rejoice. Lord's Supper is too sacred to speed through the motions. So look back, forward, up, down, in, and around, and you will be prepared for a miracle that only Jesus can do.

Scared or prepared?
Clark Schultz

My five-year-old son came home from kindergarten saying, "I'm not scared; I'm prepared." He then went on to tell me that he practiced hiding from the wolf today in school. *Hmm.* Is this like new math (what was wrong with the old math)? Are they bringing live animals into the classroom now?

My wife and I deduced that the teacher was preparing her students for an active shooter drill. Yes, this is the world we live in, and sadly we need to teach these lessons to our children. This got me thinking about Matthew 10:28: **"Do not be afraid of those who kill the body but cannot kill the soul. Rather, be afraid of the One who can destroy both soul and body in hell."** When the end of the world or last days become a topic of discussion, what is your reaction? Are you scared or prepared?

Jesus spoke these words when he was sending out his disciples on their intern mission trips, not to be confused with the Great Commission, which came later. He was preparing his disciples, as well as preparing us. When the end comes, we DO NOT need to be scared. Why? **"Even the very hairs of your head are all numbered. So don't be afraid; you are worth more than many sparrows"** (Matthew 10:30,31).

We thank the school and teachers for their teaching and preparing our children for all situations. We thank our pastors, teachers, parents, and grandparents for showing us that ONLY JESUS can destroy the wolf.

Are you a confident Christian?

Mike Novotny

Feeling confident (a.k.a. hopeful, optimistic, etc.) comes down to a simple equation: Confidence = Resources > Needs. For example, you feel confident about passing a class when your resources (like your intelligence, previous grades, study habits) are greater than the needed knowledge for the class. You feel confident you can afford something (that house, car, phone) when your resources (savings and income) are greater than the needed price. That's the confidence equation.

Based on that definition, you, I, and every Christian can be supremely confident. Will you make it to heaven? Does God like you? Is God for you? Will he use (your learning disability/health dilemma/chronic pain) for some higher purpose? To all these questions and more, we shout, "Absolutely!" Because Jesus is always greater than any and every need.

When we have Jesus, we have the ultimate resource, a source of forgiveness, salvation, and power. Instead of looking in the mirror and trying to find enough inner resources to meet the needs of life, Jesus turns us toward the cross, where we find everything we need, freely given in his blood.

Paul wrote, **"In [Jesus] and through faith in him we may approach God with freedom and confidence"** (Ephesians 3:12). Tell your insecurity to take a hike. You have Jesus Christ, which is all you need to be a confident Christian.

God's operator's manual
Andrea Delwiche

This won't surprise you, but there's no long-lost recipe for a trouble-free life. Jesus told his followers, **"In this world you will have trouble"** (John 16:33). The sweet, untroubled face of a sleeping child stirs us in part because children are largely free from worry, including the reality that we won't be able to protect them from tears.

We persevere because we have hope in Christ. We can also *thrive* if we choose to follow the operator's manual of sorts that God laid out for us in Scripture. God's commands are *practical.* He hasn't handed down his laws and guidelines to trip us up. He has given them to provide a road map and the best preventative care manual ever printed.

"Blessed are all who fear the Lord, who walk in obedience to him. You will eat the fruit of your labor; blessing and prosperity will be yours" (Psalm 128:1,2).

This is no recipe for financial wealth or earning our way to heaven. It's a realization of the facts of existence. God created us, loves us, and knows best how, under his care and blessing, we can succeed.

"[God's] commands are not burdensome," writes the apostle John in 1 John 5:3. We show love for God by obeying his commands, and then *we* are the ones who reap the benefits of living a life of love for God.

This too is part of the saving message of Jesus. We are saved for eternity, but we are also saved for a life of meaning, purpose, and joy in the here and now.

Jesus will heal you
Mike Novotny

You can't read the Bible and deny that Jesus cares about our bodies. Jesus didn't just teach; he also touched. He didn't just preach; he put his hands on sick and blind and dead bodies and gave them health, sight, and life. In fact, most of Jesus' miracles were about physical bodies that needed to be healed.

Since Jesus is the same yesterday, today, and forever, I want you to be confident that he can do the same for you. He can heal you. More than that, Jesus will heal you.

Sooner or later, Jesus will heal your body. Your migraines, arthritis, anxiety, cramps, and cancer are all like those hourglass sand timers, and every day is one day closer to your pain being gone for good. Through medicine or surgery or a miraculous snap of his fingers, either today or next year or on the day when he returns, Jesus will heal your body. Do you believe that?

The apostle Paul, who both experienced miracles and lived with an excruciating "thorn" in his flesh, confidently wrote, "[The Lord Jesus] **will transform our lowly bodies so that they will be like his glorious body**" (Philippians 3:21). Jesus *will!* Not might. Not maybe. Not depending on how he feels. No, Jesus will transform our lowly, broken bodies. We won't ache or hurt forever. One day soon, Jesus will return with power and love to transform these lowly bodies into something glorious and new.

You are one day closer to the healing you have ached for. Pray with me—Come quickly, Lord Jesus!

HELP WANTED!
Clark Schultz

Perhaps HELP WANTED signs litter the sidewalks on your daily commute. Maybe you're the one looking for help or a job.

As a teen, my parents encouraged me to find a job that paid well, and if I didn't like it, to stick with it and not quit. It's advice I pass on to this generation of "I need to find the perfect job" workers. Working at a place that is difficult gives perspective on what real work is and teaches life lessons of pain, struggle, and an appreciation for the people and the work done at the business.

When it comes to our salvation, we too need big HELP WANTED signs on our heads and hearts. By nature, our sinful condition means we should not be hired but fired into the pit of hell. But then came Jesus. **"Jesus began to explain to his disciples that he must go to Jerusalem and suffer many things . . . and that he must be killed and on the third day be raised to life"** (Matthew 16:21). Jesus took the job that we could never do. He did all the tasks the Father asked him to do, and he did them perfectly. He did not quit. In turn, he gave his life for our lives, he paid the ransom for our sins, and he gave us the paycheck of eternity.

Help wanted? Yes! Help given in Jesus! That's a sign we can proudly display!

Why religious people are afraid
Mike Novotny

The other day I asked ChatGPT why people who believe in God still become afraid. In impressive time, the artificial intelligence typed out a list of answers that I, as a Christian, found fascinating. Reason #1: "People may fear the unknown, death, or the afterlife." Reason #2: "Religious individuals often adhere to a set of moral and ethical principles outlined by their faith. Fear of deviating from these principles or facing divine judgment for perceived wrongdoing can contribute to anxiety or fear." Catch that? The top reasons for fear are uncertainty about the afterlife and being judged for our sins.

I wonder who could help with that (insert knowing smile here)? Speaking of Jesus, the apostle Paul declares, **"He was delivered over to death for our sins and was raised to life for our justification"** (Romans 4:25). If Jesus died for our sins, then we don't need to fear God judging us for our wrongs. We are completely forgiven for every time we have deviated from the moral principles outlined by Jesus. And if Jesus rose to life, then we know precisely what happens after death. We open our eyes to see the perfect face of our forgiving Father in heaven.

Friend, too many people forget the fear-erasing power of the cross and the empty tomb. Today, I urge you to remember Jesus. Your fear doesn't stand a chance next to him!

JOY.
Katrina Harrmann

I sat in my living room after having a rough day. I was surrounded by twinkle lights and listening to Christmas music, just getting a chance to relax. I glanced down at my cocoa mug and saw the word inscribed on it—JOY.

I laughed at the period that followed the word JOY. It wasn't JOY! It was JOY. Period.

JOY. is very different than JOY!

JOY. is a call to action. An imperative.

As I held that mug, the music I was listening to wailed about glad tidings of great joy, and I thought about how for many people, joy doesn't come in an obvious way, like the shepherds—their quiet night rent with angel fire, the heavenly shrapnel of which literally smacked them upside their heads. (That was JOY!)

For many people, JOY of any kind is an effort.

For families dealing with sickness or loss . . . or joblessness or strain . . . no JOY! For people who are emotionally strained . . . no JOY!

But, perhaps, still . . . JOY.

If we choose to hunt it down like the wise men, dedicated and curious and longing for that speck of light . . . JOY.

A search. A command.

A baby in a manger.

Who gives JOY. to countless without JOY!

"Consider it pure joy, my brothers and sisters, whenever you face trials of many kinds, because you know that the testing of your faith produces perseverance" (James 1:2,3).

We are prayer warriors
Christine Wentzel

I confess that in the past, when I read on social media that someone needed a "prayer warrior" to pray for their health or loved one or struggle, my first thought was, "That counts me out."

For years I struggled with my prayer life. To tell someone I would pray for them often meant I would save it until I could do it privately if I remembered. I rarely prayed on the spot, let alone face-to-face with that person.

"I'll pray for you" has become a cliché to the world and even in some Christian circles because it is either taken as a platitude that people just say but don't mean or with skepticism—especially if it's not backed up with actions such as actual prayer and then follow-up to see how the person is doing.

I've learned to push past my fears of not having the right words to say or even believing the lie that my prayers are too little for God to bother with. How did I do that? I remembered what God says about my prayers.

He says, **"Therefore confess your sins to each other and pray for each other so that you may be healed. The prayer of a righteous person is powerful and effective."** (James 5:16).

God promises my prayers and yours are powerful and effective! Improving our prayer lives is an ongoing process. We can't let our fears of messing up or feeling self-conscious prevent a chance to open a door to the power of God. We ARE prayer warriors!

A God with skin on
Jan Gompper

A visiting pastor at church told the story of a little girl who cried out in fear after having a bad dream. Her mother rushed to comfort her, assuring her that God was with her and that he would take care of her. To the mother's surprise, her daughter replied, "I know that God is with me, Mommy, and that he'll take care of me, but I want somebody here with skin on."

Have you ever wanted "a God with skin on"? Maybe you wished you could've held Jesus' hand physically from your hospital bed. Perhaps you ached for a hug from Jesus when you learned of the death of a loved one or when your spouse wanted a divorce. Though we know God is with us, sometimes a God with skin on would help, wouldn't it?

The disciples *did* experience a God with skin on, yet they still had doubts and fears, even after hearing of Jesus' resurrection. While they huddled behind closed doors, Jesus appeared to them, saying, **"Why are you troubled, and why do doubts rise in your minds? Look at my hands and my feet. It is I myself! Touch me and see; a ghost does not have flesh and bones, as you see I have"** (Luke 24:38,39).

How do people experience a God with skin on today? **"Now *you* are the body of Christ, and each one is a part of it"** (1 Corinthians 12:27). So whenever you bring a word or touch of comfort to hurting or frightened souls, they see and feel Jesus.

Storing up
Linda Buxa

"Mary treasured up all these things and pondered them in her heart" (Luke 2:19).

When I'm feeling ungrateful about my blessings, I think about my grandma. I go to bed with the dishwasher running. She washed dishes by hand. My laundry is washed and dried after a few pushes of buttons. She washed hers by hand and hung them on a clothesline. I can drive to the store, and in minutes my freezers and refrigerators (note the plural) are full. She stockpiled her abundance by canning and storing the vegetables from her garden. She knew she needed to store up when there was an abundance so the family would have provisions when conditions weren't as favorable.

The same is true for our faith. Mary treasured up—stored up, canned up—all the moments of Jesus' life, including when the shepherds visited her baby and the wise men later brought him gifts. Then when a sword was piercing her soul because a sword was piercing his side, she could go back to those stored-up moments and know he was fulfilling his mission.

Your stored-up provisions might not be as dramatic, but they are just as important.

When life is good, store up the goodness of God in your heart. When you feel his peace, can it in the jars of your heart so that when life hurts—and it will—you can go back to that abundance and know that he has provided in the past, provides in the present, and will provide in the future.

Right-on-time delivery
Liz Schroeder

As a kid, I remember Christmas gift labels that read, "Do not open until December 25." Oh, the thrill of anticipation that coursed through my eight-year-old body! What could be under the wrapping? And please, God, let it be the stuffed unicorn I circled in the Sears catalog!

When God promised Adam and Eve that a Savior would be born, they didn't understand God's timeline. He didn't tell them when they could open the gift, only that the Gift would come. So when Eve became pregnant, she assumed her baby was the Messiah. In truth, she gave birth to Cain, who would grow up to become a murderer (see Genesis 4).

If God had put a gift label on the promised Messiah, it would have read, "Do not open for four thousand years." That's a long time to sustain anticipation!

"But when the set time had fully come, God sent his Son, born of a woman, born under the law, to redeem those under the law, that we might receive adoption to sonship" (Galatians 4:4,5).

As a parent, it's hard for me to wait until Christmas to give our kids their gifts. When it's the perfect gift, I can't contain my excitement. I wonder if that's a taste of how my heavenly Father felt during those four thousand years?

God has a Christmas gift for you: an adoption certificate signed in the blood of his Son. Go ahead and rip off the wrapping. His forgiveness, love, and acceptance are yours to enjoy right now.

Decorations doing their job
Daron Lindemann

What are your Christmas decorations telling you? The evergreen tree. The glistening lights. The nativity scene. It is all symbolism that helps you celebrate. Just like the number of candles on a birthday cake symbolizes your age.

Typically, however, symbolism tends to lose its meaning over time, and the symbol becomes the thing instead of pointing to the thing. Like when Christmas dinner makes everybody so stressed out that they forget about the peace of Jesus.

The Bible reports an epic event as the Israelites crossed the Jordan River and entered their new land. To commemorate the event, God commanded Joshua to set up 12 stones at their camp. He wanted that pile of stones to be a reminder in the future. He wanted the Israelites to ask, "What do these stones mean?" (Joshua 4:21).

Take an inventory of your Christmas decorations and ask, "What does this mean?" Do this as you take down the decorations. Write down notes for next Christmas, perhaps doing this same exercise as you take the decorations out of the box and display them next year. Teach your children.

The evergreen Christmas tree symbolizes everlasting life, and it points up like an arrow to heaven. The candy cane represents Jesus, white because he is holy with red stripes for the blood he shed to save us. Wrapped gifts remind us that God wrapped himself in flesh and became the gift of salvation for sinners. And more!

Do some research about the symbolism of Christmas, and help your decorations do their job.

God's positive thinking
Dave Scharf

Positive thinking can sometimes just be pretending. The philosophy of "Ignore a problem, and it will go away" or "It's only a problem if you treat it like one" sounds comical until the sad reality dawns on you that this is the approach to spiritual needs for many.

The apostle Paul said, **"Finally, brothers and sisters, whatever is true, whatever is noble, whatever is right, whatever is pure, whatever is lovely, whatever is admirable—if anything is excellent or praiseworthy—think about such things"** (Philippians 4:8). Notice what the first qualification for positive thoughts is: They have to be true.

This is the truth: I am a great sinner, but I have a greater Savior in Jesus, who died and rose for me. He won for me forgiveness and a guaranteed life in heaven! Now I wake up every day as a forgiven child of God, knowing that my Jesus is with me, he loves me, he is guiding all things for my good, he is blessing my life beyond what I can possibly imagine, he is preparing a mansion for me in heaven, he has freed me to give him glory in my life and in countless ways to thank him for his goodness to me, and I have all I need in him. The next time you start thinking negatively, ask yourself who is the epitome of everything Paul lists in this verse? It's Jesus. That is true positive thinking!

The story ends (kind of) like it began
Mike Novotny

The final chapter of the Bible says, **"Then the angel showed me the river of the water of life, as clear as crystal, flowing from the throne of God and of the Lamb down the middle of the great street of the city. On each side of the river stood the tree of life, bearing twelve crops of fruit, yielding its fruit every month. And the leaves of the tree are for the healing of the nations. No longer will there be any curse"** (Revelation 22:1-3). Sound familiar?

Back in the beginning, there was a *river* that flowed from Eden. And there was *fruit* and *the tree of life* and people who walked with *God*. The Bible's final verses are meant to take us back to the original world before the curse of sin corrupted it.

Except this version of paradise is even better, an upgraded Eden. Because the devil doesn't slither in this garden (he was tossed into the lake of fire in Revelation 20) and God promises, "No longer will there be any curse." Never again will work hurt or marriage be messy. Never again will we sin or feel shame or hide from God.

Your story, because of Jesus, ends with all blessing and no curse, a new kind of Eden. Except this paradise will not end in a page or two. It will endure forever.

Today you are one day closer to what the Bible's final pages promise. Hold on tight, child of God. You are so close to experiencing what Adam and Eve did, only better!

Are you good enough for God?
Mike Novotny

Recently, my friend went to a funeral of a man who was dearly loved by his community because he had served his community deeply. But during the service, the priest admitted that the deceased had not been confident he could make it to heaven. Was he good enough? Had he done enough good? The priest went on to say, "The saints in heaven are those who do good on Earth."

Let's think about that for a second. How good is good enough to be with God? It takes a lot to get into Harvard, and heaven is way better than Harvard, so what spiritual test score is required? You can try your best, but is your best enough for God? (And how often do you actually try your best?) No wonder so many people are not confident they are going to heaven.

Forgive me for judging another man's funeral sermon, but that priest was wrong. You don't get to God by being good. None of us are good enough. I'm not. You aren't either.

But Jesus is. Paul's words on this subject are classic for a reason: **"For it is by grace you have been saved, through faith—and this is not from yourselves, it is the gift of God—not by works, so that no one can boast"** (Ephesians 2:8,9). Salvation is all about God's grace, about faith in Jesus, about the gift the Lord gives when he declares, "I forgive you at the cross!"

Believe in Jesus. He is all you need to be good enough for God.

How can I know God's will?

Daron Lindemann

A man hiking at night fell off a cliff. He managed to grab a branch that stopped him from tumbling to his death. But he knew he wouldn't be able to hold on for long. He called out, "Is anyone up there?"

After what seemed like an eternity of silence, he heard God's response, "I can help."

The man eagerly waited for his miraculous deliverance. "Let go of the branch!" God commanded.

The man questioned why God would tell him to do something so foolish. This wasn't deliverance at all. There had to be a better option. "Is anyone else up there?" the man inquired. All the while, as he dangled from the branch, his feet were only six inches off the ground.

We often wish that we knew more about God's will. We pray and struggle trying to figure out the right way. All the while, however, God has clearly revealed his will to us. Printed plainly in the Bible.

Jesus once said, **"My Father's will is that everyone who looks to the Son and believes in him will have eternal life"** (John 6:40). The apostle Paul wrote, **"We instructed you how to live in order to please God. . . . It is God's will that you should be sanctified"** (1 Thessalonians 4:1,3).

The Bible gives us God's perfect promises to live by and God's guidance to make life even better. What would change in your life if you started paying more attention to God's will that he already reveals?

Piercing wisdom
Matt Trotter

"Then Simeon blessed them and said to Mary, his mother: 'This child is destined to cause the falling and rising of many in Israel, and to be a sign that will be spoken against, so that the thoughts of many hearts will be revealed. And a sword will pierce your own soul too'" (Luke 2:34,35).

Have you wondered what to say to someone who's grieving? It's hard to muster more than, "I'm sorry." And that's okay; expressing sorrow is a good thing. Even though Mary knew what the future held for her Son, she felt sorry too.

It was not until the tragic death of my daughter that the pointedness of the sword Simeon wrote of stung me. When my daughter had her last MRI, I could see it in the faces of the nurses and staff as a sharp pain started in my chest. It felt like panic and dread, like a heart attack—but it was my soul being pierced.

Losing a child is a piercing of a parent's soul. It's a scar that never fully goes away. When people ask me what it felt like to lose a child, I say, "It still feels as if a pen was stuck into my chest." It still hurts. I think of this more as I age and realize other people are wounded in this way too.

Next time you meet someone in grief, think no further than Mary, the mother of Jesus, a perfect Son, and yet her soul was pierced. It's okay to be sorrow-full, to be sorry.

Abide
Katrina Harrmann

At the close of every year, I like to pick out a word for my coming year.

I enjoy this more than trying to decide on a resolution for the year because, let's face it, resolutions are easy to make but pretty hard to stick to.

Instead, if I choose a word, I can often think about it and pray over it and ruminate about what it means in my life.

This past year, my word was *Abide*.

We happened to be singing a song in church at the close of last year, and the lyrics talked about asking God to teach us to abide.

I love the idea of abiding. Of "learning" to abide.

It doesn't mean that life is perfect.

It means that I am learning to "BE" where God has placed me.

It means that I am learning to lean into him . . . depend on him.

This was a great thought for me to bring to mind during high and low moments of the year.

Consider choosing a word that means something to you and that you think you'd enjoy holding close or considering! Words like *faith, trust, patience,* and *joy* are good places to start. Or choose an entire Bible verse that you can bring to mind throughout the year!

"Abide in me, and I in you. As the branch cannot bear fruit by itself, unless it abides in the vine, neither can you, unless you abide in me" (John 15:4 ESV).

DEVOTIONS FOR SPECIAL DAYS

Death should bother you
Mike Novotny

If the thought of death bothers you, I don't blame you. In the beginning, God didn't create things to die or say goodbye. Visitations and funerals and graveside services weren't what our Father intended when he made the universe "very good." That's why in the Bible, death is called our "enemy" (1 Corinthians 15:26). That's why when Jesus himself went to a funeral, he wept (John 11:35). Death bothered him too.

In this broken world, things die. Dreams, hopes, and friendships die. Flowers wilt, bread grows stale, and divorce kills sacred vows. Widows walk into church every week. Miscarriages happen every month. A time will come when you will attend far more funerals than weddings. How will you handle the death that is everywhere in this life?

What about Easter? The same Jesus who rose on Easter morning once said, **"I am the resurrection and the life. The one who believes in me will live, even though they die; and whoever lives by believing in me will never die"** (John 11:25,26). In the blink of an eye, your post-death life will get unbelievably wonderful.

Heavenly paradise, by comparison, makes spring break stink and the Florida sun seem lame. In heaven you get to see God. God!! Some people are terrified to die. Not us. We have Jesus, the Son of God, the resurrection and the life. And every day from now until then is not just one day closer to death; it's one day closer to the best life you can imagine.

Going on an adventure
Katrina Harrmann

One of my favorite books (and movies) is the *Hobbit* by J. R. R. Tolkien.

I love the part when Bilbo finally decides to go with Gandalf and the dwarves, and he runs out of his house as he shouts, "I'M GOING ON AN ADVENTURE!"

How exciting! What would it be like to go on a real adventure?! All too often, I finish watching this scene and then come crashing back to earth as I look around my house . . . the dirty dishes in the sink, the laundry on the floor, or the list of events I need to drive my kids to. As a parent, it seems like adventure has passed me by.

Sometimes it seems that when we choose motherhood, we miss out on some of life's BIG adventures—let alone the adventures of *biblical* proportions like slaying giants like David or leading an army like Deborah or saving a nation like Esther.

But it's important to remember that God gives mothers a huge and important task—to prepare our own children for the adventures of life.

"Start children off on the way they should go, and even when they are old they will not turn from it" (Proverbs 22:6).

The good news is that this journey with our children is also full of adventure, if we choose to see it. The adventure of teaching and laughing and loving. It is perhaps the greatest adventure of our lives—protecting and guiding these little lambs.

Follow in his steps
Clark Schultz

This past winter after a snowstorm (no school!), our entire family went outside to exercise. First there was the drill of dressing our boys (yes, that took more time than the actual hike), and then we set out into the shin-deep snow.

Like clockwork, our three boys had different approaches to attacking the snow. The middle child bolted ahead to where we couldn't see him on the trail. The oldest trudged behind about 25 yards, complaining about how cold he was. Meanwhile, the youngest stayed close to Mom and Dad and then begged to be carried after he got snow in his boots. Finally, we got some momentum from all three boys when we said, "Follow in Daddy's footprints!"

Peter said something similar to a group of persecuted Christians who were suffering for loving Jesus: **"To this you were called, because Christ suffered for you, leaving you an example, that you should follow in his steps"** (1 Peter 2:21).

Are you trudging through struggles right now? Are you bolting ahead, leaving behind the comfort of your church family? Maybe you're lagging back in your faith, complaining about the struggle. Or maybe you're amid the muck and can't seem to get traction. Peter's encouragement rings true today: "Follow in Jesus' steps."

Dear friend, you step with a Savior who suffered for you so you won't suffer eternally. He is there to pick you up, ahead of you to lead you, and beside you to carry you. Happy hiking!

Today is a gift
Ann Jahns

On my bed sits a decorative pillow. In gold script, it elegantly declares, "Today is a gift." I treasure this pillow for two reasons: It was a gift from my youngest son, and it is a daily reminder of God's unchanging goodness.

Thanksgiving Day is a day when it's easy to remember to be grateful for God's gifts. If you are spending the day with loved ones, you may even list the ways that God has blessed you.

Yes, today is a gift from God. But what about the days that don't feel like a gift? Days when you would like to take my inspirational pillow and throw it against the wall? Like the day you get the news you've been dreading? Or the day you finally admit that your marriage is over? Or the day you are so weary—physically, emotionally, and even spiritually—that you just want to give up?

In his book, James talks about finding "pure joy" in those types of days. He reminds us, **"Every good and perfect gift is from above, coming down from the Father of the heavenly lights, who does not change like shifting shadows"** (1:17). I love that final reminder of God's immutability—he *does not change like shifting shadows.* This world offers us false, fleeting gifts. Only the gifts from our heavenly Father are perfect. And through those, he blesses us.

Today is a gift. And tomorrow. And every day that God gives us. *Lord, help us to recognize each day as the perfect gift it is. Amen.*

About the Authors

Pastor Mike Novotny pours his Jesus-based joy into his ministry as a pastor at The CORE (Appleton, Wisconsin) and as the lead speaker for Time of Grace, a global media ministry that points people to Jesus through television, print, and digital resources. Unafraid to bring grace and truth to the toughest topics of our time, he has written numerous books, including *3 Words That Will Change Your Life*, *When Life Hurts*, *Lonely Less*, and *Taboo: Topics Christians Should Be Talking About but Don't*. Mike lives with his wife, Kim, and their two daughters, Brooklyn and Maya; runs long distances; and plays soccer with other middle-aged men whose best days are long behind them. To find more books by Pastor Mike, go to timeofgrace.store.

Linda Buxa is a freelance communications professional as well as a regular blogger and contributing writer for Time of Grace Ministry. Linda is the author of *Dig In! Family Devotions to Feed Your Faith*, *Parenting by Prayer*, *Made for Friendship*, *Visible Faith*, and *How to Fight Anxiety With Joy*. She and her husband, Greg, have lived in Alaska, Washington D.C., and California. After Greg retired from the military, they moved to Wisconsin, where they settled on 11.7 acres and now keep track of chickens, multiple cats, and 1 black Lab. Their 3 children insisted on getting older and exploring what God has planned for their lives, so Greg and Linda are now empty nesters. The sign in her kitchen sums up their lives: "You call it chaos; we call it family."

Andrea Delwiche lives in Wisconsin with her husband, three kids, dog, cat, and a goldfish pond full of fish.

She enjoys reading, knitting, and road-tripping with her family. Although a lifelong believer, she began to come into a deeper understanding of what it means to follow Christ far into adulthood (always a beginner on that journey!). Andrea has facilitated a Christian discussion group for women at her church for many years and recently published a book of poetry—*The Book of Burning Questions.*

Pastor Jon Enter served as a pastor in West Palm Beach, Florida, for ten years. He is now a campus pastor and instructor at St. Croix Lutheran Academy in St. Paul, Minnesota. Jon also serves as a regular speaker and a contributing writer to Time of Grace. He once led a tour at his college, and the Lord had him meet his future wife, Debbi. They have four daughters: Violet, Lydia, Eden, and Maggie.

Pastor Matt Ewart and his wife, Amy, have been blessed with three children who keep life interesting. Matt is currently a pastor in Lakeville, Minnesota, and has previously served as a pastor in Colorado and Arizona.

Jan Gompper spent most of her career teaching theatre at Wisconsin Lutheran College in Milwaukee. She also served six years as a cohost for *Time of Grace* during its start-up years. She has collaborated on two faith-based musicals, numerous Christian songs, and has written and codirected scripts for a Christian video series. She and her husband now reside in the Tampa area, where she continues to practice her acting craft and coach aspiring acting students as opportunities arise. She also assists with Sunday school and other church-related activities.

Katrina Harrmann lives in southwest Michigan with her photographer husband, Nathan, and their three kids. A lifelong Christian, she attended journalism school at the University of Missouri, Columbia, and worked at the *Green Bay Press-Gazette* and the *Sheboygan Press* before taking on the full-time job of motherhood. Currently, she is an editor for Whirlpool and lives along the shores of Lake Michigan and enjoys gardening, hiking, camping, doing puzzles, and playing with her chihuahua in her free time.

Ann Jahns and her husband live in Wisconsin as empty nesters, having had the joy of raising three boys to adulthood. She is a marketing coordinator for a Christian church body and a freelance proofreader and copy editor. Ann has been privileged to teach Sunday school and lead Bible studies for women of all ages. One of her passions is supporting women in the "sandwich generation" as they experience the unique joys and challenges of raising children while supporting aging parents.

Pastor Daron Lindemann loves the journey—exploring God's paths in life with his wife or discovering even more about Jesus and the Bible. He serves as a pastor in Pflugerville, Texas, with a passion for life-changing faith and for smoking brisket.

Paul Mattek is a development director at Time of Grace. His great passions are design and Jesus, and as such his personal mission is to show people God's beauty in whatever way possible. He loves that at Time of Grace he gets to grow the ministry by meeting people and reminding them about the incredible love of Jesus—the best "sales" job ever. Paul and his wife, Julia, have four children—June, Louis, Elias, and Penelope (Penny)—and a pet guinea pig, Cinnamon.

Pastor Nathan Nass serves at Christ the King Lutheran Church in Tulsa, Oklahoma. Prior to moving to Oklahoma, he served at churches in Wisconsin, Minnesota, Texas, and Georgia. He and his wife, Emily, have four children. You can find more sermons and devotions on his blog: upsidedownsavior.home.blog.

Jason Nelson had a career as a teacher, counselor, and leader. He has a bachelor's degree in education, did graduate work in theology, and has a master's degree in counseling psychology. After his career ended in disabling back pain, he wrote the book *Miserable Joy: Chronic Pain in My Christian Life*. He has written and spoken extensively on a variety of topics related to the Christian life. Jason has been a contributing writer for Time of Grace since 2010. He has authored many Grace Moments devotions and several books. Jason lives with his wife, Nancy, in Wisconsin.

Pastor Dave Scharf served as a pastor in Greenville, Wisconsin, and now serves as a professor of theology at Martin Luther College in Minnesota. He has presented at numerous leadership, outreach, and missionary conferences across the country. He is a contributing writer and speaker for Time of Grace. Dave and his wife have six children.

Liz Schroeder is a Resilient Recovery coach, a ministry that allows her to go into sober living homes and share the love and hope of Jesus with men and women recently out of rehab or prison. It has been a dream of hers to write Grace Moments, a resource she has used for years in homeschooling her five children. After going on a mission trip to Malawi through an organization called Kingdom Workers, she now serves on its U.S. board of directors. She and her husband, John, are privileged to live in Phoenix and call CrossWalk their church home.

Pastor Clark Schultz loves Jesus; his wife, Kristin, and their three boys; the Green Bay Packers; Milwaukee Brewers; Wisconsin Badgers; and—of course—Batman. His ministry stops are all in Wisconsin and include a vicar year in Green Bay, tutoring and recruiting for Christian ministry at a high school in Watertown, teacher/coach at a Christian high school in Lake Mills, and a pastor in Cedar Grove. He currently serves as a pastor in West Bend and is the author of the book *5-Minute Bible Studies: For Teens.* Pastor Clark's favorite quote is, "Find something you love to do and you will never work a day in your life."

Karen Spiegelberg lives in Wisconsin with her husband, Jim. She has three married daughters, six grandchildren, and has been a foster mom to many. Years ago she was encouraged to start a women's ministry but was unsure of the timing. When her brother died suddenly, it hit her hard—that we can't wait until the time seems right for our ministry; the time is now. And so in 2009, with God's direction, A Word for Women was born. Karen finds great comfort in Psalm 31:14,15: "But I trust in you, O Lord. . . . My times are in your hands."

Matt Trotter is the president and CEO of Time of Grace Ministry. His responsibilities include ensuring the ministry stays true to its vision/mission, overseeing the business aspects of the ministry, shaping the strategic direction, and creating a culture in the organization that makes it the "best job ever" for every employee. Matt and his wife, MJ, have been blessed with five daughters of resplendent beauty and boundless energy. Together the family enjoys school, volleyball, swimming, and training their faithful dog, Mars.

Christine Wentzel, a native of Milwaukee, lives in Norfolk, Virginia, with her husband, James, and their rescue dogs. After two lost decades as a prodigal, Christine worships and serves at Resurrection Lutheran in Chesapeake, Virginia. In 2009 she served as writer and coadministrator for an online Christian women's ministry, A Word for Women. In 2022 she accepted a position to become the social media director for the WELS military ministry that sees to the spiritual needs of active duty members serving in the armed forces.

About Time of Grace

The mission of Time of Grace is to point people to what matters most: Jesus. Using a variety of media (television, podcasts, print publications, and digital), Time of Grace teaches tough topics in an approachable and relatable way, accessible in multiple languages, making the Bible clear and understandable for those who need encouragement in their walks of faith and for those who don't yet know Jesus at all.

To discover more, please visit
timeofgrace.org or call 800.661.3311.

Help share God's message of grace!

Every gift you give helps Time of Grace reach people around the world with the good news of Jesus. Your generosity and prayer support take the gospel of grace to others through our ministry outreach and help them experience a satisfied life as they see God all around them.

Give today at timeofgrace.org/give
or by calling 800.661.3311.

Thank you!

Made in the USA
Monee, IL
29 September 2024

66894060R00229